Metaphor AND Masculinity IN Hosea

Studies in Biblical Literature

Hemchand Gossai
General Editor

Vol. 141

PETER LANG
New York • Washington, D.C./Baltimore • Bern
Frankfurt • Berlin • Brussels • Vienna • Oxford

Susan E. Haddox

Metaphor AND Masculinity IN Hosea

PETER LANG
New York • Washington, D.C./Baltimore • Bern
Frankfurt • Berlin • Brussels • Vienna • Oxford

Library of Congress Cataloging-in-Publication Data

Haddox, Susan E.
Metaphor and masculinity in Hosea / Susan E. Haddox.
p. cm. — (Studies in biblical literature; v. 141)
Includes bibliographical references.
1. Bible. O.T. Hosea—Criticism, interpretation, etc.
2. Metaphor in the Bible. 3. Men—Biblical teaching. I. Title.
BS1565.52.H33   224'.606—dc23   2011027217
ISBN 978-1-4331-1356-7
ISSN 1089-0645

Bibliographic information published by **Die Deutsche Nationalbibliothek**.
Die Deutsche Nationalbibliothek lists this publication in the "Deutsche
Nationalbibliografie"; detailed bibliographic data is available
on the Internet at http://dnb.d-nb.de/.

© 2011 Peter Lang Publishing, Inc., New York
29 Broadway, 18th floor, New York, NY 10006
www.peterlang.com

❖CONTENTS❖

More than ever the horizons in biblical literature are being expanded beyond that which is immediately imagined; important new methodological, theological, and hermeneutical directions are being explored, often resulting in significant contributions to the world of biblical scholarship. It is an exciting time for the academy as engagement in biblical studies continues to be heightened.

This series seeks to make available to scholars and institutions, scholarship of a high order, and which will make a significant contribution to the ongoing biblical discourse. This series includes established and innovative directions, covering general and particular areas in biblical study. For every volume considered for this series, we explore the question as to whether the study will push the horizons of biblical scholarship. The answer must be yes for inclusion.

In this volume Susan Haddox examines the use of metaphor in Hosea with a particular focus on the emphasis and language of masculinity as it pervades political apostasy in Hosea. The author observes correctly that while in many ways masculinity dominates the Hosea text, there is a paucity of scholarship in this area. She attends to this need with an extensive application of masculinity theory to Hosea, building on the limited foundation of recent scholarship that employs masculine theory. She argues that while there has been a preponderance of scholarship on female imagery in Hosea, male imagery in fact dominates the text. Using the model of social and semantic space, she evaluates the rhetorical effect of metaphors. The work of feminist scholars is acknowledged in appreciation for their importance but in this study, the angle for interpretation has been widened, and I believe that this will only enrich the scholarly discourse. Scholars will find this study instructive and sophisticated, and the ideas and arguments generated here will certainly extend the discussion in significant ways. This is an important and wide-ranging addition to the already well established body of scholarly work on Hosea, and it is one that I believe will surely expand the discourse on this text.

The horizon has been expanded.

Hemchand Gossai
Series Editor

❖ACKNOWLEDGMENTS❖

I have been thinking about metaphor and images in Hosea for a number of years, in terms of how they shape the overall rhetoric of the text. My doctoral adviser at Emory University, John H. Hayes, provided useful guidance, particularly in considering the historical context of Hosea's oracles. His humor and encouragement were always appreciated. I thank Carol Newsom of Emory University for introducing me to the work of James Fernandez and for her helpful comments on my dissertation, from which this work emerged. I also thank the other members of my committee, Martin Buss and Luke Johnson. I am grateful to Marvin Chaney at the Graduate Theological Union for bringing to my awareness the idea that the rhetoric of the book may not be primarily directed at religious apostasy and for pointing out the large number of male images in the book. As I was working on this project, masculinity studies began to emerge with increasing prominence in biblical studies and I thank Stephen Moore, not only for his pioneering work in the field, but for reviewing the sections of my work devoted to masculinity studies.

My colleagues Rob von Thaden and Brian Alderman read the early forms of the manuscript closely and provided much needed moral support through the process. I especially thank my husband Victor Lee who has always encouraged me in my endeavors and who helped with the proofreading.

A research appointment at the University of Mount Union helped me to prepare the work for publication, for which I am grateful.

❖ABBREVIATIONS❖

AB	Anchor Bible
ABD	*Anchor Bible Dictionary.* Edited by David Noel Freedman. 6 vols. New York, 1992
ACEBTSup	Amsterdamse Cahiers voor Exegese van de Bijbel en zijn Tradities: Supplement Series
ANE	Ancient Near East
ANET	*Ancient Near Eastern Texts Relating to the Old Testament.* Edited by James B. Pritchard. 3d ed. Princeton, 1969
AOAT	Alter Orient und Altes Testament
BibInt	*Biblical Interpretation*
BibOr	Biblica et orientalia
BRLAJ	Brill Reference Library of Ancient Judaism
BTB	*Biblical Theology Bulletin*
BWANT	Beiträge zur Wissenschaft vom Alten und Neuen Testament
BZ	*Biblische Zeitschrift*
BZAW	Beihefte zur Zeitschrift für die alttestamentliche Wissenschaft
CBET	Contributions to Biblical Exegesis and Theology
CBQ	*Catholic Biblical Quarterly*
CBSC	Cambridge Bible for Schools and Colleges
CLR	Cognitive Linguistics Research
ConBOT	Coniectanea biblica: Old Testament Series
CSSA	Cambridge Studies in Social Anthropology
ETL	*Ephemerides theologicae lovanienses*
FCB	Feminist Companion to the Bible
FZAT	Forschungen zum Alten Testament
GCT	Gender, Culture, Theory
HB	Hebrew Bible
HBT	*Horizons in Biblical Theology*
HSM	Harvard Semitic Monographs
ICC	International Critical Commentary
IDB	*The Interpreter's Dictionary of the Bible* Edited by G. A. Buttrick. 4 vols. Nashville, 1962

JBL	*Journal of Biblical Literature*
JBQ	*Jewish Bible Quarterly*
JCS	*Journal of Cuneiform Studies*
JNSL	*Journal of Northwest Semitic Languages*
JSOT	*Journal for the Study of the Old Testament*
JSOTSup	Journal for the Study of the Old Testament: Supplement Series
KAT	Kommentar zum Alten Testament
KHC	Kurzer Hand-Commentar zum Alten Testament
LCL	Loeb Classical Library
NAC	New American Commentary
NCBC	New Century Bible Commentary
NSKAT	Neuer Stuttgarter Kommentar: Altes Testament
NIB	*The New Interpreter's Bible*
OBO	Orbis biblicus et orientalis
OBT	Overtures to Biblical Theology
OTE	*Old Testament Essays*
OTL	Old Testament Library
OTS	Old Testament Studies
PEQ	*Palestine Exploration Quarterly*
RB	*Revue biblique*
SAA	State Archives of Assyria
SANE	Sources from the Ancient Near East
SBL	Society of Biblical Literature
SBLAB	Society of Biblical Literature Academia Biblica
SBLDS	Society of Biblical Literature Dissertation Series
SBS	Stuttgarter Bibelstudien
SJOT	*Scandinavian Journal of the Old Testament*
SSN	Studia semitica neerlandica
SwJT	*Southwestern Journal of Theology*
TCS	Texts from Cuneiform Sources
TJ	*Trinity Journal*
TOTC	Tyndale Old Testament Commentaries
TQ	*Theologische Quartalschrift*
UF	*Ugarit-Forschungen*
VT	*Vetus Testamentum*
WBC	Word Biblical Commentary
ZAW	*Zeitschrift für die alttestamentliche Wissenschaft*

CHAPTER ONE

Introduction and History of Interpretation

Introduction

Hosea is a book by men and for men. It employs a vast number of images and metaphors to address political, religious, economic, and military concerns, which in the society of ancient Israel were predominantly male concerns. Female imagery, despite the fact that it has drawn the focus of the majority of scholarship on the book, makes up only a small part of the text. After the first three chapters, male imagery predominates, but the male viewpoint prevails even with the female imagery. Although much recent scholarship has wrestled with the implications of the text for women, its implications for men, either ancient or contemporary, have not been systematically examined.

The tools for such an analysis have become available as the field of masculinity studies has emerged. In masculinity studies, as with feminist criticism, gender is not taken for granted, but is analyzed as a social construct. Social status and the distribution of power are often closely intertwined with particular forms of masculinity. Thus, examination of how masculinity is conceived and valued, and, in particular, the ways in which it governs relations between men and between men and women, reveals much about the organization of society. Because Hosea is a text and not a living society, it is possible to approach the issue of its construction of gender only through language, which in Hosea is largely figurative.

The ways in which cultures use metaphors and other types of figurative language to construct identity and to structure society is the subject of cognitive anthropology. Anthropological theories of metaphor are thus a good place to start in the analysis of a male identity in Hosea. James Fernandez developed a model that is especially useful in this task. He proposes that a culture can be conceived in terms of social space, which delineates social relationships. People use metaphors to place and to move each other within this social space. Real social space is very complex, determined by a large number of factors, but a simple, yet powerful, concept of social space can be defined by just three axes: activity, potency, and goodness. Such a construction of social space is particularly well suited to this study, because activity, potency, and goodness are important factors in the construction of masculinity. Both gender-based and non-gender-based imagery can be evaluated along these axes to examine their implications for masculinity.

In order to understand the social space represented in Hosea, it is important to consider the historical and cultural context. During the 9th and 8th centuries B.C.E., Assyria was the dominant power in the Ancient Near East, controlling the surrounding nations through vassal relationships. Vassal treaties imposed substantial tribute obligations on the vassal nation, which stressed the economic system of the subordinate nation and reduced autonomy, although they usually left the local king in power. Israel and Judah were among the nations that were vassals to Assyria. Evidence of Israel's interactions with Assyria dates back to the Omride dynasty. While no explicit treaty between the parties has been discovered, both biblical texts and Assyrian records show that Israel paid tribute, which indicates that such treaties did exist. They presumably followed the standard format of such treaties, which were witnessed by the gods of both sides and contained extensive curse lists. Because of the economic and political burden of the vassal relationships, it was common for vassal nations to revolt when they perceived that Assyria was weak or that they had sufficient allies to mount a credible campaign. The Assyrian records show that Israel vacillated between submitting to Assyria and rebelling against it, usually in alliance with Syria.[1]

Jehu appears to be the first Israelite king to take a pro-Assyrian stance, and there is the possibility that his rise to power was aided, or at least sanctioned, by the Assyrians. He seems to have remained a loyal vassal for his entire reign, and the successors in his dynasty also followed a pro-Assyrian policy. Aram was strong during this period and frequently dominated Israel.[2] When Assyria was also strong, it kept Aram in check, and Israel's status improved, meaning that Israel's strength was linked to that of Assyria.[3]

Israel's pro-Assyrian stance lasted throughout the Jehu dynasty. Its end was likely the result of the rise of an anti-Assyrian faction, which supported Shallum in his usurpation of the throne from Zechariah. Shallum may have been the choice of the general populace, but he did not gain the support of Israel's leaders and was quickly deposed in favor of Menahem.[4] Menahem evidently had difficulty establishing full control over the country and sent to Tiglath-pileser III for assistance, hiring a mercenary army, as shown in 2 Kgs 15:19–20:

> Pul, king of Assyria, came to the land and Menahem gave to Pul one thousand talents of silver, so that his hand might be with him and strengthen the kingship in his hand. Menahem sent out silver on behalf of Israel, concerning all the soldiers of the army, to give to the king of Assyria fifty shekels of silver per man, and the king of Assyria returned and did not remain there in the land.[5]

The Iran Stela, a summary inscription of Tiglath-pileser, shows that Menahem continued to pay tribute.

> The kings of Hatti, Aram on the banks of the sea of the setting sun, Qedar, and Arabia. Kuštašpi the Kummuhite, Raqyan the Ša-imerišu-ite, Menahem the Samarian, Tubail the Tyrian [several more kings and one queen are listed...] tribute and gifts, silver, gold, tin, iron, elephant hide, ivory, blue purple and red purple garments, trimmed linen garments, dromedaries, she-camels, I imposed upon them.[6]

With Pekah's coup, Israel's pro-Assyrian policy came to an end. There is much confusion about the chronology of Pekah's reign, which, according to 2 Kgs 15:27, was twenty years. Such a long reign does not fit well into the parallel Judean royal chronology. Pekah may have established a rival kingdom in about 750 B.C.E., composed of most of the territory outside of Samaria and the surrounding hills. His twenty-year reign would include both the time he ruled concurrently with other kings and the time after he seized power in Samaria from Pekahiah.[7] Pekah drew support from the anti-Assyrian contingent in Israelite society and joined Rezin of Damascus in rebelling against Assyria.[8] Their attempts to persuade Ahaz of Judah to join forces with them resulted in the Syro-Ephraimitic War. When Tiglath-pileser III responded to the rebellion in his campaign of 734–732, he destroyed Damascus, turned Syria into an Assyrian province, and took control over most of the territory of Israel outside of the hill country surrounding Samaria.[9] After Tiglath-pileser

quashed the revolt led by Rezin and Pekah, Ephraim was all that remained of the Northern kingdom. While Tiglath-pileser left Pekah in
power, his attack on the country gave impetus to the pro-Assyrian party
in Israel to depose Pekah, place Hoshea on the throne, and quickly pay
concessionary tributes to Assyria.[10]

The pro-Assyrian party did not retain power, however, and after a
few years Hoshea withheld tribute from Assyria and made overtures to
"King So" of Egypt (2 Kgs 17:4). The rebellion resulted in Hoshea's arrest, the siege of Samaria, the deportation of its intelligentsia, cultic and
political leaders, and large landholders, and the eventual conversion of
what remained of the nation into an Assyrian province.

Hosea began prophesying during the reign of Jeroboam (Hos 1:1),
the penultimate king in the Jehu dynasty, and seems to have continued at
least through the arrest of Hoshea, possibly even beyond the fall of
Samaria. The period of the oracles thus extends through the turbulent
period at the end of the northern kingdom, during which four kings were
assassinated within twenty years. The oracles have a decidedly political
focus, discussing political treachery at the domestic and international levels. The language in ch. 2 includes typical descriptions of cities ravaged
by siege and warfare, while most of the rest of the oracles share extensive
imagery with Assyrian treaties, especially with the curses.

Considering this political situation, it is my contention that Hosea's
concern with the nation's turning from YHWH relates mainly to political
apostasy. Hosea criticizes the leaders' extensive political maneuvering
and warns of the negative effects it will have on the state. Although it has
frequently been argued that Hosea opposed all foreign alliances as rebellions against YHWH,[11] I argue instead that he opposes breaking an alliance and rebelling against Assyria. A policy of non-alignment was not a
serious option in the political context. When Ephraim appeals to Egypt
and rebels against Assyria, it violates a treaty sworn in the name of
YHWH. Hosea's oracles describe YHWH's displeasure with such viola-
tions and his threats to enforce the curses listed in the vassal treaty between Israel and Assyria.[12]

The language of masculinity pervades the language of politics in the
ANE.[13] In particular, warfare is frequently presented in gendered terms.
The Assyrian king proclaims that he is a man, unequalled by rivals.[14] In
the biblical texts warriors encourage each other to be men and fight (1

Sam 4:9).[15] At the end of a battle the victors strengthen their masculinity, while the losers are feminized, as can be seen in both Assyrian reliefs and in written descriptions of battle.[16] The construction of masculinity is not limited to warfare, however, and several other components are addressed both in Assyrian and biblical texts. The ability to provide for and protect one's family is a key feature and is threatened in the treaty curses, which predict famine and destruction for the rebellious vassal king. Because imagery of politics and warfare occurs so extensively in Hosea, and those fields are closely related to gender construction, an analysis of the book in terms of masculinity provides a fruitful perspective on the text. Masculinity has components of activity (military advances, making political decisions), potency (prowess on the battlefield, providing for the protection and well-being of the family or kingdom), and goodness (upholding one's duties and honor). A social space defined by these factors, while certainly not all-inclusive, provides a basic understanding of the ways in which a variety of images affect the perception of masculinity.

This study contributes to the scholarship of Hosea in three areas. The first is the application of masculinity theory to Hosea. Masculinity theory has begun to be used in biblical studies, and recent works have explored the personification of Jerusalem in the prophetic texts from this perspective.[17] Hosea has not yet received a systematic treatment, although a few works have opened some avenues for investigation.[18] The second contribution is the identification of male imagery. Because of the extensive concentration on the female imagery in Hosea, little attention has focused on the presence of men in the text, even though the last eleven chapters mention women only in passing, while containing several types of male imagery. The third contribution is the use of an analytical model of social and semantic space to evaluate the rhetorical effect of the metaphors in Hosea. The model, which defines social space with three axes, provides a useful and easily applicable tool to compare and evaluate the identities predicated on entities by various metaphors.

My study unfolds as follows. In this chapter I briefly survey the recent literature on Hosea. I discuss some of the issues in the composition history and genre of the text before focusing on the studies of metaphor within the text. Reflecting the emphasis of studies on Hosea, most of the chapter is devoted to interpretations of the marriage metaphor in chs. 1–3. Rather than addressing individual studies, I have chosen to separate the scholarship into major interpretive perspectives and to discuss each perspective, bringing in the ideas of their major proponents as appropriate. The interpretive positions for the marriage metaphor are theological, religious, political, economic, and metaphorical. In addition, I discuss three comprehensive studies of the metaphors in the book.

Chapter 2 lays out my methodology, beginning with a discussion of masculinity theory. Gender construction in a culture is a complex process, involving issues of familial and social structure, economics, politics, and public and private interactions. In most cultures masculinity is constructed as the more public, active, powerful, and aggressive gender. Alterations in the social perception of a man's masculinity affect his social status in many areas. I argue that Hosea's audience is predominantly composed of elite males who have a very masculine social persona. The rhetoric of Hosea attacks this masculinity. In order to analyze how the rhetoric works, I use a model of social space developed by anthropologist James Fernandez, who argues that cultures use metaphors to create social identities and to establish, maintain, and alter social relationships. The effect of metaphoric predications can be assessed by plotting them onto a social space defined by the three axes of activity, potency, and goodness.

In chapter 3, I explore the gender imagery in Hosea. First, I survey how masculinity studies have been applied to biblical texts. Next, I move to an analysis of the female imagery. I discuss the traditional interpretations of the female imagery as a description of a fertility cult. I divide the imagery into the female as subject and the female as object and examine the implications of the female imagery for the masculinity of the audience. I then turn to the male imagery. I have defined seven linguistic markers of masculinity, which I compare to those found in other biblical and ANE texts. After examining how the use of the male imagery affects the perception of the audience's masculinity, I assess the imagery in terms of the axes in social space.

Chapter 4 turns to the non-gender-based imagery. I have divided it into seven categories: parent-child, sickness and healing, hunting and seeking, animal, agriculture, plant, and natural phenomena. Within each of these categories I analyze the identities predicated on Ephraim and YHWH in terms of the axes of activity, potency, and goodness. Finally, I look at how the non-gender-based imagery affects the perception of the masculinity of the audience and YHWH.

Chapter 5 provides a summary of the study and discusses the major trends. I observe the way the rhetoric places YHWH and Ephraim in the social space and indicates the proper relationship between the two. The second part of the chapter discusses subversions of the major trends, especially instability of gender in the imagery applied both to humans and to the divine. The subversions indicate that although a particular concept of masculinity is upheld by the text, it does not represent a monolithic entity.

Composition History

The book of Hosea is subject to much debate concerning its composition history and the state and form of the text. Many commentators over the centuries have found the text difficult in nearly every possible way. Hosea is one of only two prophets addressing the northern kingdom whose work is recorded in the Bible. The material was preserved in Judah, so there is considerable uncertainty about possible different editions of the text.

The first issue concerns how to determine layers of redaction. Scholars have seen different degrees of unity to the text, ranging from the concept that the book contains almost exclusively the words of the prophet to the proposal that the book had over a dozen redactors.[19] Interpreters have used various markers to try to separate redactional layers, including literary or poetic features.[20] Content has also been a popular marker, with the references to Judah, the Davidic monarchy, and the salvation oracles often considered secondary.[21] More recently many scholars have tended to find a unity in the book, even through redactional layers.[22] Others have considered the editing of the book in the context of the minor prophets as a corpus.[23]

A second issue relates to whether the work was preserved from the beginning in written form or whether there was a period of oral transmission. Those who follow the oral transmission path note the difficulty in recovering the *ipsissima verba* of the prophet. Because the oracles were adapted to the tradents' situations before they were written down, they show no redactional seams. Most of these scholars still claim, however, that the oracles are well preserved.[24] A majority of scholars thinks the oracles, though proclaimed orally, were written down fairly quickly, but then underwent various redactions at different periods in Judean history.[25]

A third issue concerns the state of preservation of the text. Most scholars consider the text poorly preserved. Many of the verses are difficult to translate and sometimes seem incomplete. To make matters worse, the book has often appeared to be a collection of short sayings with no clear connections, which adds to the difficulty in interpretation.[26] As Kuhl notes: "The very corrupt nature of the text that has come down to us and the fragmentary character of many of the oracles add considerably to the difficulty of understanding the book as a whole."[27] My study follows those discussed below who do see a coherence in the book. While the individual sayings may not connect directly with those around them, there are concentrations of themes in certain chapters, and the rhetorical force and literary construction of the book create a greater unity. The text does offer considerable translation difficulties, but some of these can be clarified by examining their relationship to these larger themes. I follow those who date most of the oracles to the time of Hosea, while holding that any later additions carry similar rhetorical force.

Genre and Rhetorical Studies

Scholars have attempted to address some of the issues of form and unity through analysis of Hosea's genre. Prophetic literature itself comprises several genres, which have various literary and institutional uses and serve particular rhetorical ends. Studies that explore the genre of Hosea thus often lead into comments on the nature of prophetic rhetoric.

Gerald Morris cautions that one should be careful about categorizing the genre of the prophetic books, noting that people often label them as both rhetoric and poetry in a rather off-hand way without paying much attention to the attributes of each of these genres.[28] He argues that rhetoric is outwardly focused, dependent on context, and functional. Poetry, on the other hand, is introspective, independent of context, and without a specific purpose.[29] While not denying that the prophetic books, including Hosea, are a mixture of the two genres of rhetoric and poetry, he places Hosea more clearly into the poetic category. In his analysis of verbal repetition and wordplay, he finds that Hosea's repetition is not typically the repetition of a rhetorical idea, meant to clarify a point of argument.

Hosea employs, rather, repetition of words and wordplays that tend to complicate more than to clarify and that lead to a less coherent form overall.[30] Morris argues that the reader picks up different features, coherencies, and literary artistry in the text when it is read as poetry rather than as rhetoric.[31] While this may be true, drawing rigid genre distinctions does not seem to be particularly useful, as even his study implies. On the one hand, Morris draws a clear distinction between poetry and rhetoric, as far as its purpose and structure. On the other hand he claims that the prophets utilize a mixture of the two.

Martin Buss also tries to tease out different genres in Hosea, but does not attempt to establish firm categories.[32] In his study of the forms of speech, the content of the oracles, and the nature of their communication as divine or human speech, he first sets out to delimit the units of the oracles. He notes that although each utterance itself may be quite short, the sayings are often assembled into larger collections through catch phrases. The book as a whole contains both poetic and narrative speech. The utterances are divided between speech purported to be divine and that attributed to the prophet. Most of the divine speech addresses the audience in the first person and second person, while the prophetic speech happens in second and third person. Buss observes that judgments and oracles from the divine tend to be more general and clothed in figurative language, whereas those of the prophet are more specific.[33] Buss identifies several forms of speech that occur in the text: threats, accusations, exhortations, parenesis, references to history, and statements of hope.

Buss also considers the types of words and images Hosea uses and compares them to similar language in the other prophets, the psalms, and comparable ANE literature. Buss argues that rather than trying to divide a prophetic book like Hosea into genres, it is more fruitful to examine the negative and positive messages of the prophet.[34] To this end he analyzes the common categories of enmity, as represented by enemies, hunting and trapping imagery, and wild animals; separation and negation, including the disownment terminology; judicial terminology; and the "Day of YHWH" language that announces destruction. Further, he looks at the types of accusations leveled, some of which are against general and moral evil, and others of which address religious evil or sins against YHWH. Positive terminology, relating to the hope for the future of Israel, is also employed, and includes language of seeking and knowing, the fear of YHWH, acting with *hesed,* healing, light, and fertility. With the negative statements, Hosea derides the weakness of the nation and condemns the ideas of self-sufficiency and pride.[35] In the positive statements, all hope of restoration is initiated by the divine, whose purpose is fulfilled despite human action. The prophet exhorts the people to acknowledge their dependence upon YHWH and to give up self-assertion.[36] Buss ultimately sees a strongly eschatological bent to Hosea's preaching.

Focusing more on the negative rhetoric, Paul Franklyn examines what he calls the curse oracles of ch. 13.[37] He places them in a predominantly cultic setting, proposing that they were uttered during the celebration of the New Moon festival. The rhetoric of the chapter consists mainly of covenant curses, which critique the apostasy of the cult of the northern kingdom. The curses bring together older traditions through figurative language and reassemble them into a new message.[38] While he acknowledges that others have seen historical references in the chapter, Franklyn does not focus on them. Instead he thinks that the liturgical nature of parts of the text points toward a cultic emphasis, so that the major focus is a critique of the syncretism of the worship of Baal with that of YHWH.

Historical and social concerns are of more interest to other interpreters, especially those who study the rhetorical aspects of Hosea's oracles. R. L. Lewis analyzes the social and historical context of the prophet, along with the figures of speech and rhetorical techniques he used. He tries to determine the style of speaking, the types of oratorical appeals he used, and the emotional impact of his preaching.[39] Richard D. Israel looks at what he calls protasis-apodosis text structures, which include prophetic conditional statements and judgments.[40] He analyzes the grammar and syntax of verses that seem to fit this two-part structure, noting that in 90% of the cases in Hosea, either the protasis is temporally assigned to the past or the apodosis is assigned to the future, so that the prophetic proclamation is situated on the temporal axis between the two.[41] In general, the protasis is related to the subject (say, Israel) and the wrongs it has committed, while the apodosis is focused on YHWH and the actions YHWH will take against the subjects.[42] Determination of the protasis-apodosis structure is more a matter of function than of grammatical or syntactical features, as the form itself can vary.[43] The main function of this pattern is that it provides an interpretation for YHWH's intervention (the outcome) and relates it to the current situation (the acts).[44] The structures thus serve the prophetic purpose of linking the actions of the people to the consequences that follow.

These studies are representative of those that have explored the possible genres and rhetorical structures of Hosea. The work has contributed to the understanding of the complexity of the text and the way it functions, but the differences in the studies underscore the difficulties of classifying it with any certainty. Because of this difficulty, in this study I will not directly address the issue of genre. I will instead focus on the metaphors and images in the book and examine the rhetorical implications of the images themselves, without considering the larger types of literary structures in which the metaphors may be embedded.

Studies of the Marriage Metaphor

The Nature of Hosea's Marriage

Hosea contains a multitude of metaphor fields, but scholarship has focused overwhelmingly on the marriage metaphor portrayed in chs. 1–3. Throughout the history of commentary on Hosea, interpreters have been obsessed with determining the nature of Hosea's marriage.[45] The question of whether it refers to an actual marriage, a vision, or an allegorical tale has generated much discussion.

A major concern in interpretation has been how to deal with the scandalous idea that God would order Hosea to marry a prostitute.[46] Patristic interpreters tried to eliminate this problem by claiming the marriage was completely allegorical, referring exclusively to the relationship between YHWH and Israel. Origen and Jerome are the most notable proponents of this view.[47] Modern interpreters are sometimes also drawn to such a perspective, although they may date the allegorization of the tale to a later redactor.[48]

Ibn Ezra promoted the position that Hosea's marriage was a prophetic vision, based on the belief that all prophecy came in nocturnal visions. He could not accept the idea that God would order Hosea to marry a prostitute in real life. Other medieval Jewish commentators followed him, as did Calvin.[49] Because the understanding that prophecies and sign acts necessarily came through visions has fallen out of favor, few modern interpreters hold this position.

The most commonly argued position in the nineteenth and twentieth centuries is that Hosea's marriage actually happened. It is clearly described in chs. 1 and 3, and, many commentators hold, in ch. 2 as well. The prophet came to see his "personal tragedy" as a symbol of the relationship between YHWH and Israel.[50] Most people who promote this understanding still resist the idea that Hosea knowingly married a woman who was promiscuous or a prostitute. The most popular explanation is that the story is told in retrospect. When Hosea married Gomer, she was "decent."[51] It was only in looking back on his experience that Hosea could characterize her as a promiscuous woman, which helped him to envision the relationship between God and the wayward Israel.[52] Only a few seriously consider the idea that God actually did order Hosea to marry a woman who Hosea knew was promiscuous before marriage.[53] Many modern commentators do not take a position on the nature of Hosea's marriage, citing the lack of evidence, but treat it as symbolic, especially ch. 2.[54]

Interpretations of the Marriage Metaphor

The discussion of the nature of Hosea's marriage has largely arisen out of the perceived need to protect the reputations of Gomer, Hosea, and YHWH, although the concern for Gomer largely relates to Hosea's status as a prophet and the rationality of YHWH's command. Regardless of what actually happened, the story itself remains and serves as a metaphor for YHWH's relationship with Samaria and Israel. There is even less consensus, however, about what the marriage means metaphorically than what it may have been literally. The interpretations of the marriage can be divided into several broad categories, which I have identified loosely as theological, religious, political, economic, and metaphorical.

Theological Interpretations
Historically most of the focus has been on the implication of the marriage metaphor for the understanding of God and the relationship between God and the people. Various commentators have interpreted the relationship positively or negatively. Generally the more negative view of God emerges in more recent studies.

YHWH as Loving Husband. Until fairly recently Hosea has often been identified as the "prophet of love."[55] God's love for Israel is reflected in the great love of the prophet for his wife. The pathos of the cuckolded prophet makes him particularly sensitive to the nature of the divine message—that of love.[56] Although the first three chapters of Hosea contain many expressions of vengeance and punishment, these indicate the feelings a husband would have for his wayward wife, and are the result of love and the desire for reconciliation, which in the end outweighs the feelings of vengeance.[57] The punishments and corrections are, in fact, evidence of God's love for Israel, used to try to make her return to him.[58] Chapter 3 shows that the husband ultimately buys her out of slavery to restore her to himself after her unfaithfulness.[59]

YHWH as Abusive Husband. The image of God as husband, justified in using any and all means of correction to express love for the people and to cause them to repent, found deep resonance in commentators for most of Hosea's interpretive history. The emergence of feminist scholarship, however, has brought to the forefront many troubling aspects of this metaphor. Of particular concern is the effect the portrayal of the divine-human relationship has for human understanding of relations between men and women. As Rut Törnqvist explains:

> What makes prophetical texts so dangerous for women is that they have been interpreted as "proof texts" and used to define and describe females and wives as generally morally and sexually corrupt, so females/women are consequently to be punished by males, i.e. husbands and other male authorities, and in the outermost instance by the husband *par preference*, Yahweh himself.[60]

The negative portrayal of the wife/woman underscores the strictly hierarchical and patriarchal nature of the relationship, and the violent depictions in these texts, which have been preserved without much question in the church canon, have been used to justify violence against women.[61]

In order to articulate these concerns more clearly, some scholars have applied methods from feminist analysis of modern pornography to the female sexual imagery in Hosea. Pornography often consists of violent depictions of desire that make a woman into a less than human object, who often is complicit in her abuse. The wayward wife in Hosea acts in such a way that she seems to bring upon herself stripping and exposure under the male gaze. Athalya Brenner labels such imagistic rhetoric "pornoprophetics." Although it was initially directed against a predominantly male audience, in order to shame them into reform,[62] the implications of the imagery have extended much farther.

Drorah Setel expands on the pornographic characteristics of the imagery. She observes that pornography is "both a description of and a tool for maintaining male domination of female sexuality."[63] The text of Hosea 1–3 shows several instances of such control. The wife is impugned and subject to punishment for acting the harlot, because her sexuality is properly under the control of her husband for whom she bears heirs. Chapter 2 in particular shows the complete dependence of the woman on the man for her foodstuffs and clothing, which may not be an accurate picture of reality. The passage accents her passivity. The wife is closely linked with the land and the result of her promiscuity is infertility on a large scale, showing that reproduction and fertility is under the control of the male, YHWH, not the woman. Setel notes that in this passage sexual unfaithfulness is transformed from an economic ill into an ethical ill.[64]

The negative portrayal of the wife/woman as the unfaithful and immoral partner reinforces other cultural stereotypes of the woman as Other and as the one associated with sin and evil. Alice Keefe claims that in the biblical texts female sexuality is depicted as "dangerous, derivative, and 'other'" and is associated with pollution, sin, and death. "In contrast, male sexuality is linked with God by the covenant in circumcision and protected in sacral law as inviolate (Deut. 25:11–12)."[65] Hosea's use of female sexual imagery extends this association.

Yvonne Sherwood concentrates on the "dangerous" nature of Gomer in relation to a patriarchal hierarchy. She represents the uncontrolled woman who must be boxed in, her ways "hedged up." Her existence and way of life threatens the established systems, which place women in a subservient position.

> In contrast to the conventional tableau of grace, Hosea 1–3 can also be read as a tableau of patriarchy, the establishment of a system by the systematic exclusion, entrapment and repression of the female will. The threat of the 'woman of harlotry' is that of the countervoice, the opposite which, if listened to, threatens to relativize and subvert the absolute and univocal main/male perspective.[66]

Sherwood claims that Gomer's very presence in the text is a threat, though the text also works to contain and punish her. Faced with this threat, many interpreters have chosen to "tame" her by proposing that she was chaste at betrothal, just a vision, or a symbol. Gomer's threat to the patriarchal order is also highlighted by Teresa Hornsby, who argues that Gomer, as a free-willed woman, is eventually brought under control in the text. Originally Gomer was a professional prostitute, who, as such, was economically independent, but was eventually bought (or retained for a considerable time) by an obsessive and jealous client.[67] The implication of these studies is that the writers and interpreters of the biblical text have, consciously or unconsciously, used a conception of the divine-human relationship to subordinate women.

Both the loving husband and abusive husband views are primarily theological interpretations of the book. While their proponents sometimes address historical concerns, especially with respect to the nature of Hosea's marriage, the main concerns are the implications of the text for understanding God in the present day and the continuing usefulness of the metaphor. The two views clearly lead to different conclusions about whether the text should continue to be used for theological purposes.

Religious Interpretations
In addition to providing material for contemporary theological discussions, the marriage metaphor has frequently been analyzed for information about the religious situation at the time of its proclamation. Much of its interpretation has centered on the polemic against the idols, high places, and baalim, which is intertwined with the language of "harlotry" (זנה). Until fairly recently scholars have consistently understood these references to harlotry as literal, specifically associated with a fertility cult of Baal. I will discuss the supposed fertility cult and its critics more thoroughly in ch. 3.

With or without the trappings of a sex cult, many scholars interpret Hosea's polemic as being against the worship of foreign gods, especially of Baal. The text speaks of the baalim, Baal-Peor, high places, green trees, and idols, all things commonly associated with the worship of Canaanite gods in the Bible. Scholars have treated Baal as a fertility god, which explains the many references to agricultural bounty in Hosea and the threats of its loss. The fact that the Deuteronomist often used the phrase "whore after" to indicate religious infidelity has encouraged a religious interpretation.

There is wide consensus that the "lovers" in ch. 2 allude to other gods, or at least to a syncretism between Baal and YHWH.[68] Many of these interpreters also take for granted that Hosea assumes a covenant between YHWH and Israel. The marriage thus represents the covenant, which Israel violates by going after other gods.[69] The marriage metaphor plays off the Canaanite sacred marriage ritual to symbolize religious apostasy.[70] Herbert Marks argues that Hosea is condemning a violation of the covenant in which Israel is worshipping other gods, while ignoring other aspects of covenant law, such as prohibitions of adultery, theft, and murder.[71] Stienstra argues that the religious apostasy symbolized by the wife's adultery will eventually lead to the destruction of the land.

> Hosea's metaphor may have resulted from these two separate experiences. He is thinking of the land, which will become bare, and at the same time he envisages the foreign punishment of stripping the adulteress. The punishment is especially apt precisely because it is not Israelite practice, but Israel has gone "whoring" after foreign gods, breaking the law of YHWH and thus incurring a "foreign" punishment.[72]

Because Israel has broken the covenant with YHWH, Israel will be punished by the customs of those it has pursued.

Mary Joan Winn Leith, on the other hand, understands the punishments described in ch. 2 as covenant curses, which Israel has incurred by breaking the covenant with YHWH.[73] The curses relate to the sterility of the land, in language that sounds like a reversal of creation. She argues that Hosea demythologizes one of the main creation stories in the HB, that of the divine warrior, an image also associated with Baal. Hosea's message here has three 'movements': accusation, punishment, and restoration. The accusation takes the form of the covenant curses. In the punishment section, Israel's identity is negated, and it is returned to the chaos of the wilderness. Israel is stripped naked as the day it was born. Finally, Israel is restored to a better place. A new relationship with YHWH is established and the earth will be restored to a peaceful state. Leith notes the similarities between this and rites of passage. Though she does not claim that Hosea explicitly describes a rite of passage for Israel, the use of the marriage metaphor and the naming of the children create similarities. First, Israel is isolated and its identity obscured. Then it emerges with a new identity and a new relationship to YHWH.

The creation of a new relationship, though not in explicitly mythological terms, forms the basis of another interpretation of the marriage metaphor, that Hosea attempted to usher Israel into the age of monolatry or even monotheism, proclaiming a "YHWH alone" message. Else Holt argues that Hosea used Israel's traditions of election, including the Jacob cycle and the Exodus tradition, to insist that as Israel has been chosen, it needs to commit itself exclusively to YHWH in return. According to this analysis, Israel has not abandoned a previously sworn covenant, but is emerging from a polytheistic culture into one devoted to YHWH.[74] Gale Yee also proposes that Hosea preached a YHWH-alone ideology, the need for which arose from turbulent domestic and foreign relations.[75]

Rut Törnkvist also sees an attempt to redefine the nature of Israel's identity and religious life. She proposes that the sexual metaphors, which are connected with national and religious identity, structure debate about "which God is allowed and which is not, and which woman is allowed and which is not."[76] The identity of the nation and people is as of yet fluid, in that the people think they may still belong to YHWH and someone else. Hosea tries to define Israel's identity more narrowly. Among the identities being excluded are those associated with goddess worship.

> In this sense adultery, rape, or the people "going astray" are not just violations of commandments, they are violations of various identity-constructs of "Israel."...[Chapters 1–3] reflect the anxiety and holocaust of the Goddess and her worship in the Israelite society. The text also mirrors the repression of women from the cultic sphere. The battle is fought on the cultural and symbolic level.[77]

As the cult narrows to a monolatrous worship of YHWH, it also narrows to a male-dominated system.

Margaret Odell interprets Hosea 4 (and 2) as a struggle between the levitical and Aaronide priesthood, with the added implication that the triumph of the former led to the suppression of the role of women in the cult (see also Num 12).[78] She sees evidence of the struggle in the enigmatic verse 4:5: "I will destroy your mother." Mother, she argues, refers to a cultic official, a female leader in communal festivals.[79] She observes that priests and prophets in northern Israelite narratives are sometimes called "father" (Judg 17:10; 18:9; 2 Kgs 2:12; 6:21; 13:14), so she postulates that a female cult leader would be called mother, although she admits to a paucity of evidence.[80]

A few other scholars interpret the religious polemic in Hosea's oracles as a power struggle between religious factions. Stephen Cook argues that Hosea represents a lineage-based circle of priests who had power in the pre-state period. His circle is in conflict with the centralized state cult, which arose with the monarchy.[81] The state cult incorporates syncretistic elements because of the increased concern with fertility in a centralized economy.[82] Hosea uses cultic language, revealing him as an insider, but often does so to satirize the cult, which indicates his disenfranchisement.[83]

Teresa Hornsby also sees internecine strife in the text, but from the post-exilic period, between the returning exiles and those in the land, a situation similar to that in Isa 56–66. Gomer represents Israel's former glory, as an independent prostitute. She is pursued by an obsessive client, who eventually confines her and reduces her to a "worthless thing." Hornsby's reconstruction seems unlikely, in large part because she claims that in ch. 2 YHWH represents the foreigners and the priestly class that have vitiated Israel's strength.[84] It is difficult to imagine that the author would utilize YHWH as a symbol for something else and similarly difficult to believe that Israel would be idealized as a prostitute.

Political Interpretations

While the majority of scholars contend that Hosea's main focus in chs. 1–3 is the corruption of religion in Israel, it is not the only interpretation. A second interpretive angle understands the object of the prophet's condemnation to be improper foreign and domestic politics, rather than a pursuit of foreign gods. Because of the integration of politics, religion, and economics in Israelite society, a political view does not exclude a religious interpretation of some of the imagery, it just shifts the focus. Most commentators acknowledge that many parts of the book address political issues, and a few have investigated the political themes in chs. 1–3.[85]

The political implications of the marriage metaphor feature in Julie Galambush's study of personified Jerusalem.[86] While her study focuses on Ezekiel, she discusses the marriage metaphor in the earlier texts of Jeremiah and Hosea. There are several issues to consider when interpreting the marriage metaphor from a political perspective. These include the entity that the wife represents, the nature of the lovers, and the object of Hosea's condemnation.

Identity of the Wife. When the marriage metaphor is used in Jeremiah and Ezekiel, the identity of the wife is fairly clear: Jerusalem, and in Ezekiel, Jerusalem and Samaria. The representation of the metaphor is more complicated in Hosea, because of the presence of the sign act of the marriage of Hosea and Gomer.[87] It is still probable that the wife represents the capital city of Samaria, even though it goes against the consensus that the wife represents Israel as a whole. There are several reasons to understand the wife as Samaria.[88] The first is the issue of gender. Nations and peoples take a masculine gender in Hebrew texts.[89] Cities, on the other hand, take the feminine gender. Andrew Dearman takes issue with this identification, arguing that Samaria is not mentioned in chs. 1–3 and appears relatively infrequently in the book as a whole. He also notes that the daughter Lo-Ruhamah represents Israel, so that gender is not determinative.[90] There is a qualitative difference, however, between the situation in ch. 1, which is allegorical and is largely carried out through symbolic names, and ch. 2, where the metaphor is less constrained and no names are mentioned.

Second, while the threat to strip the wife in ch. 2 is often thought to be a standard punishment for adultery in the ANE, it is not indeed the case.[91] Of the ANE texts used to testify to the practice of stripping, only one actually mentions adultery, and it is a very fragmentary text, the context of which is difficult to determine.[92] The other texts discuss divorce rather than adultery, and the practice of stripping, or rather, of leaving one's clothes behind, seems to be a concern more related to economics than to humiliation.[93] In fact, several of the texts refer to cases where the woman wants to remarry after the death of her husband, obviously not a case of adultery.[94] Brad Kelle observes that the image base of marriage and divorce does not include punishments such as the humiliation and stripping found in Hosea. Based on legal texts from the ANE and Elephantine communities it appears that property, finances, and inheritance are usually the main concerns in cases of divorces and remarriage.[95] Several verses in Hos 2 show concern with economics, mentioning grain, wine, and oil repeatedly (7, 10, 11, 14, 17, 24). The legitimacy of the children is also addressed in 2:6, suggesting that issues of divorce are important in the chapter, even if they do not relate to the sexual imagery.

The sexual imagery comes instead from the second image base, that of warfare. Language of sexual violence is common in threats to cities personified as female figures in the Bible.[96] The threats of punishments described in ch. 2 are also found in the parallel texts in Jeremiah and Ezekiel, where they clearly apply to Jerusalem and Samaria. Sexually-tinged punishment in the cognate literatures is mostly associated with the destruction of capital cities.[97] It thus seems likely that the wife in ch. 2 represents Samaria. At the time of the composition of these oracles, however, Israel was greatly reduced in territory, consisting mostly of Samaria and its immediate environs, so threats against Samaria are not significantly different from threats against the nation of Israel.

Identity of the Lovers. A second issue is the nature of the lovers in Hosea. William Moran introduced the idea that the use of the term love (אהב) in Deuteronomy has political connotations.[98] He observes that in several ANE texts, such as those found at Amarna, the vassal kings claim to love their suzerains and vice versa. A report to the king Rib-Adda, describing a revolt, reads: "Behold the city! Half of it loves the sons of 'Abd-Aširta [who fostered the rebellion], half of it (loves) my lord."[99] Assyrian texts of the 7th c. between Esarhaddon and Assurbanipal and their vassals show the same language of love.[100]

J. A. Thompson applied Moran's study of the covenantal meaning of love to the prophetic texts, suggesting that many of the references to lovers refer to political involvements (Ezek 16, 23; Hos 8:8–9; Jer 2:25, 33; 22:20–23; Lam 1:2–3, 19).[101] In suzerainty treaties, love means an unquestioning commitment of the parties involved to the covenant and its demands. Thompson pulled back from claiming this meaning of love for Hos 2, envisioning instead a related religious meaning, suggesting that Israel could be loving gods who are rival suzerains to YHWH.

The later prophetic texts make it clear that the lovers are foreign nations. Ezekiel 16:26 reads: "You played the whore with your neighbors, the Egyptians—you multiplied your harlotries to anger me." Similarly Ezek 16:28–29 accuses: "In your insatiable lust you also played the whore with the Assyrians; you played the whore with them, but were still unsatisfied. You multiplied your harlotries with Chaldea, that land of traders; yet even with this you were not satisfied." Galambush also notes that the term baalim is used in the plural, mostly with the definite article, which indicates that rather than the proper name of a god it more likely represents foreign powers.[102] Baalim is similarly used with the definite article in Hosea, and the larger context of the book suggests that the interpretation of the lovers and baalim as foreign nations is probable.[103]

Nature of the Offense. If the wife is understood to be Samaria and the lovers to be foreign nations, then the nature of the offense is clearly political, relating especially to foreign policy. Kelle argues that the oracle as a whole critiques the political actions of the rulers of Samaria, who were breaking their vassal treaties with Assyria, which would lead to their destruction. He argues that while the gender imagery does not directly address religious issues as has usually been assumed, it does use religious allusions to lend support to the seriousness of the situation.[104] Hosea's use of gender imagery thus has economic, political, and social, as well as religious connotations.

The religious language can be explained by the nature of ANE treaties. In both alliance and vassal treaties the gods of both sides were witnesses to the treaties and served as its guarantors.[105] Thus breaking a covenant sworn in the name of a god was an offense against that god, an action that impugned the power and honor of that god. The effect on the god of breaking the treaties was not unlike the loss of honor and status of the husband whose wife committed adultery. Thus, as Galambush observes, the marriage metaphor was an apt vehicle to convey the nature of the offense.

> Not only would Yahweh suffer dishonor as a king whose vassals had disobeyed, but also as a god whose name had been defiled. This aspect of Israelite apostasy—the defilement of the divine name—may have contributed more than any other to the use of the adultery metaphor to describe apostasy.[106]

The understanding that an offense against a political treaty impugned the name of the god can be seen in the writings of the time. For example, in the annals of Assurbanipal, an entry describing an Arab revolt reads:

> The People of Arubu asked one and other [*sic*] again and again, 'Why has such an evil thing as this overtaken Arubu?' (and) they say, 'Because we have not kept the mighty oaths of the god Assur, we have sinned against the favor shown us by Assurbanipal, the king beloved of Enlil.[107]

The violation of the treaty violated the oath guaranteed by the god Assur and incurred his wrath.[108]

One advantage of understanding the sin against YHWH as a violation of a political treaty is that it eliminates the issue of whether the concept of a covenant between YHWH and Israel existed in the 8th c. Despite the common consensus among Hosea scholars that such a covenant is present in Hosea, and that it is Israel's defiance of it that constitutes the adultery, there are also a significant number of scholars who argue that this concept of covenant did not develop until later. Wellhausen, who raised the issue toward the end of the 19th c., claims that the relationship between God and Israel had initially been expressed through more natural bonds, especially that of parent-child. The conception of a covenant between God and Israel developed as a result of the preaching of the prophets, rather than being an assumption of theirs.[109]

Even scholars who support the idea of an early covenant between YHWH and Israel acknowledge the role of gods in overseeing political treaties.[110] Max Weber proposes that the covenant between YHWH and the people held their political treaties to an even higher standard.

> Hence, whenever the confederate people *per se* entered a *berith*, he, the god, was an ideational party to it. All violations of the holy enactments were not merely violations of orders guaranteed by him as other gods guarantee their orders, but violations of the most solemn contractual obligations toward him personally.[111]

The connection between political and religious obligations in international treaties allows for an interpretation of the marriage metaphor that does not confine itself to religious apostasy and that fits with the political concerns expressed in chs. 4–14.

Economic Interpretations
Related to a political interpretation of the metaphors in Hosea is the economic interpretation put forth by some scholars. The economic interpretation is based on an understanding that the 8th c. marked a time of economic centralization and agricultural intensification. Economic centralization was driven in part by political centralization and the pressures of foreign tributary relations.

Gale Yee provides what she calls a Marxist-influenced materialist-ideological interpretation. Marxist theory provides the insight that "literature is grounded in historical real-life relations," while an explicitly ideological interpretation focuses on how a text is constructed in a way to promote a particular viewpoint and to hide others.[112] Thus two tasks of ideological criticism are "an *extrinsic* ideological critique that takes seriously the stages of ideological production, particularly within the socioeconomic world of the biblical text, and an *intrinsic* critique that examines the internal rhetoric of the text and how it reproduces that social world."[113] The historical context does not simply provide the background for a text, but creates the textual symbolizations. "Any analysis of the text needs to consider how the text rhetorically duplicates, legitimates, modifies, or conflicts with the ideologies that produce it."[114] The text itself offers insight into the limits of the construction of this symbolization in a given social formation. Therefore, ideological interpretations need to account for the socio-political reality of the text's production.[115]

Hosea was written in a socio-political system in which Assyria dominated. Imposition of tributes caused considerable changes in the Israelite economy. Yee argues that what was formerly a familial mode of production, in which the peasants kept most of the surplus, changed into a tributary mode that was dominated by large estates or latifundia. The elites consolidated their own power by increasing their holdings, which was facilitated by the imposition of heavy taxes that increased the indebtedness of the small farmers, who lost their land. Production shifted from diversified plantings to a concentration on cash crops: oil, wine, and grain, which could be used to pay the tributes. This trend toward monoculture made agricultural economy more vulnerable to bad weather, diseases, and insects.[116]

Four major factors influenced by foreign tributary relations contributed to the socio-economic situation addressed by Hosea:

> agricultural intensification of royal cash crops; political instability within the Israelite royal court, coupled with the external threat of Assyrian invasion; conflicts within Israelite polytheism; and socioeconomic relations among the religious and political elite: the kings, priests, and prophets.[117]

Yee argues that promiscuity in Hosea symbolizes the oppressive foreign and domestic policies resulting from these pressures.[118] Although politics and economics are the primary targets of Hosea's polemic, religion is not excluded, because of the integration of the three. Cult centers were centers of political and economic power, as well as of religious activity.[119] Priests colluded with other elites to control the flow of the cash crops and tributes. Israel, she claims, was not yet monotheistic, but Hosea promoted a "polemical monolatry."[120] Hosea's proclamation of the "YHWH alone" movement was primarily a criticism of the ways in which the Israelite cult intersected the political and economic interests of the monarchy, especially in foreign affairs. "Hosea was principally concerned with how the public male face of the cult, found in the sanctuary and priesthood, served the state."[121] The need for a strong monolatry or monotheism developed out of domestic instability and problematic foreign relations.

> [The insistence on YHWH alone] was at the same time a fight against the social and political developments of the middle and late monarchy, against a disintegration of Israelite society into competing classes and its political alliances and the foreign infiltration into it. It was only in the course of this controversy that the prohibitions against alien gods were formulated.[122]

Religious polemic thus served a larger concern with political, social, and economic changes, which Hosea saw as detrimental to society.

Alice Keefe offers a similar socio-economic analysis of Hosea. Rather than focusing on the marriage metaphor as an isolated figure, she reads it in the larger context of the family metaphor, including the children. As such it brings out the destruction of the family-centered economic and political system and the move towards centralization.

> From this perspective, it appears that Hosea's trope is not really a marriage metaphor at all, but a family metaphor, which draws upon the centrality of the family in traditional Israelite life as a way of speaking to the disintegration and impending destruction of that way of life brought about by the self-aggrandizing practices of Israel's elite establishment.[123]

As a representative of the social body, whose actions are leading toward an ever more stratified social organization, the woman pursues her lovers. Keefe reads the baalim as symbols of particular land and power structures and economic relations. The political alignments of the political elite created certain economic power structures based on moveable trade products, especially cash crops, that exploited the peasant classes.[124] References to fornication and worship of other gods "serve as alternating and intersecting tropes for inappropriate alliances or commercial 'intercourse,' and point towards the situation of Israel in the midst of a booming international market economy." [125] The social body of the nation is represented in the text as the female body, and thus the rhetoric against the wife should be viewed in socio-economic terms.

Metaphor Theoretical Interpretations

Religious, political, and economic interpretations all rely heavily on a study of the socio-historical setting of the text. Studies utilizing contemporary metaphor theory concentrate on the metaphors themselves and may or may not delve into the social context of their composition. Instead they examine the ways in which metaphors structure the way people think about the world.

While acknowledging the importance of understanding a metaphor's relation to the historical and literary contexts out of which it develops, R. Abma cautions that there is not a one-to-one correspondence between the image and the historical reality. Such caution is particularly in order when discussing metaphors for the divine, including the marriage metaphor.

> In order to understand this metaphor one must possess some knowledge of this institution....At the same time, one must be cautious not to overstress the connections between human marriage and the metaphorical marriage between Yhwh and Israel. In the interaction view of metaphor, the tenor, in this case the relation of Yhwh and Israel as depicted elsewhere, has its own characteristics. These may influence the notion of marriage and deflect it in a particular direction, highlighting some elements and disregarding others. A metaphor always involves some freedom to depart from the rules that apply to the domain of the vehicle.[126]

The marriage metaphor portrays an intimate relationship between YHWH and Israel that cannot be relayed in other ways, but the "is not" of the metaphor, the idea that the metaphor by its very definition brings together two elements that are different, must be kept in mind.

Robert Carroll focuses on the "is not" of metaphor in his attempts to downplay the negative affects of the metaphor for contemporary women. He argues that the metaphor is simply a metaphor, not reflecting real women, and thus the text is not misogynistic unless one does not treat the metaphor *as* metaphor, but instead approaches it with a feminist agenda.[127]

> There are no real women in Hosea 1–3, Jeremiah 2–3, 5, Ezekiel 16, 20 and 23, only metaphorized descriptions and representations of imaginary communities

and imagined past histories. It is all in the imagination, in the metaphors and in the ideology.[128]

He makes the point that the intended targets of the metaphor were men, and they would understand it as such, and would not have reinscribed the metaphor on their relationships with their wives. Renita Weems agrees that the target of the metaphor is men, who are cast into the role of the wife. In order for the rhetoric to be effective, however, she argues that the men have to identify with the husband in the metaphor. They have to agree that an adulterous wife is shameful and deserves punishment. Only then can they accept that their own punishment is justified.[129] Thus the male audience continues to accept the power structures presented in the metaphor.

The difficulties of the marriage imagery remain and cannot be dismissed as simply metaphor in the realm of the imagination, because metaphors have power to shape the way a society thinks and develops theological conceptions at a subconscious level. Even though contemporary marriage practices differ from those portrayed in the text, the structures that the marriage metaphor inscribes still have powerful effect today.[130] In particular, the mixture of violence and love in the marriage relationship makes the implications of the metaphor problematic.

Several scholars have examined the portrayal of metaphoric violence in the text and the functions it serves. Baumann asserts that the violence serves to show the power of the husband over the wife, the connection between the wife and the destruction of the land, and the desire on the part of the husband/YHWH to preserve the relationship at all costs.[131] Similarly Weems notes that the sexual violence shows the extent to which Hosea will go to preserve marriage.[132] She articulates two additional functions for the imagery. It first makes the point that reconciliation can only happen after punishment and second demonstrates that the punishment fits the crime. Weems relates the wife's punishment of stripping to the crime of wearing the "vulgar apparel" of adultery and promiscuity upon her face and breasts as described in 2:4.[133]

Because of the problematic elements of the marriage metaphor, Weems brings up the need to use many metaphors to try to understand the nature of the divine-human relationship. The prophet has already realized this concern, as the marriage metaphor with its female subject is only one of many metaphors in Hosea, many of which have male subjects. As Baumann notes, these serve to relativize the importance of the marriage metaphor.[134]

Studies of Other Metaphors

Although far outnumbered by the works on the marriage metaphor, some studies of the other metaphors in Hosea have recently appeared. The more comprehensive studies organize the various metaphors into image fields found throughout the text, although related images tend to cluster in particular chapters. Some of these studies also consider the rhetorical purpose of the concentrated metaphorical language.

In a study on the pictorial language of Hos 14, Bernard Oestreich treats metaphors and similes as part of various image fields with both intra- and inter-textual connections.[135] He observes that some of the metaphors, such as the marriage metaphor and the adopted child metaphor, are more extensively developed and have more emotional impact. At other points in the book, the metaphors switch around rapidly. While not as emotionally powerful, the use of multiple metaphors, rather than an extended metaphor, strengthens an argument by showing support from several different angles. According to Oestreich, Hosea thus uses clusters of metaphors to increase the effectiveness of his arguments.[136]

Oestreich focuses on the metaphors in ch. 14, where he finds several unifying themes. One of the most prominent is royal imagery, which organizes the other metaphors found in the chapter.[137] The roles of the healer, the father of orphans, the evergreen tree, and the nurturing dew are traditionally applied to kings.[138] Many of the images seem to reflect a covenant relationship, but Oestreich does not think that this requires a fully developed concept of a divine-human covenant.[139] Another prominent theme is that of paradise, with the implication that the relationship between YHWH and Israel can be restored through a re-creation. To this end the images in ch. 14 bring together metaphors used throughout the book and place them in a new perspective. Thus the plant imagery that starts in ch. 2 culminates in the image of Israel nurtured as a young plant and God as a luxuriant tree. The disobedient son from chs. 9 and 11 is adopted in 14. The images of un-creation in ch. 2 are reversed with the connotations of the paradisiacal garden and abundant vegetation. The salvation imagery dominating ch. 14 necessitates a reinterpretation of the judgment oracles that precede it.[140]

Oestreich explores the way in which the metaphors shape the rhetoric and arguments of Hosea, especially in the final chapter. Similarly, Gören Eidevall employs a method he calls "metaphorical criticism" to detect a coherency in chs. 4–14, which have often been considered only loosely connected.[141] Eidevall argues that metaphorical criticism is capable of providing insight into the ways that metaphors restructure and redescribe different areas of human experience.[142] As the reader's understanding of the metaphors increases, new insights into the ideological dimensions of the text emerge from the particular metaphorical models employed.[143] Eidevall divides the text into nine units, examines the metaphors and similes employed in each, then looks for themes and models that control the imagery used in that section and examines how they relate to those used in other sections.

As an initial step, Eidevall considers the issue of genre with respect to the oracles in chs. 4–14. He prefers a broad categorization of the types of sayings, as does Buss, who, as noted above, divides the oracles into positive and negative sayings. In addition, Eidevall finds it useful to organize these sayings in the form of a tragicomedy with its inherent ambiguity.[144] He categorizes the imagery in the book in terms of root metaphors and models, which are certain metaphorical concepts that structure the understanding of other metaphors and of the relationships between them. Metaphorical "themes," which are repetitions that do not rise to the level of a root metaphor in creating a conceptual framework, serve a subsidiary structuring function, tying together different sections of the work. They also serve to develop the metaphorical fields.[145]

Metaphors are chosen from several domains of everyday experience, but Eidevall selects the judicial, the covenantal, and the monarchical as the most important models structuring discourse in Hosea, although the agricultural and parental models are also prominent.[146] In the agricultural model, YHWH is the farmer or the landowner. The people are employees, plants, or animals. These relationships promote an understanding of mutual benefit for the parties involved, especially the benefit to the deity from the people.[147] In the parental model, a hierarchical as well as an intimate relationship is portrayed. The judicial model places the people in the role of the accused, whereas YHWH can be litigant, judge, and prosecutor. This model excludes compassion.[148] The covenantal model likewise portrays a hierarchical, largely negative relationship between the people and YHWH. Kingship, the final major model, has possibilities for positive and negative relations between the people and YHWH.[149] Eidevall observes that while the metaphorical relationships between YHWH and the people are hierarchical throughout the book, ch. 14 seems to offer a more reciprocal relationship. "Here, I suggest, the royal ideology has been 'democratized.'"[150] In general, the metaphorical models portraying YHWH as king, judge, and suzerain are used to critique human institutions and leaders.

Various themes serve to create a sense of narrative within the text, both within some of the individual units and as a thread throughout multiple units. Examples of the former include the "whoring" motif found mostly in 4:1–5:7 and the "heart" theme in 6:7–7:16. Other themes, such as "knowing," "healing," "eating/devouring," "returning," and "seeking," can be found in multiple sections. In addition to the themes that tie the oracles together, patterns of literary reversals, which employ a semantic element in multiple contexts that serve to bring out different, often opposite, senses of the element, create a sense of coherence.[151] The reversals often take the form of a switch from threat to promise or from promise to threat. Eidevall notes that the theme of (re)turning is a prime exemplar of this rhetorical device.[152] The reversal process is initiated by YHWH. Some particularly important reversals that form larger patterns in the text are fertility vs. sterility, sacrifice vs. victimization, and the disappearing deity vs. those who seek him. In the final chapter these reversals are resolved in a predicted paradise of lush fertility, a communal meal between people and deity, and the return of the people to a present god.[153]

Emmanuel Nwaoru undertakes a similar comprehensive study of the imagery in Hosea.[154] He observes that metaphors are used to describe YHWH, Israel, and inanimate objects or abstract concepts such as iniquity, the land, wind, and pride, and he seeks to explore the literary and exegetical value of these many images. The images are often related to one another through repetition and through metaphor fields, including family, agriculture, hunting, plants, animals, and healing. Nwaoru points out the hierarchical nature of many of the images relating YHWH and Israel (wife/husband, hunter/prey, physician/patient). Contrasting images are used to describe the two at different points in the book. For example,

YHWH appears as both as shepherd and lion, as a healer and as disease.[155]

Particular themes unify sections of the book. The first three chapters are tied together through the imagery of marriage and promiscuity. The possibility of reconciliation is present, but is, for the most part, initiated by YHWH.[156] Chapters 4–14 are related by the recurring themes of "knowledge," "love," "return," and the verb "to go." Nwaoru argues that the overriding model of the second half of the book is a legal one, with YHWH as the plaintiff and the people as defendants.[157] Nwaoru relates some of the image fields in Hosea with those in other parts of the Bible, as well as ANE texts, and ends his study with a close reading of several of the image fields, including animals, plants, birds, family, and harlotry. For each metaphor field he considers what message Hosea may be trying to communicate through the use of that image. Nwaoru argues that the metaphors serve to express the relationship between YHWH and the people, to relay the complex message of YHWH's judgment and forgiveness, and to create a bond between Hosea and the audience.

Both Eidevall and Nwaoru offer the kind of comprehensive examination of imagery that this study undertakes. Rather than duplicating their careful analyses of specific metaphors, I will focus my analysis on how the various metaphors craft identities for Israel and YHWH and the relationship between them. I propose that the prophet critiques Israel by using metaphors that ascribe to it a socially inferior identity, often parodying images associated with masculinity and power. The ways in which the different metaphorical fields in Hosea work to shape how Israel and YHWH are perceived can be analyzed through a model of social space. To facilitate the analysis I group the metaphors into broad categories and look for trends within the same category (to see, for example, whether Hosea consistently uses certain types of animal imagery for Israel) and between categories (to see if Israel portrayed as an animal and as a child may share similar components of identity or relationship to YHWH). While this procedure removes the images from their surrounding context and loses the nuances of the rhetoric of the individual oracles, which often shift rapidly between metaphorical fields, it allows one both to ascertain the distinctiveness of an individual image in comparison to other images in the same metaphorical field, and to detect more easily broader trends in the rhetoric of metaphors from different fields.

❖CHAPTER TWO❖

Masculinity and Metaphor
An Approach to Analysis

There may even be reason for believing, if we can learn from frogs in this regard, that what our ears, eyes, mouths are really telling our brains—or what the brain finally understands from what it is told—about the bloom and buzz of experience is the essential qualitative pattern of potency, activity, and goodness (edibility) of the things which catch our attention.

James W. Fernandez, *Persuasions and Performances*

Masculinity Theory

In this chapter I will introduce some of the basic ideas of masculinity theory and propose a model of social space developed in the field of cognitive anthropology as helpful ways to analyze the function of the figurative language in Hosea. Masculinity theory is useful for analyzing both the imagery that is obviously related to gender and that which is not, because the majority of figurative language in Hosea reflects an understanding of masculinity similar to the language directly addressing gender. Both types of imagery rhetorically move the audience in the same directions. In order to analyze both the gender and non-gender imagery and their relation to the construction of masculinity in the text, I will utilize the model of anthropologist James Fernandez. His studies explore how societies use metaphorical language to establish, maintain, and change identities and relationships within a particular social setting.[1] Using information from computational linguistics, he has developed a model that can evaluate the movements metaphors cause along the axes of action, potency, and goodness, which are factors directly applicable to an assessment of masculinity.

Audience

To establish the relevance of masculinity theory to the study of Hosea, it is helpful to consider the nature of the implied audience. I am working under the assumption that Hosea's intended audience was predominantly composed of elite males. Several factors support this contention. First, elite men are the primary addressees. Priests, prophets, and rulers are specifically mentioned and their actions and thoughts are discussed (4:5–9; 5:1, 10; 6:9; 7:3, 5, 7, 16; 8:4, 10; 9:15). Second, when women occur in the oracles outside of chs. 1–3, their fathers or husbands are the ones spoken to and held accountable, not the women themselves. For example, in 4:13–14 Hosea complains about the seeming idolatry of the people and continues: "That is why your daughters fornicate and your daughters-in-law commit adultery. I will not punish your daughters for their fornication and your daughters-in-law for their adultery, because they [m] turn aside with prostitutes and sacrifice with the holy women." Third, even in chs. 1–3, where the woman is directly addressed, the wife is identified as a representative of a larger political entity, rather than as an individual woman.[2] Fourth, most of the oracles address issues that concern leaders, rather than common men or women. These topics include foreign alliances, cult matters, political coups, and appointments. Therefore, I argue, along with many other scholars, that even when female imagery is used, it is directed towards males.[3]

Anthropological Perspectives on Masculinity Theory

Because the implied audience is male, examining the nature of masculinity portrayed in the text provides insight into its rhetoric. The field of masculinity studies shares with feminist studies the goal of bringing ideas about gender and sex roles into consciousness.[4] What distinguishes the relatively recent interest in masculinity studies from the centuries of scholarship that focused almost exclusively on men is the degree of self-awareness. Rather than assuming that men and the masculine are the norm for analysis, it looks specifically at the role and expectations for men in a given culture.[5]

It is important not to conflate masculinity studies with studies about men.[6] The latter looks at particular, variable individuals or groups, while the former is concerned with social constructions. Construction of masculinity is usually associated with construction of power in a society.

Masculinity studies examine the ways in which masculine elements and ideals pervade the scaffolding of society as a whole. Andrea Cornwall and Nancy Lindisfarne observe:

> interpretations of maleness, manhood or masculinity are not neutral, but rather all such attributions and labels have political entailments....the processes of gendering produce difference and inequality: and nowhere more obviously than in the versions of masculinity associated with (masculinized) notions of power.[7]

Masculinized power as a social structure can be further distinguished from that of individual men because it is usually presented as "hegemonic masculinity." Again from Cornwall and Lindisfarne: "In our borrowed use of 'hegemonic masculinity,' our interest is in understanding how relations of power and powerlessness are gendered, and how, in any particular setting, attributions of masculinity are assumed or imposed."[8]

There are two elements of this hegemony that are of interest here. One is the promotion of a particular kind of masculinity at the expense of other expressions.

> The ability to impose a particular definition on other kinds of masculinity is part of what we mean by "hegemony." Hegemonic masculinity is far more complex than the accounts of essences in the masculinity books would suggest....It is, rather, a question of how particular groups of men inhabit positions of power and wealth, and how they legitimate and reproduce the social relationships that generate their dominance. An immediate consequence of this is that the culturally exalted form of masculinity, the hegemonic model so to speak, may only correspond to the actual characters of a small number of men....Yet very large numbers of men are complicit in sustaining the hegemonic model.[9]

This dominant type of masculinity then makes itself known through the institutions and power structures of society, which is the second element of hegemony.

> "Hegemony," then, always refers to a historical situation, a set of circumstances in which power is won and held. The construction of hegemony is not a matter of pushing and pulling between ready-formed groupings but is partly a matter of the *formation* of those groupings. To understand the different kinds of masculinity demands, above all, an examination of the practices in which hegemony is constituted and contested—in short, the political techniques of the patriarchal social order.[10]

Those who "win" the power dictate the norms of masculinity. Once the elements of a particular hegemonic masculinity are embedded in the power structures, however, they become self-perpetuating, although not static. R. W. Connell notes that hegemony is always contextual: "'Hegemonic masculinity' is not a fixed character type, always and everywhere the same. It is, rather, the masculinity that occupies the hegemonic position in a given pattern of gender relations, a position always contestable."[11]

In such a system, gender comes to symbolize particular aspects of power and social organization. Strathern notes that in Melanesia gender represents the contrast between domestic production and public activity, traditionally female and male realms, respectively, so that when men encourage each other to be involved in public activity, they say not to "behave like women."[12] Becoming like women or feminized is a frequent metaphor used by men to represent loss of social prestige or power across various cultures.[13]

In addition to Strathern's studies in Melanesia, several studies in the Mediterranean region have noted similar conceptions. Stanley Brandes has worked in Andalusia studying male folklore—jokes, pranks, skits, stories, as well as ritualized activities, such as the olive harvest. Many jokes, not surprisingly, revolve around sex and issues between men and women. The jokes often seem a way to play with anxieties around masculinity and emasculation. The butt of the joke is often the male character who is put in the position of a woman sexually. The jokes and skits are also laced with elements of class anxiety, which are sometimes couched in gender terminology.[14]

David Gilmore, who also worked in this area of Spain, highlights the up and down orientation of many of the issues of class and gender. Political weakness and lack of social status are often expressed in sexual or gender-linked language. "Andalusian men often perceive political weakness, being in the lower position in relation to other men, as a feminized position analogous to the position of the sexes in copulation, giving rise to fears of emasculation and sexual violation."[15] Losing, be it in the area of politics, economics, or class issues, is equated with feminization, that is, with moving down in the gender hierarchy. Gilmore observes:

> We see in this conflation of experiences the power of orientational metaphors to define the inchoate subject....Ramifying throughout the linked system of im-

ages, this fear of losing control, of "falling down," in any one dimension thus magnifies as a fear of extinguishment, of bodily diminishment in all dimensions—social, sexual, moral.[16]

Being feminized through sexual penetration is a metaphor for subordination in the Greek community studied by Peter Loizos. In this context, the negative connotations of a male being penetrated are not associated with the idea of homosexual sex itself, but are clearly related to feminization. The active partner retains his masculinity, and perhaps even gains some perception of power by subordinating the passive partner. The passive partner, however, loses status by being placed in the female position.[17]

Anthropological masculinity studies have thus shown that across many cultures, conceptions of gender relations and gendered language signify complex relations of power, economics, and social status. In these relations it is usually the masculine that comes out on top, so to speak, at least in public arenas. Because of this there is great concern among men with maintaining and building up their masculinity and keeping themselves from becoming feminized, which would lower their status in many aspects of social life.

Applying Masculinity Theory to Hosea

In this study I am utilizing anthropological observations and theories about gender and gender relations, such as those discussed above, to provide insight into the rhetoric of Hosea.[18] Some cautions about taking an anthropological approach are in order, however. First, I am not observing real people; I am examining a text. Second, Hosea does not represent relations between real men and women. Even descriptions of relations between men and women in the world of the text are extremely limited, occurring only between Gomer and Hosea in ch. 1, the husband and the wife in ch. 2, Hosea and the woman in ch. 3, and the men and their daughters and daughters-in-law in ch. 4. The relationship between Hosea and Gomer is not developed. Gomer never speaks and the only activity mentioned is the conception and bearing of children. The marriage is presented in symbolic terms. Chapter 2 appears to expand on this relationship, but the wife is clearly a metaphorical entity rather than an actual person. Chapter 3 is also highly symbolic and not useful as an example of a real relationship. The relationships of father-in-law and daughter-in-law in ch. 4 are even less developed. While these verses are suggestive of particular social structures and expectations, the men and women never interact. Third, the text often does not refer to individual men, but instead addresses Ephraim or Israel as a personified nation. Therefore, rather than working in the realm of observation of actual people and relationships, I am working with a text that has encoded cultural perceptions and expectations of these relations. Further complicating the matter is that Hosea is a prophetic text. Not only am I looking at a text rather than at actual people, but also I am looking at polemical, rhetorically-shaped oracles, not at a set of observations, or even a narrative text that describes and develops relationships. Thus I am at least two or three levels removed from the reality of actual relationships between living people.[19]

Understanding real relationships, however, is not of concern in this project. Rather, I am interested in how gender is encoded in the text and how it is used in the rhetoric of power and politics. In other words, it is not necessary to my project that I understand how gender relations actually functioned in ancient Israel. In fact, real gender relations would not be particularly useful, because they are complex and often differ from normative statements about such relations.[20] In public venues, such as the delivery of prophecy, normative ideas tend to predominate. To make an analogy, what is important in the interpretation of metaphors is not the actual properties of the image, but rather the perceived qualities.[21] The rhetoric in Hosea employs social perceptions of gender relations, which are much less slippery than real relations, to address particular political and historical situations.[22]

An additional concern is that there is a certain circularity in deriving conceptions of gender and gender relations from a text, which one then uses to interpret that text. Portrayals of gender in other biblical texts of various genres provide some insight into the concept of masculinity in ancient Israel. Unfortunately, "ethnography" is not a genre present in the Bible. If used carefully, however, comparative anthropological studies can be helpful to reconstruct the conceptions of gender underlying the rhetoric of Hosea. Although anthropological ethnographies describe particular, unique cultures, comparative analysis of these studies reveals elements that are characteristic of multiple cultures. Cultures displaying particular forms of gender hierarchy often show similar relationships between gender, politics, power, and social status. I will be utilizing anthropological studies of cultures that seem to share certain elements of gender relations with ancient Israel to help with understanding the intersections of gender, power, and politics.

Keeping these cautions in mind, I place some constraints on my analysis. Rather than looking broadly at gender or gender relations, I focus on masculinity. There are several reasons for this. First, the few times when women are mentioned in the text, the focus is on the ways in which women affect the construction of masculinity.[23] Second, the text does not try to justify, explain, or even uphold gender relations, but uses them to accomplish particular rhetorical purposes, making it difficult to extract information about the nature of these relations. Third, because the audience was presumably predominantly composed of elite males, who were at the top of the masculine food chain, the oracles are geared to them, addressing their (mis)understanding of the socio-political situation.[24] Finally, I will focus on masculinity because there is a dearth of information about the construction of femininity in the text, and it is too simplistic to place masculinity and femininity in opposition. The relationship is usually much more complex. Eve Sedgwick notes: "Masculinity and Femininity are in many respects orthogonal to each other. Orthogonal: that is, instead of being at opposite poles of the same axis, they are actually in different, perpendicular dimensions, and therefore are independently variable."[25] The orthogonal nature of gender construction means that femininity is not simply the negative of the masculinity portrayed in Hosea.[26]

The issue is complicated, however, by the fact that hegemonic masculinity tends to create what may be called a straw-woman femininity, which is closer to being the inverse of masculinity. Thus rhetoric that accuses men of being women implies that they have non-masculine characteristics or are acting in ways opposite to how men should act. A femininity as defined by hegemonic masculinity is a different construction than one would find if one were looking at femininity by itself. Because Hosea is a short text focused almost exclusively on the masculine perspective, it only barely sketches a straw-woman femininity, much less a broader conception of femininity as it may have functioned in society as a whole. I will thus concentrate on masculinity.[27]

Anthropological Theories of Metaphor

Symbolic Language

The construction of masculinity is accessible in Hosea only through language. Most of that language is figurative. It is necessary, therefore, to have an approach that is sufficient to analyze the tropes and rhetoric of the text. The field of metaphor studies is vast and growing and encompasses a variety of perspectives ranging from philosophical to cognitive to rhetorical.[28] Because I am taking an anthropological perspective on masculinity, an anthropological perspective on language seems apropos.

Anthropologists have long been interested in the ways in which cultures use language. Systems of classification and symbolic systems are particularly prominent in the literature, describing how cultures consciously create a sense of identity and establish and change social relationships using non-human images. While the symbols and metaphors used and the relationship between them are specific to a particular culture, similar phenomena can be observed in a wide range of cultures, from primitive to industrial.

One type of identity formation occurs through totemism. Lévi-Strauss's discussion is one of many that note the frequency with which individuals or groups take on the identity or particular characteristics of animals or plants.[29] As Lévi-Strauss observes, however, what has been called totemism is not a simple transfer of identity from animal to human, but part of a complex system of organizing and transforming a society's understanding of itself and the world in which it exists.

> In other words, the operative value of the systems of naming and classifying commonly called totemic derives from their formal character: they are codes suitable for conveying messages which can be transposed into other codes, and for expressing messages received by means of different codes in terms of their own system. The mistake of classical ethnologists was to reify this form and to tie it to a determinate content when in fact what it provides is a method for assimilating any kind of content. Far from being an autonomous institution definable by its intrinsic characteristic, totemism, or what is referred to as such, corresponds to certain modalities arbitrarily isolated from a formal system, the function of which is to guarantee the convertibility of ideas between different levels of social reality.[30]

The type of system of transformations that Lévi-Strauss describes is applicable to a wide variety of areas of classification, not just to humans and human relationships.[31] It also shows that cultural identity and social structure are not determined separately from other aspects of society. The ways in which humans organize themselves often correspond to the ways in which they organize their world.

Most cultures expand the symbolic system exemplified by totemism through figurative language. Tropes provide the means to play with identity and to organize elements of a culture. Paul Friedrich, through what he calls "anthropological poetics" studies how creativity, language and culture constantly interact. He observes that "tropes are a basic means of synthesizing with language and for relating language to experience and practice."[32]

A particular focus on the play between language and culture characterizes the anthropological perspective on metaphor and serves to distinguish it from the typical linguistic and semantic approaches. Philosophers of language are most concerned with how metaphors are identified, how they affect word and sentence meaning, the relationship between the parts of a metaphor, and how they convey truth.[33] Cognitive linguists take a step back and consider the ways in which language relates to the patterns of a culture's thinking, if not to some innate human characteristics.[34] Rhetorical approaches are obviously sensitive to context.[35] All of these approaches illuminate the various elements of language under study, but despite the differences among them, their primary focus is on language itself and how context and culture affect the meaning and comprehension of language. Anthropologists, on the other hand, tend to take a different perspective, focusing rather on culture and asking how language acts in and affects a particular culture.

The anthropologist's approach assumes that metaphor is a common and powerful means of expressing and changing societal dynamics. Fernandez argues that especially rich sources of metaphor are the interactions that take place between people and entities in different positions in society, e.g. different genders, classes, and ages. Such interactions have a particular potential for what he calls "revelatory incidents…those especially charged moments in human relationships which are pregnant with meaning."[36] In order to express this excess of meaning, figurative language must be employed.

Definitions of Metaphor

Since Fernandez sees human interaction as a primary generator of metaphor, his definition of metaphor is rooted firmly within the realm of human social relationships.[37] Rather than providing a linguistic definition, Fernandez discusses metaphor in terms of how it functions in human identity formation and human society.[38]

> [Metaphor is defined] simply as a strategic predication upon an inchoate pronoun (an I, a you, a we, a they) which makes a movement and leads to performance.[39]

Despite Fernandez's assertion that metaphor is thus "simply" defined, his statement requires a bit of unpacking. It may be helpful to compare this definition with some more traditional definitions. Janet Soskice, emphasizing the linguistic nature of metaphor, defines it as "that figure of speech whereby we speak about one thing in terms which are seen to be suggestive of another."[40] Lakoff and Johnson provide a more cognitive definition, focusing on the mental processes involved: "The essence of metaphor is understanding and experiencing one kind of thing in terms of another."[41] Fernandez's definition is predominantly social. He understands an inchoate pronoun as a human, or a group of humans, who is searching for identity. The human forms one part of the metaphor, the "one thing" in Lakoff and Johnson's and Soskice's definitions, while the "other thing" or "terms suggestive of another" are predicated upon him/her, creating some sort of social identity. For example, in the metaphor "Ephraim is a cake not turned" (Hos 7:8b), Ephraim is the pronoun, and the unturned cake is the identity that is placed upon him by the prophet.[42]

Fernandez's claim that the pronoun is inchoate is important to the relevance of metaphor as a means of establishing identity and relationship. If the pronoun already had a strong identity, there would be no room for metaphoric social movement. According to Fernandez, humans are by nature inchoate to a greater or lesser extent.

> To be human is to have, to one degree or another, a problem of identity for it is to have, sooner or later, a gnawing sense of uncertainty—what I call here "the inchoate"—which lies at the heart of the human condition and which energizes the search for identity through predications. 'Dubito ergo sum!'[43]

Examples of the use of metaphor to define people are prevalent. One of the commentators covering the Tour de France bicycling race repeatedly refers to one of the top competitors as "a great diesel engine."[44] Lawyers are not uncommonly referred to as snakes. Calling a political strategist an attack dog succinctly expresses the role of that person to bring down the opponent. Some have been used so often that the connotations of the metaphors are effectively reduced to one dimension. Sedentary people are called couch potatoes, without extensive reflection on other tuber-like properties. Calling someone a hawk or a dove is effectively limited to that person's position on the use of military force.

Social Quality Space

Metaphor predications are of a variety of different types, as Fernandez observes:

> metaphors can serve a variety of functions: informative, expressive, declarative, directive, and so forth. I do not pretend that what I want to say about metaphor here encompasses all these uses. The point is that there is an important social use of metaphor involving the occupancy of various continua which in sum constitute a cultural quality space.[45]

Fernandez utilizes a spatial model of society in his analyses. A cultural quality space is defined by a number of parameters, determined by a particular society's values and differentiating factors. These parameters are set up as continua in the model. The continua represent axes which are important in the way a society situates, judges, and places people in respect to one another. In contemporary American society, some examples of continua may include rich/poor, young/old, educated/illiterate, beautiful/ugly, and powerful/disenfranchised, among others.[46] A poor, illiterate, old, disenfranchised, ugly person in our society occupies an unfavorable position in the social space. The beautiful, young, rich people tend to be in the optimal places—where the majority of the people in society would like to be. The multi-dimensional spatial analysis is most useful when trying to assess the relative positions of people characterized by different mixes of values.[47] People can be in different points in space, having a different mix of positions along the various continua, but still be situated in relatively better or worse places in society. Who would be placed more optimally: an old, ugly, and rich person, or a young, beautiful, and poor person?[48]

Fernandez sums up the idea of quality space and its relation to metaphor as follows:

> The items belonging to any domain can be arranged (if we know enough about them) on various scales....The sum total of these continua defines the quality space of a culture. Metaphor is the chief means by which pronouns take their places and move about in that quality space. Society, in simple, is the movement of pronouns about within quality space.[49]

Fernandez defines two general categories of metaphor that work in social quality space: those that set the framework of society, arranging the various continua with respect to one another, and those that work to change people's relative positions within that social grid.

> I am going to define the uses of several kinds of metaphor, persuasive or colocative metaphor in the first place, and performative or organizing metaphor in the second. I am then going to ask how these metaphors operate in respect to culture conceived of as a "quality space."[50]

Performative Metaphors

Performative or organizing metaphors are those that form the basis of particular cultural understandings and rituals. Such organizing metaphors serve to establish people's positions in the cultural quality space, rather than to change these positions. Different groups' interpretations of the metaphor, however, may establish people in different positions. The metaphors then lead to performances, or ways to act within the frame that has been structured.

In contemporary America the metaphor of pulling oneself up by one's own bootstraps shapes the national psyche around the concept that in this country if a person works hard, then that person can become anything he or she wants to be. The self-made man (or woman) is a cultural ideal. As an organizing metaphor it leads to performances in public policy, although like most metaphors, it can be interpreted in different ways. On the one hand, the metaphor can be used to portray unsuccessful people (at least according to the standard measures of the culture) as lazy. Since these people's problems are basically their own fault, the government has no obligation to help them. Others may accept the same metaphor with its connotations of individual responsibility, but perform it differently. They may look at an unsuccessful person and question how one is supposed to pull oneself up with one's bootstraps if one has no boots. These people think the government should ensure that everyone at least has access to the same opportunities.

Metaphor is also frequently used to organize performance in religious practice. In the context of the Christian church, one of those metaphors is Christ as the slain lamb, which organizes concepts of salvation and parts of the ritual of the Eucharist with the idea of cleansing blood and sacrifice. Different Christian communities interpret this metaphor in different ways, so that some describe it as substitutionary atonement, the idea that Christ the lamb was sacrificed in place of the believer, whereas others focus more on the idea of self-sacrifice as an action that Christians can and should emulate.

A person's or group's position in cultural quality space is usually defined through multiple metaphors, which can lead to different performances at different times. Fernandez gives the example of the Apostle's Revelation Society in Ghana. When the members use the metaphoric predication, "We are Christian soldiers," the performative consequence might be, "Our church activities must show our militance in fighting against the forces of the devil." If they use, however, the predication "We are the voices of God," this could lead to the consequence, "We must study the Bible so that we can learn God's language. We must concentrate our attention on sermons and seek speaking in tongues."[51] Neither one of these metaphors alone can structure the whole of the church's self-understanding. In fact, many other metaphors are brought into play.

Persuasive Metaphors

The second type, persuasive or co-locative metaphor, attempts to change the place of people within the cultural quality space. By definition metaphor brings together images from two different domains, so that any predication of an identity on a pronoun causes one to look differently at the pronoun, and often at the predicate as well.[52] In the definition of metaphor given above, Fernandez calls predication "strategic" because the identities placed upon a pronoun are rarely neutral.[53] The pronoun is given a different self-perception and/or a different identity in the perception of others. This may, in turn, lead to the pronoun occupying a different relative position in society. Metaphor moves people or groups by either taking them from a less defined state (inchoate) to a more defined state (or at least to a somewhat differently defined state) or by changing their positions along a particular continuum, such as intelligence or power.

> Language has devices of representation at its disposal, mainly metaphor, by which pronouns can be moved about—into better or worse position—in quality space....The point is that there is an important social use of metaphor involving the occupancy of various continua which in sum constitute a cultural quality space. Persuasive metaphors situate us and others with whom we interact in that space.[54]

People use persuasive metaphors to define identities (both their own and that of others) within a broader culture and to explore and optimize their societal positions with respect to other people or groups.

Metaphors work to move people and social entities by associating them with vehicles that have particular culturally assigned values. Aristotle observed that "if we wish to ornament our subject, we must derive our metaphor from the better species under the same genus; if to depreciate it, from the worse."[55] The principle of rhetorical movement can be expanded beyond comparison with the same genus. If the leader of one country calls some other countries, for example, the "Axis of Evil," he intends to move these countries into a less esteemed place in the social quality space.

Popular sociologists have recognized this power of metaphor to shape identity and alter relationships. In *Wild at Heart,* a book focused on male spirituality, John Eldredge discusses how contemporary American culture has tried to redefine "goodness" for men with more "feminine" qualities, including passivity. Metaphors, often in the form of nicknames, have emasculated boys and have caused them to lose their true identities as fighters and to feel impotent. By redefining what is good, the more liberal elements in society, Eldredge believes, have moved men and boys to a worse position in the social grid. To optimize their placement in the social quality space, boys need to be named "tiger," not "little lamb."[56]

The abilities to establish identity within a community and to move pronouns within quality space are among what Fernandez has identified as the "missions" of metaphor. The first mission is to provide an identity for subjects that were formerly amorphous. ("Boys are little lambs.") The second mission allows for movement of these subjects in the cultural framework. ("Boys are not little lambs; boys are tigers.") The third helps position the subjects optimally within that quality space. ("Boys are tigers; girls are kittens.")[57]

Responses to Predications

Persuasive metaphors not only move pronouns about in the cultural space, but can lead to performance, in part through how the pronoun responds to a particular predication. One response is for the pronoun to accept the predication unaltered and perform accordingly. We can see this in cases of people "living up" or "living down" to expectations. A child told continually that he or she is a star, may perform to fulfill this predication by practicing harder, studying more, trying out for more sports, etc. (Sometimes, however, such expectations lead to a rejection of this predication later in life.) On the other hand, a child told that he or she is trash may feel that any effort is wasted because he or she is not worth anything.

A second response is to accept the predication, but to alter its meaning. A prime example of this is the patriotic children's song "Yankee Doodle." The British sang this song during the American Revolution to mock the Americans, predicating this identity of a fool onto the rebels. The Americans, however, embraced this image, but transformed it into an upstart, vibrant image thumbing its nose at the aristocracy. This image is now so thoroughly engrained in American culture that millions of schoolchildren sing it without having any idea of its initial derogatory connotations.[58]

A third response is to reject the predication and act on that rejection. The aforementioned denigrated child, rather than accepting the metaphorical identity, may say, "I am not a piece of trash, and I'll prove it." Or the subject of the predication may simply ignore it, which is itself a kind of performance, because it conveys something about the subject's estimation of the predicator. Often the rejection of the predication involves the subject predicating a different identity on itself. "I'm not a piece of trash; I'm a hidden treasure." The rejection can also take the form of throwing the predication or a similar one back on the speaker. This can be seen in the children's exchange: "You're a slimy booger!" "I know you are, but what am I?"

One of the difficulties in studying metaphoric predication in a text is that the response of the audience, especially the original audience, is extremely difficult to ascertain. Hosea predicates several different identities onto the audience, but it is impossible to know how the audience responded to those predications. My analysis therefore must be limited to identifying the movement that the prophet was likely trying to accomplish rather than evaluating how it was received.

Axes for analysis

In order to assess the movement that a pronoun makes through social quality space, it is necessary to identify some axes that define that space. As noted above, cultures employ many different continua to establish social identity and relationships. While increasing the number of axes more accurately describes a complex social space, it also makes more difficult a comparison of relative positions of pronouns within that space. For that reason, Fernandez suggests that the concept of semantic space developed by Charles Osgood can be a helpful place to begin an analysis of quality space. As a computational linguist, Osgood analyzed how people differentiate the meanings of words using concepts represented by several ·continua: good-bad, complete-incomplete, timely-untimely, weak-strong, heavy-light, constrained-free, fast-slow, etc. In particular he was interested in the connotations of words—how people feel about them. His project included study of undergraduate student responses, thesaurus analysis, and review of other studies. He then identified three continua that account for a large proportion of the variance of meaning judgments. These three are evaluation, potency, and activity.[59] While many other continua play a role in the determination of meaning, the three factors accounted for more than 70% of the variance.[60] Thus a three-dimensional semantic space constructed from these three axes will provide a simplified but still powerful way to examine metaphoric predication.[61] The continua of evaluation, potency, and activity are also useful in correlating the linguistic space analyzed by Osgood to social quality space. First, evaluative judgments (I will call this an assessment of "goodness" following Fernandez), activity, and potency (or power) are common judgments applied to people, especially in the social sphere.

The topographic model proposed here would suggest that in cultural life pronouns come to possess appropriate or inappropriate feelings of potency, activity, and goodness attached to them....Social life from the perspective of this model is the set of those transactions by which pronouns, the foci of identity, change their feeling tone—the sense of potency, activity, and goodness attached to them.[62]

Second, unlike some of the other continua one might chose to define cultural space, such as beauty, wealth, and lineage, these are axes along which an individual can make considerable movement.

In the case of Hosea, whose audience I have argued is composed of elite, relatively powerful males, these issues seem to be of much concern. Many of the metaphors in Hosea attempt to move people along these axes, and also to change the relationships between the axes. A conflict of ideas about who should be powerful, the value of action, and the definition of goodness pervades the book.

Tropes Related to Metaphor

Having laid out the basic method I employ, I now turn to a discussion of some tropes related to metaphor, including simile, metonym and synecdoche, because Hosea utilizes many such figures of speech. I place these tropes within a broad definition of metaphor and follow Fernandez in considering them functionally equivalent in many ways. As such a claim is by no means universally accepted, I will discuss my rationale below.

Simile

Simile is the most important trope in Hosea, as it appears more frequently than does metaphor, strictly defined. Nearly all of the references to YHWH occur through simile, and it is the most common way to refer to the personified nation as well. The similes introduce a wide range of image fields and often appear in clusters or as thematic elements throughout the book to develop an image.

There is some argument about the degree of distinction between the categories of simile and metaphor. Many philosophical linguists argue for a clear distinction between the two tropes. Max Black states that similes are literal comparisons between two objects and thus have a limited effect on the reader, whereas metaphor is much more complex. In part this is because metaphor makes the reader wrestle with the meaning of the juxtaposition of the two terms, the points of comparison, and the interaction of the two terms. In arguing this way, Black contrasts his interaction view of metaphor with the comparison view, which treats a metaphor as an "elliptical simile."[63] Yet Black notes that the distinction sometimes blurs, and not all similes are limited to particular concrete comparisons.

> A comparison is often a prelude to an explicit statement of the grounds of re-semblance; whereas we do not expect a metaphor to explain itself. (Cf. the difference between *comparing* a man's face with a wolf mask, by looking for points of resemblance – and seeing the human face *as* vulpine). But no doubt the line between *some* metaphors and *some* similes is not a sharp one.[64]

Indeed it is not necessary to think of similes as simple literal comparisons. Like metaphors, complex similes also create similarities and interactions between two realms. Nelson Goodman notes that the difference between metaphor and simile is not significant, because even with simile the reader must determine what is important about the comparison and draw out the implications.[65] Janice Soskice argues that a more useful contrast is between "illustrative" similes which tend to be simpler, straightforward comparisons and "modelling" similes, which function more like metaphors, by creating an interaction capable of considerable development.[66] She thus changes the point of comparison from the general category of simile versus metaphor to modelling simile versus metaphor. In this latter case, the grammatical form of the simile does not necessarily limit its scope of meaning. As she observes, "we can say that metaphor and simile share the same function and differ primarily in their grammatical form."[67] Simile in Hosea is often of the modelling type, partly because the book does not usually use isolated figures of speech, but clusters images together, developing a model.

More importantly, when employed for rhetorical purposes, the difference between the two tropes may be insignificant. Aristotle argued that there is no significant difference between the two: "A simile is also a metaphor; for there is little difference: when the poet says, 'He rushed as a lion,' it is a simile, but 'The lion rushed' [with lion referring to a man] would be a metaphor; since both are brave, he used a metaphor [i.e. a simile] and spoke of Achilles as a lion....[Similes] should be brought in like metaphors; for they *are* metaphors, differing in the form of expression."[68] On the other hand, he finds simile somewhat "less pleasant because it is longer; it does not say that this *is* that, so that the mind does not even examine this."[69] While the general effect is the same, metaphor is somewhat more attractive rhetorically. Similarly, Wayne Booth observes:

> It is curious that the difference between metaphor and simile, essential in the study of some kinds of metaphor, seems here to become extremely unimportant. It is perhaps true that adding a "like" or "as"...will weaken it somewhat. But this addition does not change the nature of the picture, and one is not surprised to find that classical theorists, unlike many modern philosophers with different purposes in view, have seen the choice between simile and metaphor as minor.[70]

When the rhetorical and social effect, rather than the cognitive effect, is what is important, differences between metaphor and simile matter little.

Metonym and Synecdoche
While simile is the most common individual trope in Hosea, metonym also appears frequently, especially in the development and interaction of clusters of images. A metonym is a trope in which a word is used figuratively for a word or concept closely associated with it, often an attribute used to represent its subject. For example, the term threshing floor can represent agricultural yield, as in Hos 9:2: "Threshing floor and winepress will not feed them." Similarly, the United Methodist Church's advertising slogan, "Our hearts, our minds, and our doors are open," represents the concept of inclusive acceptance and love. The closely related trope synecdoche occurs when one substitutes a part for the whole or a whole for the part. An example of both is "the eyes of the nation were on him." The sentence really means that the citizens of the nation were paying attention, neither that there were disembodied eyes (part for whole) nor that the abstract notion of nation had eyes (whole for part). In contrast, metaphor is defined as the linking of two unrelated terms.

The relationship between metaphor and metonymy has been the subject of much discussion.[71] On one side of the discussion are those stressing that the two types of tropes represent different types of cognition. Metonym involves reasoning by contiguity within the same domain of reference and metaphor requires reasoning by similarity linking two different domains.[72] Soskice claims that by linking two domains metaphor is more cognitively complex than metonymy or synecdoche.

Instances of metonymy and synecdoche point one directly to the absent term; it would be a failure in comprehension if, on hearing the phrase 'the White House said today', one wondered if shutters and doors opened like mouths; or of [*sic*], on hearing that 'twenty sails entered the harbour', one wondered how the sails got there without the ships. Metonymy and synecdoche function as oblique reference and as such they, if any of the tropes, fit the bill for being primarily ornamental ways of naming.[73]

Metaphor, in contrast, by linking two domains, opens up a range of associations that can create a new vision of their relationship.[74]

On the other side of the discussion are those who, while acknowledging the difference in cognitive function, observe that the uses of metaphor and metonym sometimes overlap. Lakoff and Johnson explain that as cognitive processes, metaphor, or the conception of one thing in terms of another, has primarily a function of understanding, whereas metonym primarily uses one thing to refer to another. The functions are not always discrete, however.

But metonymy is not merely a referential device. It also serves the function of providing understanding....Which part we pick out determines which aspect of the whole we are focusing on....Thus metonymy serves some of the same purposes that metaphor does, and in somewhat the same way, but allows us to focus more specifically on certain aspects of what is being referred to.[75]

The framing provided by metonym can reorient the understanding of a subject much as does the juxtaposition of a concept from a different domain, as occurs in metaphor.

Focusing on this overlap of functions, Fernandez groups metonyms and synecdoche with metaphors as a means of organizing and making movements within cultural quality space. The two categories can share functions because metaphor and metonym occur within particular cultural frameworks and associated contexts, which are created by both paradigmatic and syntagmatic relationships. Fernandez describes this overlap as follows:

Metaphors give rise to a syntax of scenes designed to put them into effect, and in that sense they do take over the mission of metonyms (which is to represent and bring into association a larger context). Metonyms, on the other hand, take over the mission of metaphor in the sense that the elements of a syntagmatic progression can suggest themselves as a metaphor for the pronomial subjects of that progression.[76]

Metonyms and metaphors interact to create more networks of images for describing and understanding social space.

Both figures can be used to move people in the cultural quality space. When applied to people metonymy often serves the purpose of depersonalization. It focuses attention on particular characteristics while ignoring others. Hence metonymy is often, though not always, used in a derogatory fashion. Calling bodyguards hired guns tends to make people discount their intelligence. The schoolyard taunt "four eyes" has connotations of physical weakness. Metonyms like these function to move a person to a less optimal position in the cultural quality space.

Metaphorical Domains

Another way in which metaphors, metonyms, and other tropes function in a culture is through their role in developing concepts and conceptual domains. Renate Bartsch defines a concept as a stabilized set of experiences and expressions. Concepts can be linked by relations of similarity (generally through metaphor) or contiguity (generally through metonymy). Concepts can be extended in two major ways: through broadening or narrowing and through metaphor or metonym. Broadening or narrowing does not involve a major change in the way one views a concept—it just focuses attention on different parts of the concept. Metaphor and metonymy on the other hand cause a change in perspective.[77] Perspective, used as a technical term in cognitive linguistics, is a second-order concept that organizes individual concepts. For example, the perspective of education contains the concepts of earning grades, writing papers, and studying for exams. Metaphors and metonyms can change the way concepts are organized into perspectives and can create new similarity or contiguity relationships between concepts.

Fernandez translates this idea from the realm of abstract concepts into its societal implications. He discusses "domains of belonging," which refer to social dynamics and the formation and dissolution of social groups. In particular Fernandez emphasizes the constant flux in these groups as people redefine their relationships or have redefinition imposed upon them.

> It is my view that the study of the 'play of tropes' is one important way to help us to understand that dynamic. For the 'play of tropes' is essentially a play of mind within domains (by metonym principally) and between domains (by

metaphor principally). It is a play of mind that emerges out of our sense of the world's predominant classifications and collections of significant being—the predominant 'domains of belonging'—while it also affects these classifications and collections. Likewise, it is a play of mind that is energized by social situations even as it is influential in shaping them.[78]

Domains thus interact on multiple levels. They can be ways of organizing thoughts and concepts that range from the mundane to the most intricate social relationships. The dynamics of domains of belonging play out in all levels of society. Individuals exist at different times in various domains: work, family, physicality, musicality, etc. Metaphor can serve to bridge those domains. "Metaphor is, like synesthesia, the translation of experience from one domain into another by virtue of a common factor which can be generalized between the experiences in the two domains."[79] Metaphor is, of course, not the only way such bridges can be built, but it is a very powerful way.

The interplay between metaphor and metonym, that is, between similarity and contiguous relationships, can, in its simplest form, be illustrated by the classic form of analogy, A:B::C:D. For example, a tree is to a forest as a man is to his tribe. On each side of the analogy we have contiguous relationships that could be represented by metonym or synecdoche. Tree and forest are in the same domain, as are man and tribe. The connection between the two sides of the analogy is a metaphoric predication, a bridging of domains: a man is a tree. The two types of relationships can be used to develop a concept. A portrayal of YHWH as a bereaved bear is a metaphoric predication crossing domains. The image invites intra-domain expansion, however. A bereaved bear draws up many connotations—dead cubs, blind rage, danger, vicious attacks. Developing the domain of the bear leads directly to the victim of the bear's rage, which it mauls and mutilates. The image of the victim again causes a metaphoric leap to the nation of Israel, subject to a bloody defeat by the Assyrians.

Metaphor, the Inchoate, and Masculinity

The play of tropes is unavoidable in the metaphoric description of society, because humans are by nature inchoate, constantly searching for identity, both in individual and social realms.[80] The use of tropes proves fruitful in the search for identity for several reasons. First, as figurative language they can approach the indefinable in ways that literal or analytic language cannot express. Second, the inchoate is polyvalent. It cannot be defined by one image, but requires multiple, shifting images even to begin to touch its core. The interactions between metaphors and metonyms generate multiple ways to conceptualize a pronoun. Third, because of the shifting quality of the inchoate, any predication of identity is particular to an individual, a time, and a place. The inchoate continually fuels the quest for identity, which a play of tropes has the capacity to explore. Fourth, even the most successful attempts to define the inchoate are not absolute, but can only be expressed in relation to other domains.[81]

The shifting nature of the inchoate may contribute to the large and shifting number of tropes used in Hosea. The audience cannot be defined by a single image, but requires multiple predications. To make matters more complex, the identity that I argue Hosea is attempting to predicate comes largely from a domain that is also ill-defined—masculinity.[82] Similar to Fernandez's assessment of the inchoate, Cornwall and Lindisfarne argue that gender identities are constantly shifting:

> Indigenous notions of gendered difference are constantly created and transformed in everyday interactions....Multiple gendered (and other) identities, each of which depends on context and the specific and immediate relations between actors and audience, are fluid and they are often subversive of dominant forms.[83]

Fernandez's concept of social space can help to elucidate how the various metaphors in Hosea construct a conception of masculinity. David Gilmore has already employed such a spatial analysis in his study of Andalusian peasants. His social geometry of gender takes into account axes of power, spatial separation, and "norms about status and place, sexuality, morality, and the associated comparative semantics of 'aboveness' and 'belowness.'"[84]

> Domains like sex and politics are not bounded "things" but two-way informational conduits. Rather than seeing a ranking of variables, or a series of epiphenomena, or black box operations, it may make sense to regard sets of social facts as equally privileged. The social-geometry approach that I propose here seeks to position the different sensory experiences not side by side, but three-dimensionally, "montage-like," in Lock's phrase. There emerges through such a cultural architectonics a more complete image of what people sense.[85]

Formulating a social geometry of gender allows for the incorporation of several elements pertinent to the construction of gender and does not require that they all correlate with one another. A more complex understanding of gender can emerge. For my study of Hosea, it also provides a way to compare the strategic movement used in the gender imagery to that of the imagery that is not explicitly related to gender.

I have divided the images in Hosea into nine categories: female imagery, male imagery, parent-child, sickness-healing, hunting, animal, agriculture, plant, and natural phenomena. Some images belong to multiple realms and transfer connotations between realms. In chapter 3, I will examine the construction of masculinity in the gender imagery, while in chapter 4, I will analyze the non-gender imagery along the three axes of potency, activity, and goodness, which help relate these images to concepts of masculinity.

CHAPTER THREE

Predications of Gender-Based Imagery

> The first strategy of anyone who puts forth a metaphor in predication about a pronoun is to pick a domain of equivalence whose members have some apt shock value when applied to a pronoun and give perspective by incongruity.
>
> James W. Fernandez, *Persuasions and Performances*

Gender-based imagery is the most common metaphorical category in Hosea. Both female and male imagery are present in the text, but while the female imagery has received considerable attention, the male imagery has been neglected. Both types, however, can be illuminated by the application of masculinity studies. After providing a brief survey of the ways masculinity theory has begun to be used within biblical studies, I will look closely at the gender imagery in Hosea. The female imagery divides into two sub-categories: female as subject and female as object. I analyze the male imagery with respect to seven different markers, which can be divided into sexual relationships and potency images. With both female and male imagery I focus on their implications for the construction of masculinity. Finally, I examine how the predication of the gender imagery on the male audience affects its position in social space, as defined by the three axes of activity, potency, and goodness.

Masculinity Studies of the Bible

Biblical scholars have begun to see masculinity studies as a useful way to probe the text. Ancient Israel shares characteristics with some of the societies mentioned in the previous chapter, which have been the focus of much anthropological work on masculinity: clear distinctions of gender roles, power based in a patriarchal system, and an emphasis on honor and shame, among others. In biblical studies, as in masculinity studies in general, much of the concern with the construction of masculinity arose in response to feminist interpretations. Rather than being a reactionary movement, however, it has mostly reflected an increase of interest in broader gender issues. I will focus on those studies of the Hebrew Bible, particularly of the prophetic texts.[1]

Psychoanalytic Studies

Many of the masculinity studies of biblical texts follow a psychoanalytic model, rather than an anthropological model, which I employ, but they raise some important issues in biblical constructions of gender. Howard Eilberg-Schwartz, in his provocatively titled work, *God's Phallus*, provides a rather extreme example of this approach in an exploration of some of the difficulties that he proposes a male deity causes for male worshippers.[2] He asserts that with respect to a male god, men must be feminized, because the natural assumed relationship between parties is heterosexual. If god is male, the people must be female. This means that men must also be female. Consequently, if the men are female, then the women must be excluded from cult entirely, because their natural complementarity with the male deity would threaten the male position. "To come face to face with God is to see oneself in the position of wife."[3] Eilberg-Schwartz argues that this explains the commandment that the men abstain from sexual relations before approaching God. They have to remove themselves from the position of husband and prepare to be wives.[4] Furthermore, they link women with impurity and thus exclude their natural wifeness from the cult.[5]

The image of YHWH as the husband of Israel, however, is not typically found outside of the prophets. There is no general indication in the biblical texts that worshipping a male god presented that much of a problem for male worshippers. Even more overtly sexual gods were worshipped in the area and there is no evidence that natural complementarity prevailed. While in some cases priestesses attended the temples of male gods and priests those of female gods, this was not universal.[6] Even in the prophetic texts, placing the male audience in the position of the wife seems to be more rhetorically shocking than one would expect if this conception were widespread. Despite these difficulties, Eilberg-Schwartz does raise some interesting points for consideration. In a society in which masculinity was a common representation of power, YHWH had to be perceived as the most masculine. Everyone else was in a subordinate position. This idea is the basis of Eilberg-Schwartz's explanation of the odd episode in Exod 4:24–26, in which YHWH seeks to slay Moses after sending him back to Egypt. Zipporah saves him by circumcising their son and touching his genitals with the blood.

> God's attack on Moses is in part an attack on his masculinity. That is why circumcision appeases God. The blood of circumcision is a symbolic acknowledgment that a man's masculinity belongs to God. Submitting to God and surrendering one's masculinity amounts to the same thing.[7]

Similarly, Eilberg-Schwartz interprets Jacob's wresting with the angel in Gen 32:25–33 as resulting in a genital injury, understanding hip as a euphemism.[8] Jacob has to subordinate his masculinity to YHWH. When he does, his name is changed to Israel, and he becomes a patriarch. He notes that in Hosea's version of the story, Jacob is explicitly described as wrestling in his manhood (אונו).[9]

Jan Tarlin proposes a somewhat similar interpretation of the relationship between human and divine masculinities in Ezekiel. In his interactions with God, Ezekiel subjects himself to domination by the divine, becoming feminized, though not female. His masculinity has in effect been shattered. "The return onto male subjectivity of the lack, weakness, and fragmentation males usually project onto females has, for Ezekiel, created a new form of subjectivity: a person with a penis who has renounced any claim to possessing the phallus."[10] Submitting to God requires relinquishing one's masculinity.[11]

Studies of Individual Masculinities

Other studies have focused on identifying various masculine characteristics of prominent men in the Bible. In particular, David Clines has studied David and some of the prophets. He identifies several traits possessed by David that he categorizes as particularly masculine characteristics.[12] He is an active warrior, killing or supervising the killing of some 140,000 men in all. He displays verbal prowess and persuasiveness, especially in his encounters with Saul.[13] He has great beauty, which is also positively attributed to several prominent men in the Bible.[14] Comments about his beauty are particularly associated with his anointing and succession. He shows bonding with other men, particularly with Jonathan, and, despite having several wives, is mostly portrayed without women.[15] Clines also notes David's musical abilities, observing that stringed instruments are typically associated with male players.[16] David is not necessarily the ideal ancient Israelite man, however, as some of his actions seem to go against masculine norms.[17]

Clines also detects several characteristic masculine traits in the prophets, similar to the ones he identified for David.[18] He lists characteristics that may apply both to the men and to their prophecies. These include exhibiting strength and violence,[19] serving as standard bearers who hold people and nations (including foreign nations) accountable through their oracles, and showing a concern for honor, holiness, and preserving the tradition. They possess great verbal prowess, including the use of satire to dispense praise and blame. An important characteristic is that they place politics in the ethical realm, often using gendered language. Clines argues that they are, by and large, portrayed as womanless, while some appear in the company of men (2 Kgs 6). Women are either portrayed negatively or not at all. The few neutral mentions of women are undeveloped. While most of the prophets are married, their wives and children only enter the picture as symbols. Most notable is Hosea's wife Gomer and his unfortunately named children. Isaiah's wife is also mentioned in the context of bearing children with symbolic names. Ezekiel is told not to mourn his dead wife, while Jeremiah is told not to marry at all.

While Clines attempts to draw these elements of masculinity from the texts, the method is not entirely free of problems. By focusing on particular persons, Clines obtains particular masculinities. There is no guarantee that the traits are representative of masculinity in the society.[20] He notes, in fact, that David seems to act against masculine norms at different points.[21] Likewise the prophets are hardly typical men, and while the classical prophets do seem to be portrayed as ideal figures, the writing prophets appear to act against cultural norms. This is particularly true of their relationship with women, which makes it difficult to make a reliable claim that the ideal man is womanless. Some of these difficulties may be resolved with analysis of additional texts. Clines's analysis also does not address how possession or lack of these masculine traits affects the perception or power of the men he studies.

I examine the masculinity of the brothers in Genesis, focusing on Abraham, Ishmael and Isaac, and Jacob and Esau. These men represent some features of normative masculinity, but go against them in other ways. In the pairs of brothers, one is generally more characteristically masculine than the other. The brother who is less masculine is the one ultimately chosen by God to bear the covenant. I argue that this is because the less masculine man is more willing to submit to God.[22]

Studies of Normative Masculinity

Most of the above studies focus on specific masculine characters in the Bible and explore the explicitly masculine traits attributed to these characters. My approach is more abstract, focusing on the traits themselves, which are characteristic of a normative masculinity. These characteristics are not necessarily attributed to any particular man, although various men may display them. A few scholars have already taken this approach.

Ken Stone studied the relationship between masculinity and power in the Deuteronomistic History.[23] He reads references to sex in the Deuteronomistic History with the understanding that sex symbolizes activity in the public domain.

> These narratives are structured in relationship to cultural assumptions about sexual activity that involve the quest by males for public honor, power, and prestige. One's status as a sexual subject is seen to play a crucial (albeit complicated) role in this quest, though differently for men than for women.[24]

An important implication Stone expresses regarding the connection between sex and public power is that the relations between men and women in the narratives are at their root power struggles between men.[25] The illicit sex between Amnon and Tamar, Joab and Rizpah, and Absalom and David's concubines are really attacks on the masculinity of the women's guardians, who are unable to protect their women.[26] The affronted males respond in different ways. Absalom kills Amnon. Ishbaal backs down from Joab, ceding more masculinity in the process. David eventually returns and defeats Absalom. David's masculinity is severely questioned in this whole saga, however, because in the first place he is fooled by Amnon's plot, and thus puts Tamar in jeopardy, and then, once he finds out, he takes no action to punish Amnon. Likewise he does not punish Absalom for killing Amnon, although he was angry at both episodes.[27] He is a father unable to control or discipline his children, fore-shadowing his lack of control over his kingdom.

Another aspect of male power and prestige is developed by Harold Washington, who discusses warfare as the definitive domain of men and masculinity.[28] "The language of war in the Hebrew Bible and other Ancient Near Eastern literatures is acutely masculinist. Warfare is emblematically male and the discourse of violence is closely imbricated with that of masculine sexuality."[29] As with the Assyrian inscriptions, "being a man" is associated with dominance. The Philistines encourage each other to "be men and fight" in 1 Sam 4:9, overcoming their fear of the Ark of God and routing the Israelites. Carole Fontaine observes that this exhortation is effective because purposely subordinating oneself like a woman is worse than death: "Dread of being female outweighs dread of the Ark that smote Pharaoh and his men, and the former serves as an effective counter to the latter condition."[30] The few cases in which women kill in battle (mostly in Judges) are illuminating. Jael kills Sisera by staking him through the temple with a tent peg. Several commentators have observed that this is phallic imagery.[31] Sisera is feminized in defeat. Though Delilah does not kill Samson, she does facilitate his capture. The language used to describe her interactions with Samson is language usually associated with male sexual dominance [צחק, טחן, ענה, פתה]. Cutting his hair removes his manly strength and vigor. The greatest humiliation seems to be dying at the hand of a woman in battle. This is implied in the interaction between Deborah and Barak, when Barak is chastised for not leading the battle himself.[32] Even more explicitly, when a woman mortally wounds Abimelech by dropping a millstone on his head in Judg 9:54, he commands one of his compatriots to finish him off so that people will not say that a woman killed him.[33] The upshot of all of this is that defeated men are feminized.[34]

Cynthia Chapman addresses the military rhetoric in Assyrian and biblical sources, with particular attention to gender imagery.[35] She observes that in the Assyrian royal inscriptions various epithets for the king explicitly claim that he is a man. This statement is not an affirmation of biology, but implies power and vigor. In palace victory reliefs the king is invariably portrayed in a strictly upright posture, has a full beard, and is often carrying a drawn bow.[36] Vassal kings, in contrast, prostrate themselves before the Assyrian king, sometimes wiping the king's feet with their beards.[37] Other elements of masculinity that the Assyrian king possesses in abundance, but that the defeated kings lack, include military prowess, bravery (defeated kings are often described as fleeing in fear to save their own lives), the ability to provide for and protect his people, and the ability to leave an inheritance for his family or people. Treaty curses most often involve threats to the masculinity of the vassal kings, including the threat that they and their soldiers will become women, that they will lose their land, that their people will be deported from their inheritance, and that the king's family will become vulnerable to capture and starvation.[38] Chapman applies these observations to the account of Sennacherib's siege of Jerusalem, noting the various elements of masculinity that mark the encounter in the biblical rhetoric.

Gender Imagery in Hosea

Having provided the context of previous masculinity studies in biblical texts, I will now turn to an analysis of the imagery in Hosea that has a specific gender focus. First, I will examine the female imagery, which I argue does not provide a construction of femininity in the text, but rather focuses on issues of masculinity as defined through relationships with women. After considering the details of this imagery, I will discuss its implications for masculinity.[39]

Female Imagery

Fertility Cult Theories

Female imagery is located primarily in the first three chapters of Hosea, with a few additional references later. It is this imagery that has the most narrative development, through the portrayal of Hosea's marriage. In chapter 1, I discussed some of the literature interpreting the marriage metaphor. Here I will concentrate on the more explicitly sexual imagery, which has captured the imagination of many scholars.

The female sexual imagery has typically been lumped together with the marriage imagery and imbued with cultic meaning.[40] Israel is viewed as cheating on her husband with another god, in particular, Baal. Complex scenarios have been built around the supposed sexual fertility rites associated with the temples of Baal and Asherah. The קדשות or holy women have been frequently understood to be cult prostitutes, available to worshippers in order to insure the continued fertility of the land and the people. Canaanite rituals have also been imagined to degenerate not infrequently into drunken orgies.

> The Canaanite religion was based on nature myths which laid great stress on fertility and little if any on morality. The resulting cult was a technique for ensuring that everything that could be fruitful and multiply did so with the least difficulty and the greatest dispatch. This religion was for the Canaanites (and for most of the Israelites) what scientific humanism and technology are for people of the 20th century: essential to the means of production and for ensuring regular increase in the Gross National Product. Myths about fertility, used to foster fertility, inevitably engendered cultic techniques which gave prominence to sexual acts designed to operate with the powers of imitative magic. Male and female prostitutes thronged the shrines, making sanctuaries indistinguishable from brothels and holiness indistinguishable from harlotry.[41]

Within such a context Hosea's message appears to be concerned mainly with religious and cultic infractions. Many commentators have come to the conclusion that syncretism is the major problem here.[42] The people have not necessarily abandoned the worship of YHWH, but they are conflating him with Baal, and worshipping him with fertility rites "under every green tree."[43]

The trend has then been to examine the nature of Gomer's harlotry in light of the supposed Canaanite sex cult. "Whether her profligacy showed itself in simple adultery, or in her following the licentious rites of the consort of the Canaanitish Baal (Ashérah), we know not."[44] "[I]s she one of the temple prostitutes who were then beginning to appear in Israel under the influence of the Canaanite cult?"[45] The idea of the sex cult was so ingrained that some went so far as to associate all prostitution with cultic rites.[46] In addition to the idea of permanent cult prostitutes, another supposed feature of Canaanite religion has sometimes been associated with Gomer: the ritual defloration of virgins. In such a rite each young bride had to go to the temple to submit to a single instance of prostitution in order to gain the fertility blessings of Baal.[47]

Recent scholars have questioned the presence of a sex cult in Israel and its environs. Phyllis Bird wrote a pivotal study examining the use of זנה in biblical texts, where it refers to any kind of illicit sexual activity, not just prostitution. It is also usually distinguished from adultery [נאף]. Hosea links the images of promiscuity with illicit cult activity for rhetorical effect: improper cult worship by the males is equivalent to illicit sex by females. This was meant to catch the listeners' attention, not to imply a literal connection between the two.[48] Much of the evidence for these supposed rites comes from Herodotus, other Greek writers following Herodotus, and works like *The Testament of Judah*. These sources are unreliable, however, particularly in relation to 8th c. Israel. Sumerian texts do cite an instance of sacred marriage, but this seems to be limited to the king, not something that was practiced by the general populace.[49] The basis for the bridal defloration rite is mainly a passage in the Epic of Gilgamesh, hardly a historical text.[50] Herodotus wrote a highly polemical work telling of the degenerate nature of the Asiatics. When discussing Babylon and Cyprus (I.199) he commented: "The foulest Babylonian custom is that which compels every woman of the land once in her life to sit in the temple of Aphrodite and have intercourse with some stranger."[51] He wrote substantially after the period he describes and with the purpose of showing the superiority of Greek culture.[52] Later scholars based their accounts on Herodotus's work. Accusing one's enemies of sexual perversions is hardly unique and appears also within the Hebrew Bible.[53]

The existence of sex cults in ancient Israel is highly questionable. First, it is not clear that widespread worship of Baal existed in Israel during the 8th c.[54] Second, and more importantly, as the god of vegetative fertility, Baal is not associated with overt sexuality in the Canaanite texts, as were El and Asherah, and, in fact, repudiated sexual activity in the cult.[55] As Susan Sanders observes: "Baal was not a god of sexual fecundity and this has been one of the most common misunderstandings of his personality....Instead, the nature of Baal was about power and influence—order, rule and plenty, rather than chaos, fear and scarcity of crops."[56] His associations with fertility result more from his battles with chaos than with sexual encounters.[57] Third, there is even less evidence of sexual practices in actual worship practices. Only one mythological text contains a rubric for an accompanying ritual. While the text describes intercourse between El and Athirat and Rahmay, the rubric makes no mention of accompanying ritual intercourse, instead describing only actions such as reciting the stories, singing hymns, burning incense, and placing statues in niches.[58] The term קדשות, which many interpreters translate as cult prostitute, appears in the equivalent masculine form [קדשים] in Ugaritic texts in lists of cultic functionaries, none of which appears to have sexual connotations. Nor is there evidence of ritual de-floration occurring at the temples.[59] It appears that despite the immense scholarly efforts that have gone into finding a literal basis for the female sexual imagery in Hosea, as Alice Keefe observes: "Evidence to support the scholarly fantasy of a sex cult in Israel has found to be lacking."[60]

Female Imagery as Metaphor

Looking at the sexual imagery for its own sake and not as evidence for possible religious practices reveals some interesting patterns. The imagery divides readily into two types: the female as subject and the female as object. Instances of female imagery are distributed fairly evenly between the two types.

Female as Subject. The marriage metaphor is introduced in ch. 1. Gomer the subject appears in 1:3, 6, and 8 as a mother who conceives, bears, and weans children. These actions appear to be neutral or positive. Usually, however, the female as subject is portrayed as promiscuous. The first in-stance occurs in 1:2, where the wife is called אשת זנונים who has ילדי זנונים. The exact translation of these phrases has been hotly debated. Be-cause the substantive form זָנָה usually refers to a prostitute, some com-mentators assume that Gomer was a prostitute of some sort, most often associated with the cult of Baal, as noted above. In plural form, however, the meaning has broader implications of fornication. Many interpreters translate this as harlot, which does not have the professional connota-tions of prostitution. Bird translates this with the more rhetorically neu-tral "woman of promiscuities."[61] In any case, the text implies that the wife has sexual relations with a man other than her husband. The exact nature of the relationship is not described, however, which probably in-dicates that the details are not important to the rhetorical point of the au-thor. I propose that this is because the focus is not really on the woman, but rather on the husband and the marital relationship. It does not matter whether the wife is promiscuous by participating in a fertility cult (though this is unlikely) or in a secular relationship, or whether she gets paid for sex or not. The point is that the woman has sex outside of the marital relationship. The physical act of sex is also irrelevant, as 1:2 im-mediately brings out symbolic implications of the image, claiming that the land acts promiscuously away from YHWH. The focus on YHWH rather than the wife/land is underscored by the somewhat unusual ter-minology תזנה הארץ מאחרי יהוה כי־זנה [The land fornicates from after

YHWH]. In non-prophetic texts, Israelites are frequently accused of זנה
אחרי [whoring after] other gods,[62] where other gods are object, not
YHWH. In Hosea, other gods do not appear, and the wife rather awk-
wardly whores from after YHWH.[63] Two points can be drawn from this.
First, YHWH is the focus. Where the wife goes is insignificant, what is
important is that she is going away from YHWH. Second, because other
gods are not specifically mentioned, the phrase does not necessarily refer
to cultic matters.

The female character acts as the subject in a related set of images in
ch. 2. The wife, or rather the mother of the children with whom the husband is speaking, is accused of harlotry and acting shamelessly in 2:7,
which has resulted in the illegitimate status of the children. Further, she
pursues her lovers, attributing to them her bread, water, wool, wine, oil,
and drink. That this pursuit will be fruitless is iterated in 2:8 and 2:9. She
will not be able to find her paths; she will pursue her lovers, but will not
overtake them. She is accused of offering to the baalim, wearing her jew-
elry, and forgetting YHWH in 2:15. Finally, she will decide to return to
her husband, saying that things were better with him than they are now
(2:9). While this last action may initially appear positive, as the wife
gives up her lovers, the context shows that even the return is misdirected.
Her motivations are based in material self-interest and not repentance for
her past misdeeds. Thus the husband will continue to punish her.

A second group of images in ch. 2 projects desired future actions for
the wife as subject. These actions are relatively passive. The wife is requested to "remove her promiscuities from her face and her adulteries
from between her breasts" (2:4). Though the imagery portrays this as an
active process (removing something), the implied meaning is not really
an action, but rather a refraining from action (not being promiscuous). A
slightly different kind of passive action is hoped for in 2:17, where after
being led into the wilderness, the wife will respond as in the days of her
youth. Likewise in 2:21 the newly betrothed wife will know YHWH. The
wife appears as the subject again in 2:18, in which she will call the husband אישי and not בעלי. This form of address does not seem to be an independent action of the wife, however, but rather a response to the
husband's command.

After the first two chapters, there are two more verses in which the
female is portrayed as subject. Verse 4:13, while describing the daughters

as promiscuous and the daughters-in-law as adulterous, is addressed to the fathers, not to the women. In the next verse, these same daughters and daughters-in-law are cleared of responsibility for their actions because their fathers also fornicate. Again the emphasis is not as much on the misbehaving women as on their male relatives.[64]

Female as Object. In the second type of female sexual imagery, the female is the object of action. The first instance occurs in 1:3 when Gomer, the אשת זנונים, is married by Hosea. Chapter 2 provides the majority of the examples of female as object. Some of the examples show direct action upon the body of the wife, while others depict the removal of staple provisions. In 2:4 the wife/mother is the object of rebuke. She will be stripped naked as on the day of her birth, turned into a desert and left to die of thirst (2:5).The husband will snatch away *his* wool and flax that cover her nakedness and will expose her before the eyes of her lovers (2:11–12). The husband will also take away the food provisions. The grain, oil, and wine that the husband initially provided (2:10) will be taken away (2:11). Similarly, the wife's fig trees will be destroyed by the husband, because she thinks them her fee from her lovers (2:14). They will be left uncultivated and the wild beasts will eat them (2:14). The husband will also put an end to the wife's celebrations by removing her festivals. He will hedge up her ways so that she cannot find her lovers. In addition, not only will he punish the wife, but he will disown her children (2:6–7).

All of these actions upon the wife in the first half of ch. 2 are negative. In the second half of the chapter, she is the object of more ambiguous activities. She is seduced in the wilderness and given vineyards there (2.16). While most commentators have treated this as a positive statement, the word פתה has connotations of seduction, more than of speaking coaxingly, as the word is often translated in this particular context.[65] Similarly, "speaking to her heart" often refers to direct speech, in the sense of talking sense to her, and does not necessarily suggest tender speech, as it is frequently interpreted. There is also ambiguity about the gifts given in the wilderness. The husband promises to give the wife vineyards in the wilderness and the Valley of Achor as a plowland of hope (2:17). Achor is a valley in the plain of Jericho, but the root עכר means to bring about disaster, disorder, or ruin. It is uncertain whether these gifts are to be understood as symbols of positive transformation or as bitter irony, connected with the destruction of vineyards in 2:14. Similarly, while most interpreters assume that Hosea is hearkening back to a honeymoon phase of the relationship in the wilderness, when the wife/Israel was brought up from Egypt, the traditions preserved in Exodus show this as a period of incessant murmuring and complaints. It is impossible to know what form of the exodus tradition Hosea knew and whether or not it included murmurings, but the fact that Hosea is told to marry a promiscuous wife might support the idea that in his tradition Israel had problems from the beginning. Adding another layer of uncertainty to this passage is the word ענה which in its qal form can mean to answer/respond or to be wretched or oppressed. The piel form is a technical term for rape.[66] The ambiguity of these verses contributes to the metaphorical tension in the book. In any case, the husband will espouse the wife in righteousness and justice (2:21–22) and remove the names of the baalim from her mouth (2:19).

Chapter 3 provides more instances of the woman as object. Hosea is told to love a woman who is loved by another. This woman is then hired or purchased by Hosea (3:2) and isolated by him (3:3). The position of the woman as object is further illustrated by Susan Ackerman's analysis of the use of the term love. Noting that others have observed that love often has political implications, she undertakes a study of love in interpersonal relations. Even when it appears that emotional love is mutual, אהב is only used to refer to the more powerful person in the relationship. A husband loves a wife, but a wife never loves a husband. Likewise, a parent of either gender can love a child, but the child never loves the parent.[67] The woman taken by Hosea in 3:1 does not love another; she is loved by another, the object of both Hosea and the compatriot's love.[68]

The remaining eleven chapters of the book offer three partial examples. The previously mentioned promiscuous daughters and daughters-in-law avoid becoming the object of action, as they will not be punished (4:14). In 9:11 and 9:14 punishment takes the form of infertility, but the women themselves, who would presumably be the ones suffering this fate, are not directly mentioned, just their wombs and breasts.

Implications of Female Imagery for Masculinity
Examination of the female imagery reveals three main areas of concern: provisioning, fidelity, and reproduction. As other scholars have observed,

these are the areas that reflect most strongly on the masculinity of the husband in many patriarchal societies.

Provisioning. An important component of masculinity in the ANE was that a man should provide sufficient provisions for his wife and family. Many marriage contracts in the ANE required the husband to provide his wife with stipulated amounts of items such as clothing, oil, and food-stuffs.[69] Failure to do so could be grounds for divorce in the Middle Assyrian Laws.[70] The same is true in at least one set of circumstances in biblical law: "If he takes another [wife], he shall not diminish her food, clothing, or marital rights. If he does not do these three things for her, she may go out freely, without [paying] money" (Exod 21:10–11).

In addition to these cases, many of the curses in Assyrian treaties relate to the provisioning/protecting features of masculinity, as Chapman has observed.[71] The curses contain threats to the vassal king's personal family, as well as the larger population. One common curse predicts that if the king violates the treaty, his inability to provide food for his people will result in cannibalism. For example, the Treaty of Aššur-nerari V with Mati'-ilu, King of Arpad, curses the violator, saying: "May Adad, the canal inspector of heaven and earth, put an end to Mati'-ilu's land, and the people of his land through hunger, want, and famine, may they eat the flesh of their sons and daughters, and may it taste as good to them as the flesh of spring lambs."[72] Similar curses occur in Esarhaddon's Succession Treaty, which phrases the predicted cannibalism in more personal terms for the rebellious king. In the most developed example:

> May Adad, the canal inspector of heaven and earth, cut off sea[sonal flooding] from your land and deprive your fields of [grain], may he [submerge] your land with a great flood; may the locust who diminishes the land devour your harvest; may the sound of mill or oven be lacking from your houses, may the grain for grinding disappear from you; instead of grain may your sons and your daughters grind your bones; may not (even) your (first) finger-joint dip in the dough, may the [...] of your bowls eat up the dough. May a mother [bar the door] to her daughter. In your hunger eat the flesh of your sons! In want and famine may one man eat the flesh of another; may one man clothe himself in another's skin.[73]

The curses stipulate that the king will not be able to provide for his people, either for his immediate family or for the country as a whole. This is a great dishonor.

In light of these expectations of provisioning, by misattributing the provisions of the grain, oil, wine, and clothing in Hosea, the wife insults her husband's honor, in effect stating that her husband did not provide for her, but rather another man did. Ken Stone argues that this misattribution in Hos 2 affronts the husband's masculinity just as much as the sexual straying.[74]

Fidelity. The second area of concern, the threat of the wife's infidelity, has been discussed more thoroughly in scholarship. Such studies have frequently employed the so-called honor/shame model, derived from anthropological work mostly in the Mediterranean region, but to some extent in other areas of the world. In the classic honor/shame model, women are constantly under the close control of men, initially their fathers and brothers and later their husbands. They are expected to remain virgins before marriage and to be faithful after marriage. Outside sexual activity is a threat to the honor of the males responsible for the women. An important component of this model is that honor of men is largely dependent on the shame, that is, the chastity, of the women in their household.[75] Competition between males is quite high, with challenges requiring a strong response.[76] Although the model has been criticized as overly simplistic for linking honor and shame too closely to gender and for glossing over differences between the cultures, it has proved a useful way to look at certain features of social relations.[77]

Such a strongly gender bound model has limitations.[78] The traditional linkage of male honor to female shame ignores the broader aspects of honor not explicitly related to the sexuality of female relatives, including honesty and hospitality, and the fact that the lack of these virtues causes men to be thought shameless, not only lacking in honor.[79] A broader conception of honor and shame can be found throughout the HB, with the David narratives having received particular scholarly attention.[80] The focus of this broader conception tends to be on men and masculinity rather than on the relations between men and women. Although the latter are still important, proper relations and respect between men in the public arena are of foremost concern. Relations of honor and shame thus form an important part of the construction of masculinity in the biblical text.

Even in the looser form of the honor/shame concept, the fidelity of a man's wife is necessary for his honor and thus his masculinity. If a man's wife strays, it affects masculinity in multiple ways. First, the husband faces the shame of not controlling his wife. Julie Galambush applies this idea to her analysis of the marriage metaphor in the prophetic texts. "Although adultery did not defile the name of the husband, the shame created by Yahweh's failure to keep his subjects 'at home' would have found powerful expression in the image of the god as cuckolded, and therefore shamed, husband."[81] Second, adultery may suggest to other people that the husband has failed to provide the necessities of life: sufficient food, clothing, and other provisions, or sufficient virility.[82] In such a case, the shame falls on the husband rather than the wife. Third, the lover himself may be seen as challenging the husband's masculinity. In a society in which male relatives are responsible for the protection of a female, provisionally and sexually, the making and breaking of relationships between men and women are in large part relations between men, with the woman as the focal point.[83]

The treaty curses bring out another aspect of the infidelity of the wife. A curse in the Esarhaddon Succession treaty reads: "May Venus, the brightest of the stars, before your eyes make your wives lie in the lap of your enemy."[84] While it is possible that this curse threatens the rape of the wife, another interpretation corresponds closely to the situation in Hos 2, that she is unfaithful, and the husband knows about it. Because it is a goddess who brings about the unfaithfulness of the wives, from the perspective of the husband, they may appear to choose to be unfaithful. A curse in the Aramaic treaty between Mati'el, king of Arpad, and Bar-Ga'yah, king of KTK, also relates the wives of the kings and nobles to promiscuous activity: "[And just as] a [har]lot [is stripped naked], so may the wives of Mati'el be stripped naked, and the wives of his offspring, and the wives of [his] no[bles]!"[85] While this curse is often used to illuminate the punishment of the stripping of the wife in 2:5, it is perhaps also useful to consider the parallel with the harlot. The wives become like harlots, at least in some aspects. Looking at the image of the unfaithful wife from this perspective does raise questions about the tenor of the metaphor, especially that of the husband. If the audience is the wife and the husband is YHWH, then the wife must be at fault. In these treaty curses, however, it is the husband's disobedience that leads to the punishments to the wives, which are in turn punishments for the husbands.[86] The image of the adulterous wife in ch. 2 may thus have a dual resonance with the audience: one in which they must identify with the wife and one in which they are faced with concern about their own wives.

Reproduction. The strong emphasis on female fidelity in marriage is often justified by a concern with paternity. In order for a man to know that his offspring are indeed his own, he must ensure that he is the only one having intercourse with his wife. The children themselves, especially sons, serve, among other things, as proof of their father's virility. Although the female who is childless is often castigated as barren, in many areas of the world, the male is considered the real source of the child, while the mother serves as an incubator. The language of seed, sowing, insemination, and so forth is quite common cross-culturally, including ancient Israel.[87] In this model the male provides the seed, while the female is the soil. Soil can be fertile or barren, but it ultimately plays a passive role.[88] The active role of the male must be continually proved.[89] In Hosea, the presence of children vouches for the virility of the husband, but the possibility that they are not his threatens this element of his masculinity.[90]

Responses to Challenged Masculinity

The husband's response in chs. 2 and 3 indicates his desire to defend and reaffirm his masculinity. As several scholars have noted, part of the irony of an honor/shame or other system of hegemonic masculinity is that the subordinated female has considerable control over the reputation of the dominant male.[91] Considerable pressure is put on the male relatives to ensure their reputations through their females' chastity.[92] While a cuckolded man is dishonored, the man who is potentially in the position of the most shame is one who knows about his wife's infidelity, but does nothing about it. To avoid this ultimate shame, the men of Andalusia, when informally discussing their wives, would be sure to say that *as far as they knew*, their wives were faithful, so that if this should not prove the case, they were absolved of responsibility.[93]

The husband in Hosea does not want to suffer this fate of shame from inaction in the face of infidelity. He threatens to disown the children and to punish the wife.[94] In addition to reclaiming his masculinity through his direct actions on his wife and children, the husband makes a counterattack on the masculinity of the lovers.

Stripping her naked before her lovers will not only expose her body and the foolishness of her ways, it will also prove, contrary to her claims, how feeble and
impotent are her lovers to protect and provide for her (v. 12).[95]

Showing that the lovers are incapable of saving the woman from the punishment of her husband places the blame for the straying back on the
woman. The wife did not leave because her lovers were more manly than
her husband.

Male Imagery

I have so far analyzed the implications the female imagery has for the
masculinity of the husband in the text. I will address the implications that
being portrayed as the wife, a woman, has for the male audience below.
At this point, however, I will stay within the plane of the text to consider
the male imagery. To understand the context of the images Hosea uses, it
is helpful to look at literature from surrounding areas in the ANE, as well
as other biblical texts. In particular I will examine treaties and incantations from Assyria, which was the dominant power in the region during
the time of Hosea's prophecies. These texts will help to illuminate the
types of images used for gender and sexuality in the area. I will also consider the rhetoric of Hosea's sexual metaphors and compare it with the
rhetoric of the Assyrian treaties.

Virility as Power

Many of the images in Hosea relate to virility. Sexual potency is an important symbol of power in a patriarchal society, such as found in 8th c.
Israel, and the ability to display one's sexual virility was an important
component of male honor.[96] This concept finds support in several biblical
texts, particularly in the Deuteronomistic History.

Second Samuel 10 describes an episode in which the Ammonites
mistreat a group of envoys sent by David. The Ammonites shaved the
beards of the envoys and cut off their robes "in half, up to their hips"
[בחצי עד שתותיהם], which probably left their genitals exposed, or nearly
so. These particular actions were a direct assault on the men's masculinity, causing them shame. David recognized this and let them stay in
Jericho until their beards could grow back. As an attack on his messengers' masculinity and honor translated into an attack on David's own
honor, he was motivated to protect himself as well as the men. Since the

act was intended to shame David and his messengers, and not merely to rebuff them, the Ammonites became odious [כי נבאשו] to David.[97]

The same terminology of shame is used in 2 Sam 16. After Absalom has claimed his father David's kingdom, he proves his potency as a potential king by having intercourse with his father's concubines one after another in the view of "all Israel" (2 Sam. 16:22). Through this action he not only displays his own potency, but also demonstrates David's impotence, evidenced by his inability to protect his household, an important aspect of masculinity.[98] Ahithophel advises Absalom to perform this act so that Israel may hear that he has become odious [כי-נבאשת] to David.

The use of the term נבאש thus underscores the idea that Absalom's assault of David's concubines was a direct challenge to his masculinity in several ways.[99] First, he caused David to flee, leaving his family behind. As noted above, in the Assyrian curses and chronicles, the shamed and defeated king flees to save his own life, but leaves his family to fend for themselves. Second, Absalom's actions underline the fact that David left his concubines to guard the house. Not only did he flee himself, but he did not even appoint another man to protect his family. Instead he left his concubines in charge, people who were toward the lower end of the prestige ranking in the royal household, women with even lower status than his principal wives. Third, Absalom had intercourse with David's wives, cuckolding him. He thus made himself odious to David, while at the same time raising the status of his own masculinity.

The inverse situation occurs in I Kgs 1, where the symbol of David's final decline and his loss of political control is his impotency in the presence of Abishag, the most beautiful virgin in the land (1 Kgs 1:4). His impotence extends to matters of state, as he remains out of the loop in the battle for succession and is informed of the situation by his wife (1 Kgs 1:18). While he ultimately shows the power to name his successor, he does not take a direct role in the announcement, which is made public by his servants, and he makes Solomon king in his place before he dies (1 Kgs 1:48), showing that his own power to rule has diminished.

Solomon's potency as king is, in turn, partially expressed through his harem, which comprises 700 princesses and 300 concubines (1 Kgs 11:3). The princesses display his political power, representing the many alliances he has made with other nations. The concubines represent his sexual potency. While these many wives ultimately lead to Solomon's downfall, in his prime they symbolize the great extent of his power.

As shown by the examples above, male sexual imagery is intertwined with images of male vigor and implications of power. I will thus use the term "potency" to represent this mixture of sexual, social, and political power and "impotency" to represent the lack thereof.

Comparative Texts

Much of the male imagery in Hosea has been overlooked, because it is not as obvious to contemporary eyes as is the female imagery. An examination of ANE texts that have more overt sexual and gender connotations, however, reveals a common image base. These texts are useful for bringing to light some of the more obscure metaphors in Hosea.[100] I will use several comparative materials, including Assyrian treaties and other documents, Canaanite myths, and other biblical texts. One source that has proved of particular use in illuminating the male imagery in Hosea is a collection of 7th c. Akkadian potency incantations with accompanying rituals called the *ŠÀ.ZI.GA* ("Rising of the Heart").[101] While Hosea may or may not have been aware of these or similar texts, they serve to illustrate the types of images for male sexuality that were present in the cultural milieu of the ANE, which was politically dominated by the Assyrians.[102]

Categories of Male Imagery in Hosea

In contrast with the female sexual imagery, in which the references to female as subject and as object are roughly equal in number, slightly favoring the female as object, the male sexual imagery predominantly shows the male as subject. The imagery in which the male is the object often appears as an inverse to the male as subject, so I will not separate the imagery into these categories. I will instead treat particular imagistic words or themes, which divide into two categories. Illicit sexual relationships, which associate men with treachery and deceit, are represented by the terms זנה and נאף, while potency images, which form an important component of masculine identity, include sticks and staffs, און, lifting up and גאון, baking imagery, and bow imagery.

זנה. The first category of illicit sexual relationships is זנה. Forms of זנה occur in nine verses in chs. 4–14 with a male subject or implied subject. Israel and Ephraim are not only grammatically gendered as males, but are clearly personified as such in the text (4:10, 11, 12, 15, 18; 5:3, 4; 6:10; 9:1). The significance of the male subject has largely been ignored. Even those commentators who look at promiscuity imagery beyond the first three chapters often see these references as a return to female imagery. Among the few who have recognized that these are clearly males being discussed, Bird proposes that the hiphil form, which appears three times in Hosea (4:10, 18; 5:3), could indicate the male role in prostitution. Despite the male subject, however, she characterizes the other references as still playing on female imagery.[103] When זנה is used with female subjects in Hosea, there has been much debate about whether or not the references are literal or figurative. Most feminist scholars conclude that they are figurative, while, as noted above, many previous scholars have taken at least some of the images literally. When the male is the subject, however, the jump to figurative is immediate.[104] The result of this is that the metaphor is treated as if it were dead.[105] While this may be true of the non-prophetic material, in Hosea, at least, the metaphor seems to be very much alive, and as such, has broader rhetorical implications.

The first time the verb appears in the masculine is 4:10: "They will eat, but not be sated, they will fornicate but not break out/through" [ואכלו ולא ישבעו הזנו ולא יפרצו].[106] The verb פרץ has two basic meanings: to break through, as in breaching a wall, and to break out, or to multiply quickly and spread out in space. There is thus a possible double entendre in the verse. One relates to infertility, in which the man will be promiscuous, but will not have offspring. Loss of fertility even with much effort is a common treaty curse. The treaty between Mati'-ilu and Aššur-nerari V reads: "may Mati'ilu's (sex) life be that of a mule's."[107] Similar curses come from Esarhaddon's Succession Treaty: "May Belet-ili, the lady of creation, cut off birth from your land; may she deprive your nurses of the cries of little children in the streets and squares."[108] "Just as a m[ule has n]o offspring, may your name, your seed, and the seed of your sons and daughters disappear from the land."[109]

The second connotation relates to lack of satisfaction in the sexual act itself. The male will fornicate, but will not breach the female's "wall."[110] The imagery of breaking through is sometimes used in the military defeat of cities, which are often portrayed as female. Breaching the wall is the symbolic equivalent of sexual penetration.[111] Either of these

two connotations parallels the preceding colon expressing the lack of satisfaction from food.

While this example links fornication with futility, the two other
verses employing the hiphil form link fornication with shamefulness or
impurity. In 4:18 fornication is paired with drinking rather than eating:
Their drink turns aside, they indeed fornicate" [סר סבאם הזנה הזנו].[112] It
is followed by an allusion to some misbegotten love: "they indeed love
disgrace, her gift" [אהבו הבו קלון מגניה].[113] The final hiphil form comes
in 5:3 in parallel with impurity: "Because now you have fornicated,
Ephraim, Israel is defiled" [כי עתה הזנית אפרים נטמא ישראל]. The result of this fornication, described in 5:5, is that their pride will be humbled [ענה], and they will stumble in their iniquity [עון].

The qal perfect appears in 4:12 and 9:1 and the masculine singular
participle in 4:15. Twice Ephraim is associated with the nominal form
זנות (4:11 and 6:10). In both of the qal perfect cases, the fornication occurs in some sense away from God. The prepositions are noteworthy,
however. The last part of 4:12 reads: "They fornicated from under their
God" [ויזנו מתחת אלהיהם]. While the semantic context here is clearly
masculine, as shown by the masculine singular possessive suffixes in the
first half of the verse, the preposition תחת places the males in the female
position, underneath.[114] In 9:1, however, the preposition is a compound
with על: "Because you [Israel] have fornicated from upon your God"
[כי זנית מעל אלהיך]. While the meaning is presumably similar, as על
has a semantic range including "with" or "over against" the change in
terminology is interesting.[115] It parallels the use of על in the second half
of the verse, in which "you have loved hire (prostitute's wages) upon
every threshing floor of grain" [אהבת אתנן על כל-גרנות דגן]. Nevertheless it remains an unexpected choice of preposition, contrasting with the
more clearly submissive תחת or אחרי found elsewhere in Hosea. In any
event, the promiscuity here will result in deportation and the inability to
provide pure food (9:3), another failure in masculinity.[116]

The masculine singular participial form זנה occurs in 4:15, where
Judah is warned not to follow Israel's example of fornicating. Verse 4:11
is grammatically difficult, and זנות should probably be joined to 4:10 to
read: "because they abandoned YHWH to observe fornication" [כי-את
יהוה עזבו לשמר זנות]. Joining the two resolves the problem of the otherwise objectless לשמר, but זנות itself could just as well be read with the

following verse, joining wine and new wine in taking away the people's heart. In 6:10 Ephraim's fornication is found in its house, parallel with the uncleanness of Israel.

Twice Ephraim is afflicted with a רוח זנונים (4:12 and 5:4). While רוח is grammatically feminine, the construction is found in the context of a discussion about a male audience being led astray. Following a spirit of fornication clearly refers to the men's motives. In addition to the direct attribution of זנה to men, the males are criticized for going apart [פרד] with prostitutes (4:14),[117] hiring lovers (Ephraim—8:9),[118] and becoming detestable like their love (Israel—9:10). The references to male illicit sexual activity keeps the rhetorical focus on the wrongdoing of the audience as males, excluding the possibility of evading responsibility through the construction of a female "other."[119]

נאף. The men are also characterized as adulterers (7:4).[120] Adultery in the time period is defined as sexual relations with or by a married woman, regardless of the marital status of the man. Adultery is thus a crime against a husband rather than against a wife. In the context of a chapter filled with political intrigue and apparent conspiracy against the king, characterizing the plotters as adulterers is interesting.[121] One possible explanation is that the men are once again being cast into the position of adulterous women, albeit indirectly, shown as betraying their king by plotting to assassinate him. Despite the emphasis on the adulterous woman in the prophetic books, however, of which Hosea gives the earliest example, adultery is a term more often associated with men than with women in the biblical texts.[122] Thus it would seem unlikely to immediately place the male audience in a female role. Another possibility is that the conspirators are committing adultery against the king as men, making a direct challenge to his masculinity. It is more difficult in this latter case to figure out the role of the wife. Because this is a metaphor rather than an allegory, however, the absence of the wife may be irrelevant. The strong masculine images in ch. 7 clearly suggest that the issue is the contest between men.

In addition to the use of adultery as a trope for competing potencies, it also implies treachery and deceit.[123] An analogous passage in Jer 9:1b pairs adulterers and bands of traitors, who tell lies and forsake truth: "because they are all adulterers, an assembly of traitors" [כי כלם מנאפים עצרת בגדים]. What makes this an especially telling parallel is the presence of a raiding band and treachery in Hosea 7:1. In addition, in 7:3 these treacherous ones make the king merry. The word עצרה used in Jeremiah has a primary meaning of a holiday or a festive assembly. Thus in both passages adultery, deceit, and celebrations are linked, while women are conspicuously absent. The adultery imagery emphasizes the treacherous competition between men.

Sticks and Staffs. In addition to the fields of illicit sexual relations there are several more categories of masculine imagery relating to potency. One of the more obvious cases is in 4:12, which reads: "my people asks his stick and his staff tells him" [עמי בעצו ישאל ומקלו יגיד לו]. The majority of commentators have interpreted the stick and staff as cultic items, which fits with the usual interpretation that Hosea has primarily religious concerns. For example, NRSV translates the verse as "My people consult a piece of wood and their divining rod gives them oracles."[124] Another way to interpret the verse, however, is through phallic imagery, where the rod and staff are euphemisms for penis.[125] The likelihood that this is phallic imagery is increased by its immediate context in an oracle describing promiscuity and adultery. It is preceded by vv. 10b–11: "Because they abandoned YHWH to observe fornication, and wine and new wine takes away [their] heart" [כי־את־יהוה עזבו לשמר זנות ויין ותירוש יקח־לב] and followed by v. 12b: "For a spirit of fornication leads them astray, and they fornicate from under their God" [כי רוח זנונים התעה ויזנו מתחת אלהיהם].[126] In other words, wine has taken away the men's minds and they are thinking with another part of their anatomy.[127] The chapter as a whole is quite dense with sexual imagery, especially with excessive or illegitimate sex, so the phallic nature of the rods and staffs is appropriate in the context.

Cognate literature provides several examples of rods and staffs as phallic imagery. One is found in the Canaanite text of "Shachar and Shalim." After having intercourse with his two wives (with his "hand" as long as the sea), El evidently needs a break before resuming activities with his passionate wives:

> Surely El entices two women; lo! the two women cry out:
> "Oh husband, husband, thy sceptre is lowered, the staff of thy hand laid aside (?)
> Lo! the bird is roasted at the fire; scorching hot at the coals are
> the two women, wives of El—wives of El (now) and for evermore!"[128]

אוֹן. The word אוֹן is an equivalent term to potency in English, with connotations of sexual, physical, economic, and political power.[129] The term appears twice in ch. 12. Jacob exerts himself with God in his אוֹן "manly vigor" in 12:4. Eilberg-Schwarz comments on the allusion to Jacob in this passage and its implications of unwarranted pride:

> Hosea's retelling emphasizes that Jacob's struggle with God occurred in his manhood ('ono). Furthermore, it makes Jacob's supplanting of Esau parallel Jacob's struggle with God. Hosea views the struggle with God as part of Jacob's (Israel's) hubris. He is so defiant that he is willing to stand against God.[130]

The economic connotations of אוֹן appear a few verses later in 12:9, still in a context of unwarranted hubris, where Ephraim says: "Surely I have become rich. I have found potency for myself" [אַךְ עָשַׁרְתִּי מָצָאתִי אוֹן לִי]. This is followed by the enigmatically worded justification: "all of my acquisitions do not find for me iniquity that is sin" [כָּל־יְגִיעַי לֹא יִמְצְאוּ־לִי עָוֹן אֲשֶׁר־חֵטְא]. There is a play here between what Ephraim has found for himself (אוֹן) and what his acquisitions have not found for him (עָוֹן).[131] Of course, the implication of the passage is that iniquity has indeed been found.

Lifting Up and גָּאוֹן. More examples of hubris viewed in spatial terms, perhaps including anatomical space, include 13:1, in which Ephraim "lifts up" in Israel, and 13:6, in which the people's "heart lifted up," and therefore they forgot God. It is worth noting that in the ŠÀ.ZI.GA texts "heart" (ŠÀ) is the primary euphemism for the phallus, and the "lifting of the heart" is the hoped for result upon using the potency incantations.[132] Here again is the possibility that pride is symbolized by sexual potency. The opposite seems to occur in 11:7, where the people do not "lift up together" when called. This verse is difficult to translate, and it is not clear who is doing the calling and what is being lifted, but the people seem impotent to respond to the call.[133] Lifting up in a figurative sense is represented by גָּאוֹן or pride. The word occurs in the same phrase twice in 5:5 and 7:10: "Israel's pride is humbled" [וְעָנָה גְאוֹן־יִשְׂרָאֵל].

Baking Imagery. Another group of male sexual images, especially prevalent in ch. 7, is related to baking. The relationship between food and sex is common in Hebrew and other literatures and vernaculars.[134] Song of Songs provides particularly obvious food linkages. Some examples are:

2:4: "He brought me to the banquet house" [הביאני אל־בית היין]; 4:11: "sweetness drops from your lips, bride; honey and milk are under your tongue" [נפת תטפנה שפתותיך כלה דבש וחלב תחת לשונך]; 4:16: "Let my beloved come to his garden and eat its delightful fruits" [יבא דודי לגנו ויאכל פרי מגדיו]; 5:1: "I have eaten my honeycomb with its honey. I drank my wine with my milk. Eat, lovers, and drink, drink deep of love" [אכלתי יערי עם־דבשי שתיתי ייני עם־הלבי אכלו רעים שתו ושכרו דודים]. Judges 14, which recounts the tale of Samson and his Philistine fiancée, also associates honey with marriage and sex.

Negative connections between food and sex are found in Proverbs. Proverbs 30:20 describes an adulteress with implications of eating: "Thus are the ways of an adulterous woman: She eats and wipes her mouth and says, 'I have done no wrong'" [כן דרך אשה מנאפת אכלה ומחתה פיה ואמרה לא־פעלתי און]. An association of bread with illicit sexual activity also occurs in Prov 6:26: "Indeed the price of a prostitute is up to a loaf of bread" [כי בעד־אשה זונה עד־ככר לחם]. Connections between food and sex in Hosea are found in ch. 2, where the promiscuity of the wife is rewarded or punished through the giving and taking away of foodstuffs.[135]

Hosea 7 develops an extensive baking metaphor. First, there is the oven itself, a תנור, which is mentioned three times in vv. 4, 6, and 7. It is an upright cylindrical oven with a fire at the bottom, and the food, usually bread, is placed through a hole in the top.[136] The image has obvious phallic possibilities, which are exploited by the context of sexual and political potency. Verse 7:4 most clearly puts the oven in the realm of sexual symbolism: "They are all adulterers, like an oven stoked by a baker" [כלם מנאפים כמו תנור בערה מאפה]. The verse connects the heat of the oven and the heat of illicit sex, an association underscored by the play between מנאפים [adulterers] and מאפה [baker].[137] All of this heat in turn symbolizes political treachery and regicide. The next use of תנור is in 7:6: "They brought near their hearts like an oven in their ambush" [כי־קרבו כתנור לבם בארבם]. The remainder of the verse describes how their baker slept all night, then in the morning flares up like a blazing fire. Subsequently in 7:7: "All of them burned like an oven and consumed their rulers. All their kings have fallen" [כלם יחמו כתנור ואכלו את־שפטיהם כל־מלכיהם נפלו]. The conspirators assert their own potency over that of the kings and princes, who have fallen, a description of impotency in all of its various senses.[138]

A second group of baking images concerns dough and bread. Verse 7:4, which also contains the oven and adultery references mentioned above, states: "he stops stoking from the kneading of the dough until its leavening" [ישבות מעיר מלוש בצק עד־חמצתו]. Before causing the oven to blaze up to full strength, the conspirators wait for their potency to rise. The first stage of bread preparation has shown the conspirators' assessment of their own potency as growing and consuming their rulers. Hosea then develops the imagery further in order to show that their self-image is delusional. The people are not kneaded into potency, rather in 7:8: "Ephraim is kneaded/mixed up among the peoples" [אפרים בעמים הוא יתבולל].[139] The related Akkadian root is used in Assyrian texts to indicate the mixing of peoples for trade and other purposes.[140] Thus the implication may be that the conspirators will not gain independent political power, but will be subject to Assyrian control.

Moving onto the next phase of baking, in 7:8 Ephraim is compared to an unturned cake: "Ephraim is a cake not turned" [אפרים היה עגה בלי הפוכה]. Such a cake would be raw and doughy on one side and burned on the other, not useful for human consumption.[141] Here Ephraim thinks he is potent, like risen bread, but turns out to be simultaneously burned and squishy: impotent.[142] In political terms, Ephraim is caught between two nations. His appeals to Egypt are unsuccessful, and his revolt against Assyria has dire consequences. In the terms of the imagery, Ephraim is unsupported by Egypt (squishy) and burned by Assyria.

Finally, there are images relating to the finished bread in 7:9: "Strangers consume his strength, but he does not know. Also gray hairs/mold sprout on him, but he does not know" [אכלו זרים כחו והוא לא ידע גם־שיבה זרקה בו והוא לא ידע]. Ephraim is unaware that strangers consume his "strength."[143] כח like און connotes virility as well as physical strength, power, and the produce of the land. Ephraim's lack of knowledge about being eaten has multiple implications. First, in the symbolic realm, Ephraim has lost his virility and is no longer able to "know," i.e. to perform sexually, and not only this, he does not even realize it. Second, in the political and economic realm, Ephraim has lost his potency, being mixed up among the nations, but does not realize this. Third, Ephraim's military might has been eviscerated, but he does not realize this, as evidenced by the multiple rebellions against Assyria.

The subsequent line has similar connotations. The translation is somewhat difficult, being either "gray hairs sprout on him" or "mold sprouts on him." The latter meaning is supported by Shalom Paul, who notes that the phrase שיבה זרקה has an Akkadian equivalent in the Gilgamesh epic: šîba ittadi [it had thrown off a mold], although šîba means literally "white hairs."[144] It is possible that a pun is intended, playing off both meanings. Mold, of course, sprouts on bread and denotes decay, the opposite of potency. Gray hair symbolizes old age, with its attendant loss of virility.

Some have noted that such a negative view of old age does not seem appropriate, because it was generally revered in ancient Israel as a time of wisdom.[145] This only adds to the irony of the passage. At an age when wisdom is supposed to be present, Ephraim does not even know his own condition.[146] Rivkah Harris observes that although old age was theoretically respected in many cultures, in actual practice elderly men were probably marginalized, because of the loss of virility and military prowess.[147] The loss of virility with old age is alluded to in Genesis 18:12, where Sarah laughs when the visiting men tell Abraham that she will bear a child. She questions, "After I am worn out shall I have pleasure, and my husband is old?" Sarah's question, interestingly enough, does not concern whether or not she can bear a child, which is the question the visitors say she asked in the next verse. Her concerns, rather, were of the preceding circumstance: could her old and impotent husband have intercourse with her and give her sexual pleasure.

Bow Imagery. A significant field of male sexual imagery that finds many analogies in ANE literature revolves around military might. In particular, the image of the bow as a symbol of potency is widespread. As an instrument of power in military situations and in hunting, it is a natural symbol for masculinity in general.[148] In both biblical and ANE texts and reliefs, bows and archers represent strength and dominance. Assyrian reliefs often show the king standing upright, holding a bow, signifying his power and dominance.[149] The bow was a common weapon and a symbol of might in warfare in ancient Israel, as evidenced by the many occurrences of קשת throughout the biblical texts as a descriptor of warriors, both Israelite and foreign. The bow as a metonym for a mighty warrior appears in 2 Sam 1:17–27, David's lament over Saul and Jonathan, appropriately titled "Bow." Jonathan's bow had never turned back from the blood or fat of the slain warriors, nor had Saul's sword returned empty (1:22). But then in 1:27: "How the mighty have fallen, the weapons of war have perished" [איך נפלו גבורים ואבדו כלי מלחמה].[150] In other texts, the vanquished flee before the bow (e.g. Jer 4:29; Isa 21:15; Ps 11:2). If a warrior is particularly blessed and strengthened he will bend an extra strong bow. David praises God for strengthening his hands for battle so that he can bend a bow of bronze (2 Sam 22:35), as does the singer of Ps 18:35. A broken bow, on the other hand, indicates total defeat. In the biblical texts it is often YHWH who breaks the bows, as a symbol of YHWH's dominion. The nations whose bows are broken are no longer the powerful actors, and in the particular contexts of the verses, this signals a significant reversal of power. In Hannah's song in 1 Sam 2:4, a text describing the overturning of the expected order, where the powerful are dethroned, she sings: "the bows of the mighty are broken, and the faltering are girded with strength" [קשת גברים חתים ונכשלים אזרו חיל]. YHWH defeats the enemies and breaks their bows (unspecified—Ps 76:4; Elam—Jer 49:35; Babylon—Jer 51:56 [through agents]). Broken bows also signify peace under the dominion of YHWH (*e.g.*, Ps 46:9; Zech 9:10). The first reference to the bow in Hosea 1:5 concerns divine bow breaking: "I will break the bow of Israel in the valley of Jezreel" [ושברתי את־קשת ישראל בעמק יזרעאל].

In addition to appearing in biblical references, bow breaking was a fairly common symbol of defeat and humiliation in the surrounding context. The Assyrian reliefs mentioned above, which show the kings as armed and upright, show the defeated parties with their bows down and loose, abandoned, and sometimes forced to cut their own bows by the victor. One particular relief depicts a prisoner kneeling next to a stack of bows he has surrendered, while Aššurbanipal is standing upright with a fully drawn bow, testing the newly confiscated equipment.[151] The victor, epitomizing masculinity, is upright and armed, while the loser is prostrate and bowless. Likewise, in Gen 49:23–24, Joseph (as a tribe) is blessed and is described as prevailing in battle, for while the archers assailed him severely with arrows, "his bow remained taut, and (the arms of) his hands were made agile" [ותשב באיתן קשתו ויפזו זרעי ידיו].

The bow is a multifaceted symbol, incorporating several elements of masculinity. Some of these features appear in Neo-Assyrian treaties of the time, especially in the extensive curse lists. In addition to military might, the bow's connotations of sexuality and fertility emerge in the curses. The threat to break bows thus symbolizes the crushing of both military might and sexual power. Violating the treaty engenders punishments in which the military, protective, provisional, and procreative aspects of the rebel are destroyed, all of which are important elements in the construction of masculinity. The Sefire inscriptions contain curses that extensively describe how the land, as well as its inhabitants, will become barren and how the fields will be sown with salt and weeds, adding: "Just as (this) bow and these arrows are broken, so may Inurta and Hadad break [the bow of Mati'el] and the bow of his nobles!"[152] Likewise a treaty between Aššur-nerari V and Mati'-ilu reads:

> May Mati'-ilu's (sex) life be that of a mule, his wives extremely old; may Ištar, the goddess of men, the lady of women, take away their bow, bring them to shame, and make them bitterly weep: "Woe, we have sinned against the treaty of Aššur-nerari, king of Assyria."[153]

The association between having one's bow broken and being forced to crouch, as in the relief mentioned above, also appears in treaty curses.[154] Esarhaddon's Succession treaty provides some examples:

> [May Ištar, lady of warfare, break his bow in] the thick of battle, and have him crouch as a captive [under his enemy]."[155]

> May Astarte break your bow in the thick of battle and have you crouch at the feet of your enemy, may a foreign enemy divide your belongings.[156]

> [May] Ištar, lady of battle and war, smash your bow in the thick of ba[ttle], may she bind your arms, and have you crouch under your enemy.[157]

The humiliation of breaking a man's bow and forcing him to crouch takes on special significance when one considers the sexual connotations of the bow image. Bows appear in the Ugaritic poem, "The Birth of the Gods of Dawn and Dusk," as a symbol of sexual potency:

> 'El bends his bowstave, He drew his mighty shaft, He lifts (it), he shoots skyward. He shoots a bird in the sky, He plucks (it), he sets (it) on coals. 'El

seduces his wives, Lo, the two women cry: O husband! Husband! Stretched is
your bowstave, Taut is your mighty shaft.[158]

Bows are also used in the ŠÀ.ZI.GA incantations. For example, from
No. 3, line 20: "And who has made you fall limp like slack cords?"[159] and
No.18, lines 3'–4': "May the [qu]iver not become e[mp]ty! May the bow
not become slack! Let the batt[le of] my love-making be waged! Let us lie
down by night!"[160] A further example comes from a Hittite impotency
ritual of the sorceress Paškuwatti which involves taking a spindle, a mirror, and women's clothing from the impotent man and giving him the
bow and arrow.[161] Psalm 127:3–5 provides a particularly relevant example, as it incorporates fertility, protection, and military might.

הנה נחלת יהוה בנים שכר פרי הבטן
כחצים ביד־גבור כן בני הנעורים
אשרי הגבר אשר מלא את־אשפתו מהם
לא־יבשו כי־ידברו את־אויבים בשער

Sons are the heritage of YHWH, a reward is the fruit of the womb
Like arrows in the hand of a warrior thus are the sons of youth
Happy is the man who fills his quiver with them.
He will not be ashamed when they drive away the enemy at the gate.

The image has proved enduring, stretching from the Ugaritic and Hittite
texts through at least Ben Sira, who categorizes the headstrong daughter
thus: "As a thirsty traveler opens his mouth and drinks from any water
near him, so she will sit down in front of every tent peg and open her
quiver to the arrow" (26:12, NRSV).

The above material suggests a possible solution to the translation of
7:16, Hosea's second reference to the bow, which has proved difficult.
The first line is quite terse: "they will return but not up(ward)" [לא ישובו
על]. One interpretation sees "upward" as a reference to YHWH.[162] A
second takes the last two words together as "Not High," a disparaging
reference to Baal, while some go ahead and emend the text to לבעל.[163]
Another proposal is to emend further or reverse the words to get something along the lines of "turn to what is nothing/useless."[164]

I propose translating it as it stands: "not up"[165] and read it with the
following colon (היו כקשת רמיה) as a potency image. "They return, not
'up'—they are like a slack bow!" The surrounding context supports this

understanding, in the light of the bow imagery I have been discussing. YHWH complains that the people have been deceitful. YHWH had strengthened their arms (another potential military image) but they plot evil against him. Then they return, not up—they are like a slack bow, and their officials will fall by the sword. (vv. 15–16). They are defeated and (symbolically) emasculated.[166]

Implications of Male Imagery for Masculinity

As I have shown, the instances of male and masculine imagery far out-number the instances of female and feminine imagery, except in the first three chapters. The several types of male imagery contribute to a multi-dimensional picture of masculinity. Even those cases that may appear to be female imagery, such as 9:1, which associates זנה with threshing floors and prostitute's fees, are addressed to a masculine subject. The repeated use of זנה with a masculine subject emphasizes the actions of the male audience. While the female imagery in the first three chapters is also di-rected toward men, placing them in position of the wife, the direct male language allows no avoidance of the accusations of fornication, a rhetor-ically charged offense.

With the נאף imagery the field of discourse changes slightly. Rather than drawing on an image field of sexual promiscuity, which has less def-inite boundaries as far as the nature of the offense, it draws on the field of adultery, which is an offense against the husband. As developed above, adultery is more clearly a question of conflict between men. Thus adul-tery images speak more directly to issues of masculinity. The connota-tions of treachery and intrigue add another facet to this picture. The adulterer clearly challenges the masculinity of the cuckold, but the mas-culinity of the offender is also affected through the association with treachery and violation of social mores.[167]

The next groups of images relate more directly to general characteris-tics of masculinity. The phallic imagery of the sticks and staffs has a vis-ceral connection to masculine understanding, which is then ridiculed. The general, multi-faceted term for masculine virility, און, is played upon, showing that the source of masculine pride can lead into hubris and self-delusion, which is also communicated through the use of גאון. The effort to place oneself in a position of "aboveness" to use Gilmore's term, by lifting oneself up, often leads one into iniquity and forgetting the true top of the power structure, YHWH.

The baking imagery allows for the development of several aspects of masculinity. The initial association of men with food reminds one of the provisioning aspect of male honor. Sexual heat and power are mixed with political intrigue and power structures, which rise like dough before breaking forth into lawlessness and murder. Inappropriate mixing with foreign nations leads to political and economic impotence. Finally decay sets in for old bread and old men, leaving them useless and weak, consumed by others.

The bow imagery brings together sexual and military prowess, two important aspects of masculinity. Symbolizing military might, bow imagery includes protecting one's family and property, as well as representing bravery on the battlefield. The breaking of a man's bow is a symbol of a polyvalent defeat of his masculinity. This particular image was used frequently in the Assyrian empire and elsewhere. In Hosea, the men are never depicted in the strong position with drawn bows. Instead their bows are broken or slack.

The rhetorical effect of the fairly dogged assault on the audience's masculinity is to move them down the social scaffolding, into a different, less desirable sector of social quality space. YHWH appears as the most powerful being, which means that everyone else must move to a less optimal place. The males in the text strive after the normal attributes of masculinity, including power, self-directed activity, and potency, but they are criticized for the way in which they are pursuing them. Hosea does not directly criticize the power structure itself, but rather the men's perception of their place within it.[168] In general the oracles suggest that they are not as manly as they think they are.

Mixed Gender Imagery

One important concept that I have not yet covered in detail relates to the implications of the female imagery for the male audience towards whom it is directed. The rhetorical force of the marriage metaphor in chs. 1–3 is to turn the elite men who comprise the audience into women. Francis Landy makes the following observation:

> If the 'wife' is Israel, then it comprises both genders....The supplementation, or mystification, is also a displacement: the male-dominated Israelite society is characterized as female. God is the supreme patriarch before whom all the men are women: the relation of male to female is that of God to humanity. But the

metaphor is meaningless; the shift in gender of the men corresponds to no social or sacred reality.[169]

The metaphor of turning men into women is not meaningless, however. It has, rather, several powerful significations. Primary among these is the fear of men in most cultures of appearing to be feminized. Many of the studies I have cited above have dealt with this issue. Masculinity seems to be a more fragile construct than femininity and thus requires more vigilance and effort to maintain it.[170] Feminization is the figure often used to symbolize loss of power in politics, social status, and economic arenas, as well as in sexual contexts.[171] To portray the male, elite audience as a woman thus attacks many facets of their self-identity. "The marriage metaphor effectively *feminizes this male ruling hierarchy* by depicting its members collectively in the graphic image of a promiscuous wife."[172] According to Yee, this results in a loss of status, and effectively "castrates" the elite. In political terms, representing the elite as the promiscuous, penetrated wife symbolizes the nation as penetrated by foreigners.[173] By portraying the men as women, Hosea emphasizes the idea that they are not really in charge. They may think they are the potent, active partners, making and breaking alliances to control the destiny of the country, but in fact, they are getting screwed.

The shame of becoming women is well supported in both biblical and ANE texts. As noted above, warriors were encouraged to "be men" and fight (1 Sam 4:9). In contrast, the useless and fearful soldiers of the defeated Ninevah are characterized as women in Nah 3:13: "Truly your troops within you are women; the gates of your land indeed were opened to your enemies" [הנה עמך נשים בקרבך לאיביך פתוח נפתחו שערי ארצך].[174] The transformation of men into women is also a treaty curse. Esarhaddon's Succession treaty warns that if it is violated: "May all the gods who are called by name in this treaty tablet spin you around like a spindle-whorl, may they make you like a woman before your enemy."[175] Similarly, the treaty between Aššur -nerari V and Mati'-ilu, the King of Arpad threatens:

> If Mati'-ilu sins against this treaty with Aššur-nerari, king of Assyria, may Mati'-ilu become a prostitute, his soldiers women, may they receive [*a gift*] in the square of their cities like any prostitute, may one country *push* them to the next.[176]

Notable in this curse is that the king and the soldiers are not only cursed with becoming women, but with becoming prostitutes, who are near the bottom of the social status structure.[177] This curse is also the closest match with the situation in Hos 1–3, with the difference that Hosea characterizes the men as an adulterous wife rather than as a prostitute, which, in fact, may be considered worse because it represents a stronger challenge to masculinity.

Conclusions

The gender imagery portrays an understanding of masculinity in ancient Israel that includes military prowess, the ability to provide for and protect one's family, and the desire not to be perceived as feminized. It has two major rhetorical effects on the male audience. First, the female imagery feminizes them, casting them into the role of the wife. Second, the male imagery de-masculates them.[178] The main features of this construction of masculinity can be analyzed in terms of Fernandez's axes of social space: activity, potency, and goodness. In the construction of masculinity that seems to prevail in ancient Israel, the optimal place in the social space is a point with high value on all three axes. From the nature of Hosea's rhetoric, it appears that the audience perceives itself as ranking high on each of those attributes. The oracles themselves try to disabuse the audience of this conception.

The female imagery works strongly on all three axes. First, by the very portrayal of the male audience as female, the oracles attack the men's potency. Second, the audience is portrayed as a "bad" woman—promiscuous and disobedient. Third, the woman is mostly placed low on the activity axis.[179] The female appears slightly more often as the object of action than its subject. When the female is the subject, her action is misdirected, placing her low on the goodness axis as well, or thwarted by the husband, which also reduces the score on the potency axis. Most of the rhetoric of the male imagery focuses on the potency axis, particularly on military and sexual prowess and general vigor. As with the female imagery, when male activity is described, mostly with the language of illicit sex, it corresponds with a low score on the goodness axis.

Through the gender imagery, the male audience is taken from the realm of activity, potency, and goodness into the passive, impotent, and wicked octant. Hosea criticizes the improper political and economic

relations of the male elites by attacking from multiple angles their masculinity, a part of their identity that they usually use to justify their power
and prestige.

❖CHAPTER FOUR❖

Predications of Non-Gender-Based Imagery

> While it seems that the use of sexual imagery is common to human be-
> ings everywhere, as we have seen, neither the character of such images
> nor their relation to social experience are fixed or universal. Within any
> local setting, sexual images are only one among many sets of metaphors
> of identity and their use is both unpredictable *a priori* and ever-changing
> from the point of view of those who use them.
>
> Andrea Cornwall and Nancy Lindisfarne, "Dislocating Masculinity"

In the previous chapter I applied masculinity theory to the task of evaluating the gender imagery in Hosea. Hosea contains many other types of imagery, however, which I will address in this chapter.[1] I have divided these images into seven categories: parent-child, sickness and healing, hunting, animal, agriculture, plant, and natural phenomena. In each of these metaphor fields, identities are predicated upon YHWH and upon the audience. These images serve to establish YHWH's place in the social space and to move the audience into less optimal places.

In this chapter I will undertake three tasks. First, I will identify and explore the details of the imagery presented in the book in each of the categories. In addition to strictly metaphorical images, I will examine some of the more literal language that helps to fill out the categories. Next, I will evaluate implications of the imagery for the placement and movement of YHWH and the audience along the axes of activity, poten-cy, and goodness. Finally, I will assess how this placement and move-ment affects the perception of the masculinity of YHWH and the audience.

Parent-Child Imagery

Next to the gender imagery, the parent-child imagery is the most devel-oped and studied metaphor field in Hosea. The chapters that have been the focus of most previous attention, chs. 1–2 and 11, portray YHWH as the parent and Israel/Ephraim/particular groups of people as the child. In this study, however, in addition to discussing this relationship, I will examine the cases in which humans are cast in the role of parent.[2]

Ephraim/Israel as Child

Chapters 1–2

The first time the parent-child relationship appears in the text is ch. 1, where Gomer and, presumably, Hosea have three children.[3] Hosea gives each of them a symbolic name, describing the judgment of Israel. The first son is named יזרעאל, because YHWH will visit the blood of Jezreel upon the house of Jehu. There is general consensus that this refers to Jehu's massacre of Ahab's family when Jehu usurped the throne (2 Kings 9–10). The second child, a daughter, is named לא רחמה because YHWH will no longer have compassion for the house of Israel.[4] The third child is named לא עמי because Israel will no longer be YHWH's people, nor he their God.

These children are, apparently, the ילדי זנונים referred to in 1:2. The same types of questions concerning the meaning of the term זנונים arise with respect to the children as they did with the wife, except that there is more scholarly consensus in the case of the children. While the nature of Gomer's harlotries has been speculated upon to no end, as touched on in the previous chapter, the majority view concerning the children is that their labeling is a result of their mother's status. The children themselves are as yet guilty of no crime, but their mother's questionable reputation lowers their status.[5]

The children reappear in 2:1–3 with their names inverted, so that the children of Israel are proclaimed to be YHWH's people. Instead of being called לא עמי, the son will be called בני אל־חי [children of the living God]. The day of Jezreel will be declared great, and the daughter will be called רחמה. These statements are repeated with very similar language in 2:24–25. The passages differ at three points. First, in vv. 1–3 the people are commanded to call the children by their new names, whereas in vv. 24–25 YHWH personally renames the children. Second, YHWH sows Jezreel into the land in v. 25, which plays on the agricultural connotation of the name rather than the military one implied in v. 2. Third, in v. 25

the third son, לא עמי, is expected to respond to the renaming, calling YHWH אלהי [my God].

The children are also requested to respond with speech in 2:4–6, by appealing [ריב] to their mother. The husband commands the children to convince their mother to put away her fornications and adulteries, lest she suffer extreme consequences, such as being made like a desert. Likewise, the children themselves would not be pitied [רחם], because they are בני זנונים [children of fornications].

Before turning to a discussion of the role of the children, it will be helpful to consider the identity of the children. Scholars have offered three major ways to assign identity. The first is to make no distinction between the identity of the children and that of the mother, which is usually understood as Israel.[6] The second is to treat them as separate but related entities, with, for example, the mother as the collective land and the children as the individuals in it.[7] The third way is to avoid taking a firm stand, instead offering several possibilities for differences between the two.[8] I consider the children to be different from the mother. I interpret the mother as the ruling hierarchy, including the royal household, the priests, and other powerful elites, which is represented by Samaria. The children, at least in the first two chapters, are the rest of the people.[9]

In most analyses of the first two chapters, the children themselves are not of much consequence. They are rather passive, nondescript people. Even though they are named, their characters are not developed. They serve mostly as foils for the husband's contentions with their mother. Their presence, however, reveals something about the characters and relationships around them. They serve to flesh out the role of the mother, whose crimes are passed along to her children. Additionally, they may shed light on the role of the father, who names, rejects, and then restores the children. The children also mediate the relationship between the husband and wife, acting as screens or "ventriloquists."[10] Having the children address the mother in 2:4 keeps the imagery in the realm of family disputes.[11]

Perhaps because of the mediating function the children are requested to serve, their role and fate are usually subsumed into the marriage imagery. One study that concentrates on the children themselves is Laurie Braaten's dissertation on parent-child imagery. Braaten argues that much of the language in Hosea that is usually categorized as divorce language is better understood in the context of disownment.[12] Marriage and dis-ownment practices in the ANE suggest that a husband/father paid a bridewealth to his father-in-law in order to legitimate and claim his child-ren, who would then inherit in his household. If he did not pay a bride-wealth, as was common with secondary or low-status wives, the children stayed with the mother and belonged to the household of the maternal grandfather.[13]

This latter situation is what Braaten sees in chs. 1 and 2. The child-ren, whom he identifies as the inhabitants of the mother land, are the real target of the separation language. Hosea uses the disownment formulas, "You are not my people" and "Not-Pitied" to separate himself from Gomer's children.[14] The rhetoric against the mother, claiming that she is promiscuous and thus low status, serves primarily to support the case against the children.

Braaten argues that the husband gives gifts resembling a bridewealth, especially the silver and gold of 2:10, in order to remind the wife of her legal husband. She, however, does not attribute the gifts to their proper source, which casts doubt on the legitimacy of the children. Braaten fur-ther claims that the presence of the plural form עשׂו in that verse indicates that the children, as well as the mother, squandered this payment.

> More importantly, however, the bridewealth emphasizes the irony of the child-ren's behavior, and their inexcusable guilt....Yahweh's rendering of the bride-wealth was meant to make the children of his wife *his* children. Ironically enough, the very gift that was supposed to make them Yahweh's children is used to express their allegiance to another deity—they (the children [and their mother?]) 'made it into a baal'! They ungratefully waste the very gifts which evidence their membership in Yahweh's family.[15]

Because of their refusal to acknowledge their true father, the father dis-owns the children. With the re-betrothal of the wife in 2:21, however, YHWH claims the children as his own, legitimating them in 2:25.[16]

Even in Braaten's argument, however, in which the children are the focus of the attention, they remain rather passive. The only hint of activi-ty comes in the questionable reference to them in 2:10. The children are requested to speak with their mother in 2:4, but there is no record of their actually doing so. At the end of the chapter they passively accept their adoption and renaming. Only the newly denoted Ami makes any re-sponse, calling YHWH "My God."

Chapter 11

Chapter 11 contains the imagery most commonly associated with the
parent-child metaphor. The nation Israel is personified as a child whom
YHWH elects or adopts.[17] The identity of the child in this case is equivalent to that of the mother in the first two chapters: the leaders who control the political and socio-economic system of the nation, as well as the
official cult. The metaphor begins in v. 1: "When Israel was a boy I loved
him; from Egypt I called to my son" [כי נער ישראל ואהבהו וממצרים
קראתי לבני]. Braaten points out that the situation here is different from
that in ch. 1–2. The language in those chapters represents a legitimization
or disownment of the children of a man's wife. Chapter 11, on the other
hand, reflects ANE adoption language, which can occur between unrelated parties.[18]

In an adoption the status of the mother makes no difference for the
status of the child, and in most cases is not mentioned. Adoption agree-
ments specify responsibilities of both parties to the agreement. The adopter is supposed to raise the adoptee, teach him a trade, guarantee an
inheritance, and not repudiate the adoptee. In turn the adoptee is supposed to respect, obey, and serve the adopter, not leave his new household, and not repudiate the new parent.[19] If the child breaks the
agreement or repudiates his parents, he is subject to disownment or being
sold into slavery.[20]

While the interpretation of the next few verses is debated, most
people see evidence of YHWH filling the adopter's side of the agreement.
Verse 3 begins with the unusual word תרגלתי commonly translated as "I
taught to walk," which suggests a parent's care of an small child.[21] A similar, though not quite so child-specific, translation is "guide."[22] The
second part of the verse has somewhat muddled grammar, combining
singular and plural suffixes: "taking them upon his arms" [קחם על־
זרועתיו]. This is commonly emended to either "taking them in my arms"
or "taking him by his arms," either of which can relate to caring for the
child.[23] The child apparently does not appreciate this care sufficiently,
because "they did not know that I healed them" [ולא ידעו כי רפאתים].

The imagery of parental care seems to continue in v. 4, but it is beset
with a multitude of difficulties. The first half of the verse, although the
grammar is straightforward, is enigmatic: "with bonds of a man/human-
ity I led them, with cords of love" [בחבלי אדם אמשכם בעבתות אהבה].

The nature of the fetters is unclear.[24] The second half of the verse is difficult to translate, reading: ואהיה להם כמרימי על על לחיהם ואט אליו
אוכיל, and interpretations tend to fall into two groups. The first group
reads the pointing in the MT עֹל and translates "I was for them like ones
who lift a yoke [from] on their cheeks."[25] The second group repoints the
text as עֻל and translates "like ones who lift an infant to their cheeks."[26]
The farmer or the parent then bends down to feed his charge. Neither
translation solves all of the grammatical difficulties of the verse, nor does
the context provide sufficient guidance.[27] Those who follow the infant
translation see this as a continuation of the parent-child metaphor. Those
who follow the yoke translation see a return to agricultural imagery
found throughout the book.[28] Since the metaphorical field becomes more
diffuse in the rest of the chapter, it is impossible to come to a firm determination of the issue, but the expression of parental compassion in 11:8
and the calling of the children home in 11:10 may indicate that the parent-child imagery persists.[29]

Regardless of the exact translation, YHWH appears here as the good
parent, taking active care of the child.[30] The son, however, does not fulfill
his side of the adoption agreement. Although YHWH called the son in v.
1, the son listened to another call in v. 2, yet another obscure verse:
קראו להם כן הלכו מפניהם. Emendation is a popular tactic in translation, to read either, "the more I called to them, the more they went away
from me," or "they called to them and thus they went away from me."
Emendation is not necessary, however, because מפני can be causative:
"They called to them and they went because of them."[31] The antecedent
of "they" is not entirely clear, perhaps referring to the baalim and idols in
v. 2, or what they represent in terms of foreign alliances, but, as with the
wife's infidelity discussed in the previous chapter, the fact of the children's departure from YHWH is more important than where or to whom
they went.[32] Also like the wife in ch. 2, the children here do not recognize
the source of their benefits, the one who raised them and healed them.
Furthermore, these rebellious children persist in turning away, refusing to
return in v. 5, [כי מאנו לשוב] and continuing in that refusal in v. 7 [ועמי
תלואים למשובתי]. In short Israel is the son that repudiates his adopted
father and leaves him. As such, he is subject to being disowned.[33]

Chapter 9:15

Disownment language appears elsewhere in Hosea. Braaten sees this especially in 9:15. The verse reads: "All their wickedness is in Gilgal, for there I hated them [כי־שם שנאתים]. Because of the wickedness of their deeds I will drive them from my house [מביתי אגרשם]. I will no longer love them [לא אוסף אהבתם]. All their princes are rebellious." A parental relationship is not specifically mentioned here, but language of hating and driving out of the house is consistent with disownment and disinheritance.[34] Similar language is used in Judg 11:2, which describes how Jephthah's brothers disinherited him because his mother was a prostitute: "The wife of Gilead bore him sons. When they grew up the sons of the wife drove out Jephthah [ויגרשו את־יפתח], saying to him: 'You shall not inherit in the house of our father, because you are the son of another woman'" The status of Jephthah's mother led to his disownment by his brothers, as the status of the mother led to the disownment of the children in chs. 1–2. In contrast, the children seem to bear their own guilt in 9:15.[35]

Chapter 13:13

Ephraim appears as a child also in 13:13, although the relationship with the parent is minimal. The verse reads: "The pains of labor come for him. He is not a wise son, for at the right time he does not stand at the opening of the womb" [חבלי יולדה יבאו לו הוא־בן לא חכם כי־עת לא־יעמד במשבר בנים][36] One of the interesting elements of this verse is the emphasis on the son.[37] Usually when birth pangs are discussed, the woman is the focus of the attention, or if the phrase is used metaphorically, on the men portrayed as women.[38] Here the fetus is pictured as the focus, resisting birth when the time comes. The resistance shows the child's foolishness. Choon Leong Seow observes the similarity of this passage to wisdom motifs:

> The history of Ephraim's stupidity, according to the author, goes back further than one can imagine. Ephraim was born stupid. In fact, Ephraim was so stupid that he did not even know the time of his birth, nor what was expected of him then. In wisdom circles, it was believed that there was an appropriate time for everything, and people were supposed to know 'et umishpat, "time and propriety."[39]

In addition to the foolishness of not knowing the proper time for things, the stubborn child endangers its own life and the life of its mother by refusing to be born.[40] When the child should have reacted to the birth pains and emerged from the womb, he took a foolish, resistive stance.

Chapter 14:4

The final occasion in which Ephraim may be shown as a child is a passing reference in 14:4: "In you the orphan finds mercy." Besides being a general statement of the wideness of God's mercy and a marker of a good ruler, who provides for the widows and orphans,[41] the verse may be a more specific statement about the status of Ephraim. Ephraim, rebellious and disowned previously in the book, now seeks reconciliation as an orphan.[42] As an orphan, Ephraim is weak and helpless, dependent on the care of others.

Ephraim/Israel as Parent

Ephraim/Israel also assumes the role of a parent. Because humans often are parents, these relationships may or may not be seen as metaphorical. What is important about this category, however, is that it contrasts the actions and care of the Israelite parents with that of the divine parent.

Irresponsible Parents

The examples in ch. 4 demonstrate the lack of appropriate parental care. The priests in vv. 5–6 are the first objects of censure. Because the priests have stumbled [כשל], rejected knowledge [כי־אתה הדעת מאסת], and forgotten the teaching of God [ותשכח תורת אלהיך] their mother will be silenced/destroyed [דמיתי אמך] and their sons will be forgotten [אשכח בניך גם־אני]. Rather than protecting their children and mothers, who are dependent on them, the priests have doomed them through their own actions.[43]

The fathers of the daughters in 4:13–14 do not provide a better example of parenting. The daughters are accused of fornicating [תזנינה] and the daughters-in-law of committing adultery [תנאפנה], but YHWH will not punish them because "they (m) divide/turn aside with prostitutes and sacrifice with holy women" [כי־הם עם־הזנות יפרדו ועם־הקדשות יזבחו]. As with the sons, it appears that the fathers have not fulfilled their obligations to properly educate and raise their daughters. In this case, however, rather than the sons (and mother) of the priests being punished for the misdeeds of the priests, the daughters are spared punishment for their own actions, because the fathers have not acted correctly.[44]

Parents of Alien Children

The oracle in ch. 5 directly addresses the priests and royal house of Ephraim and Israel, accusing them of treachery and fornication throughout the first part of the chapter. This comes to a head in v. 7: "they have acted treacherously against YHWH because they have borne alien children" [ביהוה בגדו כי־בנים זרים ילדו]. The verb ילד in its qal form, as here, usually takes a female subject, but all of the antecedents are male. It seems, therefore, that this is another instance of the males being portrayed in a female role.

Calling the children foreign or unauthorized suggests that their paternity is in question.[45] The word בגד suggests treachery in marriage and political situations, and Eidevall suggests that the whole metaphor may be drawn from the political realm, with the בנים זרים as "alienated children" of YHWH, those who are hostile to a king they do not know.[46] It is also possible to take that metaphorical interpretation in a different direction. The children may not be children in relation to YHWH, but in relation to the king of Israel. The kings and priests act treacherously in 5:1–6, so the fruit of their deception, which includes treachery against YHWH in the political sphere, is a divided nation at home, a situation which sets the stage for the political intrigue and regicide that follows. זר is also used within the highly political context of ch. 8, with reference to the תורה in v. 12, where Ephraim treats YHWH's law as foreign.

Parents of Destroyed Ones

The next group of images relates to parents who are bereaved or kept from becoming parents. These images are concentrated in ch. 9. Four of the passages show Ephraim as a more or less passive recipient of bereavement, mostly at the beginning of life.

> 11: Ephraim, like a bird their glory flies away, from birth, from womb, from conception.
> 12a: Even if they raise sons, I will deprive them of men.
> 14: Give them, YHWH, give them what? Give them a miscarrying womb and shriveled breasts.
> 16b: Even if they bear, I will slay the delight of their womb.

These images suggest that the hope of Ephraim's future is gone, as there will be no future generations. Chapter 8 and the first half of ch. 9 paint a picture of political indecision and disaster which will lead to a barrenness of the land and the people.[47] Ephraim is helpless to prevent this loss of its infants and unborn. Verse 14 is often seen as a reverse blessing, and perhaps as an appeal to minimize the parents' pain by having their children die in miscarriage and infancy rather than when they are older.[48]

The fourth reference in ch. 9 intensifies the imagery of bereavement, showing the parents actively participating in the destruction of the children in 13b: Ephraim is to send out his sons to the slayer [ואפרים להוציא אל־הרג בניו]. This verse has military connotations.[49] The parents are helpless to protect their sons, and, in fact, send them out to what seems to be certain death.[50] The translation of the first half of the verse is highly disputed, and I will discuss it further in the plant imagery section.

Two more verses mention deaths of infants as consequences of war. The fate of the mothers and children dashed together at Beth-Arbel is reported in 10:15. In a similar manner, Samaria faces the prospect of its babes dashed to death and its pregnant women ripped open in 14:1. Such imagery not only exposes the brutality of war, but serves to eliminate hope for the future, as the next generation is killed even before learning to walk.

Analysis of Parent-Child Imagery

Ephraim as Child

Having described the examples of parent-child imagery, I will analyze some of the rhetorical trends. The children in chs. 1–2 appear primarily in relationship to their mother and father. They exhibit passive guilt, tainted by the misdeeds of their mother. They are objects of punishment, along with their mother, but are also the passive recipients of restoration. In the ideal world, Jezreel is sown into the earth, Lo-Ruhamah is the object of compassion, and Lo-ami is reclaimed, acting only in an appropriate response to the father, recognizing him as his god. The passive nature of the children in these images reflects the passive nature of those they represent. These are the people of the land, not responsible for instigating political or military action, but suffering the consequences nonetheless, good or bad.

Within the social space defined by activity, potency, and goodness, the children are low on the activity axes, both in the "real" situation and in the ideal situation. Because the children are unable to resist being linked to their mother's guilt, they are represented as relatively powerless. Along the goodness axis, the children seem to be somewhere in the middle, although this is an undeveloped dimension. They are disowned, which has negative connotations, but they do not bear the brunt of the blame for this action, which they suffer because of their mother's actions and status. They are moved more strongly to the good by 2:25 where they make the correct responses to YHWH.

The child in ch. 11 is a different matter. This child is portrayed as rebellious. He is active, but not exclusively. At his initial adoption, he responds to YHWH's call and passively accepts the care, learning to walk and being fed. Even when he leaves, the son's activity probably only falls in the middle of the continuum, because the action is not totally self motivated, but in response to "their" call. The child is, for the most, not very potent. Certainly the overall predication of a child onto the leading elite moves them down the potency scale, as children are under the control and authority of others. The son thinks he is powerful, as show by his rebellion, but he faces the consequence of being weakened through disownment, or even death. The son clearly scores poorly on the goodness scale. Although when he is first adopted, his goodness seems neutral, once he responds to "their" call, he moves into the bad half of the space. His lack of knowledge of the source of his healing indicates bad judgment. In a similar manner the bad judgment and wrongly directed activity of the son in 9:15 leads to his disownment, showing his impotency and wickedness.

The son of 13:13 also shows bad judgment and foolishness. This son resists the birth pangs, not presenting himself at the opening of the womb. The resistance indicates that the fetus thinks he has some power to stop the process, but, in fact, fetuses are particularly weak, completely dependent on the mother for nourishment, which is received passively through the umbilical cord. The child's resistance is futile: either he will be born against his will, or he will die in the womb. The children in 14:4 are quite passive and impotent. As orphans, they are helpless, without protection, and are seeking care. The goodness of these children is not addressed.

Ephraim as Parent

The human parents in Hosea are shown in two different, but related roles. The first is as fathers who provide a bad example for their children and neglect their education. The cases in ch. 4 fit in this category. The priests fail to protect their family, because they have neglected their leadership activities, both through their own misdirected actions and through their inaction in providing proper instruction for their sons and people. Because of this, their sons will be forgotten by YHWH. The punishment for the fathers' actions falls on their family and children. The daughters' actions in ch. 4 show the inability of the fathers to control their family members, and, even more, indicate that it was the fathers' own teaching and examples that led to their daughters' misdeeds. Thus in these instances, the parents of Ephraim clearly score low on the goodness axes. Their activity positioning is mixed, however, because negative consequences result both from their own misdirected actions and from their inaction in the necessary instruction of their children. The potency axis is not directly addressed, but the fathers appear to have not utilized the power they should have exercised to educate and protect their families.

The second role is that of the bereaved parent. While the bereavement stems from the parents' previous bad behavior, the goodness of the parent is not the focus of these images. The focus is rather on the impotence of the parents, their inability to protect their children, to raise their children, or even to bring them to term. The parents are also relatively inactive in this role, with the exception of 9:13, when Ephraim sends his sons to the slayer. Here not only is Ephraim not able to protect his children, he actively sends them to their deaths.

YHWH as Parent

God is only portrayed as a parent in Hosea, never as a child. Thus YHWH is always higher in the social hierarchy than Ephraim. As a parent, however, YHWH is multifaceted.[51] YHWH gently cares for the son in ch. 11. YHWH also acts as the disciplinarian to the children. He disowns the children in chs. 1, 2, and 9, and punishes the rebellious children. The parental bonds are not completely severed, however, and he restores the children of ch. 2 to good graces, as well as restraining the full fury of his wrath in ch. 11, calling the children home. Finally, YHWH takes in the orphan in ch. 14. YHWH is always portrayed as the active, potent parent, who rewards goodness and punishes wickedness, but who also chooses at times to be merciful. On the negative side, YHWH is also the one who takes away birth, pregnancy, and conception and promises to slay those that are born in 9:11–16. These actions show that YHWH has the ultimate power, deciding who will be parents and who will not, a role shared with other ANE gods. A curse from Esarhaddon's Succession Treaty illustrates: "May Belet-ili, the lady of creation, cut off birth from your land; may she deprive your nurses of the cries of little children in the streets and squares."[52]

Sickness and Healing Imagery

A second metaphor field that overlaps slightly with the parent-child metaphor is sickness and healing. It is much less developed, but appears in several verses, most of which emphasize the decrepit state of the people and YHWH's power to inflict and cure disease.

Cases of Sickness

Ephraim/Judah is explicitly portrayed as sick or wounded in two verses. In 5:13 Ephraim and Judah are cognizant of their unfortunate state and seek healing, but from the wrong source: "When Ephraim saw his sickness [אֶת־חָלְיוֹ] and Judah his sores [אֶת־מְזֹרוֹ], he went to Assyria and sent to the king who contends [אֶל־מֶלֶךְ יָרֵב],[53] but he will not be able to heal you [וְהוּא לֹא יוּכַל לִרְפֹּא לָכֶם] he will not cure you of sores [מִכֶּם מָזוֹר וְלֹא־יִגְהֶה]." The people are shown as recognizing their injured status and turning to the correct source of healing in 6:1–2: "Come, let us return to YHWH, for he has torn [טָרָף] and he will heal us [וְיִרְפָּאֵנוּ]; he has struck and will bind us [יַךְ וְיַחְבְּשֵׁנוּ]. He will restore us in two days [יְחַיֵּנוּ מִיֹּמָיִם] and make us arise on the third day [בַּיּוֹם הַשְּׁלִישִׁי יְקִמֵנוּ], and we will be restored in his presence [וְנִחְיֶה לְפָנָיו]." Few have interpreted these lines as indicating true repentance, however, seeing them either as the prophet's wish, or as an insincere liturgy that takes YHWH for granted, parallel to the fickle return of the wife in 2:9.[54]

One of the major issues of interpretation has been whether the language refers to healing from sickness or resurrection.[55] Wijngaards proposes that it is death and resurrection language, but in the political realm. In several Hittite texts, death refers to dethronement, and restoration to life then indicates reestablishment of power.[56] Regardless of whether the metaphor refers primarily to illness or to death, or indeed if there is much of a distinction between the two, a political interpretation does fit the context well. That ch. 5 describes the time of the Syro-Ephraimitic war and its aftermath is not greatly debated. Israel lost most of its territory to Tiglath-pileser III at that time, leaving only a small area around Samaria and would understandably want to be returned to power.

Causes of Sickness

While only humans are sick, both humans and YHWH can cause sickness and disease. YHWH acts as a wasting agent in 5:12, apparently causing the wounds that Ephraim and Judah see in 5:13, wounds that Assyria cannot cure:[57] "I am like a maggot to Ephraim [ואני כעש לאפרים] and putrefication to the house of Judah [וכרקב לבית יהודה]."[58]

The second occasion of YHWH's destructive power seen in 13:14 is more ambiguous: "From the power of Sheol should I save them, from death redeem them? Where [אהי][59] are your plagues, Death, and your pestilence, Sheol? Compassion is hidden from my eyes." The meaning of this verse is greatly debated, and the odd grammar makes it difficult to tell if it is intended positively, with YHWH ransoming the people and taunting death, or negatively. The surrounding context is entirely negative, however, so I have translated the first phrases as questions, and the second as summons to the plagues of death, or else as YHWH taking over the functions of death.[60]

Humans act as agents of sickness in 7:5, where they plot a palace coup and make the officials sick with the heat of wine [החלו שרים חמת מיין]. They are only able to make other humans ill, however, and they are not directly responsible for the illness, but rather use the instrument of alcohol. The intent is to weaken the officials so that they may be murdered.

Curers of Sickness

Humans are never portrayed as healers, and the king of Assyria is explicitly denied the role of healer in 5:13. YHWH takes on the role of healer several times, but many of these attempts are thwarted, because of lack of cooperation from the humans. YHWH wishes to heal in 7:1, but the guilt of Ephraim and the wickedness of Samaria is uncovered [ונגלה עון אפרים ורעות שמרון] and prevent this. It is not clear from the syntax whether YHWH is prevented from healing or chooses not to when faced with the sin of the nation, but the latter seems more fitting to the overall context. Verse 11:3 indicates that YHWH had healed Israel as a child, but they did not know him as the healer [ולא ידעו כי רפאתים].

YHWH again expresses the desire to heal in 14:5, perhaps with more chance of success in the context of a chapter oriented toward reconciliation. This verse focuses on figurative healing of apostasy [ארפא משובתם] and restoration of love [אהבם נדבה], which may have political connotations. While Ephraim/Israel/Judah is portrayed as particular obtuse in recognizing his true healer, 6:1–2 shows an acknowledgement of YHWH's healing power.

Analysis of Sickness and Healing Imagery

The field of sickness and healing has very established roles. Ephraim/Israel/Judah is always the sick person. YHWH is always the healer, although YHWH can also be the one to cause sickness.[61] Ephraim is never the healer and, in fact, is often a bad patient, either not recognizing his sickness or not understanding it and going to the wrong healer.

As the healer or causer of illness, YHWH has an active and potent role, in control of who will be sick and who will be cured. The goodness scale is more ambiguous. If one sees the plagues as just punishment for iniquity, however, then causing illness could still be categorized as good.[62]

Ephraim as the sick person generally has a passive and impotent role. At times he does actively seek healing, however, though not from the correct healer, and he also shows the power to refuse healing (7:1). On the goodness axis Ephraim does poorly. Verses 6:1–2 may show that Ephraim has the potential to repent and turn toward the appropriate healer. If one reads 6:1–3 in the context of the rest of the chapter, however, which describes the fickle nature of Ephraim and Judah, even these verses keep him in the negative sector. Verse 14:4, which describes the final healing and reconciliation of Israel invokes his guilt, emphasizing that his apostasy is healed. The general identity of the human in this metaphor is of the weak, misdirected, foolish person, who is eaten away by disease. The exception to this is the conspirators, who have the power to make their leaders sick and act to destroy them. This action is clearly negatively evaluated.

Hunting and Seeking Imagery

A third set of images relates to hunting and trapping. With this imagery, Israel/Ephraim appears both as hunter and hunted, but YHWH is portrayed as the hunter. When YHWH is the hunter, Israel/Ephraim is usually portrayed as an animal, so this category will lead into the next section on animal imagery.

Ephraim/Israel as Hunter and Seeker

Humans are portrayed as hunters in a few different senses. The first is hunting in the broadest definition: that of seeking or pursuing. The wife pursues her lovers in 2:9, but unsuccessfully [ורדפה את־מאהביה ולא־תשיג אתם]. She will seek them but not find [ובקשתם ולא תמצא], which is the same language used in 5:6 to describe Israel and Ephraim's unsuccessful seeking of YHWH. They also seek YHWH out of distress in 5:15 [ובקשו פני בצר להם].

The second case is that of acting as traps or snares, either as the devices themselves, or as those waiting in ambush. One example is 5:1–2: "Indeed you have been a snare to Mizpah and a net spread over Tabor [כי־פח הייתם למצפה ורשת פרושה על־תבור]. The revolters[63] have made deep the slaughter[64] [ושחטה שטים העמיקו] and I am chastisement[65] for all of them [ואני מוסר לכלם]." The subjects here, the priests, the house of Israel, and royal household appear to act both as the traps and as the hunters who come and slaughter what the trap has ensnared. A similar situation occurs in 9:9, which may employ wordplay. After setting a snare for the prophet, Ephraim makes deep and corrupts/his pit? [שחתו־העמיקו]. The link between setting traps and acting wickedly or corruptly is well established in the Psalms and other literature, especially in the context of describing the actions of an enemy.[66] Verses 6:9 and 7:6 both describe an ambush. The former portrays a band of priests as a gang of bandits waiting in ambush, who murder on the road to Shechem [גדודים חבר כהנים דרך ירצחו־שכמה וכחכי איש]. The latter describes the plotters bringing their hearts near in their ambush of the king [כתנור לבם בארבם כי־קרבו].

YHWH as Hunter

YHWH appears as a hunter of human prey, usually Israel/Ephraim, twice in a human role and several times as an animal predator, which I will discuss in the animal section. The first example is 7:12 where YHWH hunts Ephraim by spreading out his net [אפרוש עליהם רשתי] and bringing them down like birds of the sky [כעוף השמים אורידם]. The second example in 8:10 is less explicit, stating that YHWH will gather them up [עתה אקבצם], perhaps rounding up the wild asses of 8:9.[67] As with the traps and snares discussed above, net imagery is commonly used in the Psalms as a symbol of enmity.[68]

YHWH is portrayed as a hunter in other biblical texts as well, throwing a net over the house of Israel and catching him in his trap in Ezek 12:13 and 17:20, spreading a net for Pharaoh in Ezek 32:3 and for the lamenter in Lam 1:13.[69] Similar trapping imagery is found in the cognate literature, also usually describing the action of the gods against an enemy. Part of the effectiveness of this imagery is the contrast it shows between the power and wisdom of the hunting gods and the weakness of the humans, who are completely at the mercy of the gods. From the perspective of the birds, the hunting activities of the gods are "terrifying and incomprehensible."[70] Sumerian balāg songs use net imagery to convey the power and plans of the gods. One example comes from the initial section of the balāg composition *ame amašana*, which is a passage that contemplates and adores the violent power of Enlil:

> Father Enlil will lay a net: that net is a net for the enemy. The Lord of the Land will suspend a line: that line is a line for the enemy. The Great Mountain will muddy the water: he will catch fish. And the Lord of the Land will lay down a net: and he will catch small birds.[71]

Another example describing Enlil reads: "May you catch your malefactors like small birds; may you pile them up in heaps."[72]

The image of trapping birds is also common in Assyrian treaty curses, where it indicates the inability of the rebel to escape the punishment for violating the treaty. Esarhaddon's Succession treaty contains several examples. From section 80: "Just as one seizes a bird by a trap, so may they deliver you, your brothers and your sons into the hands of your mortal enemy;"[73] section 82: "Just as a...beast is caught in a snare, so may you, your [women], your brothers, your sons and your daughters be seized by the hand of your enemy;"[74] section 101: "May Šamaš clamp a bronze bird trap over you, (your sons and your [daught]ers); may he cast you into a trap from which there is no escape, and never let you out alive."[75] A common boast of an Assyrian king when he has besieged his enemy, such as this example from Tiglath-pileser III's campaign in Syria-Palestine in 734–743 B.C.E. is "Like a bird in a cage I shut him in."[76]

Humans as Prey

In addition to being hunters, humans are shown as prey of humans or other things. As noted above, the prophet is the target of Ephraim's traps in 9:8 with the fowler's snare on all this ways [פח יקוש על־כל־דרכיו]. In addition Israel is pursued by an unspecified enemy in 8:3 [אויב ירדפו].

Analysis of Hunting and Seeking Imagery

Human hunting takes two forms: pursuing and trapping. Pursuing humans show a high level of activity. Their activity is futile, however, as they are unable to find their lovers or YHWH. Their position on the goodness scale is less secure. Seeking after their lovers is negatively marked (2:9). Seeking after YHWH would seem a good thing, but as they appear to come with their sacrifices in an insincere, or at least, self-deluded attitude, that search is not portrayed favorably (5:6). The final instance of seeking is hypothetical, and the people's sincerity still seems ambiguous (5:15).

Trappers are less active than pursuers. The hunters seem to have more success in this role, lying in wait to snare the righteous. This power, however, is clearly used for ill. The language fits the classic description of evil-doers, found particularly in the Psalms. They corrupt others, ambush the prophet, and assassinate the king. They even surround YHWH with deceit. Nowhere is human hunting portrayed positively.

As prey birds, the people show some activity, trying to fly away, but cannot succeed because they are impotent, totally subject to the divine hunter. With the exception of the prophet who is assaulted by the corrupt nation, humans as prey are construed as bad, because they are being punished for their evil deeds. Carole Fontaine notes that in both Assyrian and Egyptian iconography, images of the hunt were later used for campaigns against enemies, so that the capture and defeat of animals was transferred to humans. The imagery thus serves to make human enemies into a lesser Other.[77] By portraying the elite audience as evil birds, subject to the hunt, Hosea attacks not only their masculinity, but even their humanity.

YHWH is shown as the hunter. The image of YHWH spreading out a net over Ephraim and bringing it down like birds has a few layers of meaning. First, as with the Sumerian texts, it shows the tremendous power of the god. The size differential between the mighty hunter and the small birds emphasizes the power differential.[78] Second, the imagery places YHWH as the enemy of Ephraim. In the psalms it is the enemy who casts the nets, a situation also described in the Sumerian texts. A third layer relates to the role of enforcer, as expressed in the treaties, as well as in the psalms, that YHWH should enforce justice by punishing the ones plotting treachery and evil. These layers show YHWH as unremittingly active and powerful. The goodness measure is more ambiguous, however. While on the one hand, trapping the iniquitous seems to preserve justice, on the other hand, the power is also quite destructive.

Animal Imagery

Animal imagery is another common category in Hosea, used of both YHWH and the people. YHWH is most often likened to a predator, so that this imagery ties in with the hunting imagery of the previous section. Ephraim/Israel is portrayed as prey animals and as domestic animals. The contrast between the metaphors used for the divine and the human is significant.

Ephraim/Israel as Animals

Animal metaphors predicated on humans fall into two main categories: birds and herbivores. The bird category is developed in four verses. The imagery in 7:11–12 relates directly to political actions: "Ephraim is like a silly dove without heart/mind [כיונה פותה אין לב]. They call (to) [קראו] Egypt and go (to) Assyria.[79] When they go I will spread out my net over them [אפרוש עליהם רשתי]. Like the birds of the sky I will bring them down [כעוף השמים אורידם]. I will discipline them according to the report of their testimony [איסרם כשמע לעדתם]."[80] They return home in response to YHWH-as-lion's calling in 11:11: "They shall flutter like sparrows from Egypt [יחרדו כצפור ממצרים] and like a dove from Assyria [וכיונה מארץ אשור], and I will settle them in their homes." Representing

Ephraim as a dove is interesting. Doves are not usually portrayed as stupid birds in the Bible. Other bible passages note the quick flight and
mourning sound of the dove (Isa 38:14; 59:11; Ezek 7:16; Ps 55:7–8).
Hosea plays with this to parody Ephraim's calls to Egypt and flights to
Assyria.[81] Song of Songs uses "dove" to refer to the female lover (5:2).[82]
Ephraim is thus represented here as a vacillating female bird. In the last
case, 9:11, Ephraim's glory is portrayed as a bird, rather than Ephraim
itself, although "glory" here is itself a metaphor for offspring: "Ephraim,
like a bird their glory will fly away [כעוף יתעופף כבודם], from birth,
from womb, from conception."

Ephraim's characterization as birds shares some features with portrayals of birds in other ANE literature, especially in that they represent
fleeing. A line from *Ninmešarra*, in which Inanna speaks in first person
discussing how the god Nanna drove her from her temple, demonstrates
this point: "He made me fly away like a swallow/bird from the window;
my life is consumed."[83] In the disputation between Grain and Sheep,
there is a discussion about the sad state of one of the parties: "Like fires
beaten out in houses and fields, like (a) flying swallow(s) which are flee-
ing/chased(?) from the doorway of a house, You are made like the lame
and weak of the Land."[84] Tiglath-pileser III also uses the image of a fleeing bird to describe his defeated enemies: "[…over]threw him and like a
bird […] he fled."[85]

Only certain features of birds are highlighted in much of the literature
concerning religion and war. There is no discussion of a bird's plumage
or songs, except for occasional mentions of their noisiness. Instead, as
Black remarks, "the aspects which are drawn on are the catching of small
birds (both by human fowlers and falcons); flocking together, flying or
wheeling in the air, and especially fearfully flying away; and rooks flying
up into the air in flocks."[86] Ephraim's characterization fits into this context.

The second type of animal imagery used for Ephraim is large herbivores. Ephraim is described as a wild ass solitary to himself [פרא בודד
לו] in 8:9, having gone up to Assyria. Although asses are herd animals,
wild ones stay clear of human establishment, so many interpreters view
this image as expressing the independent willfulness of Ephraim.[87] Connotations of the ass's independence and enmity emerge from Gen 16:12,
which describes Ishmael's fate: "He will be a wild ass of a man [והוא

יהיה פרא אדם]. His hand will be against everyone and everyone's hand will be against him, but he will dwell next to all his brothers."

Assyrian literature provides another perspective, that of exile. An interesting parallel is found in the inscription of Tiglath-pileser III. The inscription writer describes the fate of the queen of Arabia thus: "And she, to save her life, [...to the de]sert, an arid place, like a wild ass [...]"[88] The inscription is obviously broken and thus difficult to interpret exactly, but it is likely that the image is used here in a way analogous to the fleeing bird. The queen has been driven out of her civilized home into the desert, as a result of rebelling against the Assyrian king.[89] Similarly Esarhaddon's Succession treaty contains a curse: "May Sin, the brightness of heaven and earth, clothe you with leprosy and forbid your entering into the presence of the gods or king. Roam the desert like the wild ass and the gazelle!"[90] This characterization likely predicts Ephraim's future if it continues to violate the treaty.

Israel and Ephraim are also cast as domestic herbivores. Israel is described as a cow and a sheep in 4:16: "For Israel has been stubborn like a stubborn cow [כפרה סררה סרר], now YHWH will pasture them like a lamb [ככבש]." Ephraim is likened to a heifer in 10:11: "Ephraim is a trained heifer [עגלה מלמדה], loving to thresh. I crossed over her fair neck [ואני עברתי על־טוב צוארה]."[91] In addition, as discussed above, some interpreters see 11:4 as another reference to Israel as a cow, interpreting על as yoke. The language of hedging up the paths in 2:8 may also have as one of its connotations that of constraining the wanderings of cattle or sheep, preventing them from ruining the fields and vineyards.[92]

Bovine imagery is not unique to Hosea. In Judg 14:18 Samson complains to the Philistines compatriots of his bride: "If you had not plowed with my heifer [בעגלתי], you would not have found out my riddle."[93] In the prophetic texts, people are usually referred to as cows when they are subject to judgment. Amos refers to the rich women of Samaria as cows of Bashan [פרות הבשן] (4:1). Jeremiah uses bovine imagery to describe the punishments of the nations. Egypt is characterized in Jer 46:20–21: "Egypt is a beautiful heifer [עגלה יפה־פיה], (but) a gadfly from the north will come upon her. Even her mercenaries in her midst are like fatted calves [כעגלי מרבק], for they also turned and fled together; they did not stand." The inhabitants of Babylon are likened to cows in 50:11: "Though you rejoice, though you exalt, plunderers of my heritage, though you frolic like heifers [כעגלה] in the grass, and neigh like stallions."

Other ANE literature predicates bovine imagery on humans as well. In the Sumerian epic poem of Erra, Išum accuses Erra of having destroyed too much. She expresses the lament of the ruler of a destroyed city, complaining to his mother about her bearing him: "Since you delivered me unto a city whose wall was pulled? down? –Its people (are) the herds, and their god (is) the beater."[94] Joan Westenholz proposes that by putting humans and herds in parallel in this and other lines, the Erra in effect equates the two.[95] The Gilgamesh epic also speaks of people "lowing like cattle" (pl. 59:9).

In Akkadian literature, soldiers are portrayed as bulls. From the text "Sargon, the Conquering Hero" (ii:44): "The strong bull, the warriors he put into action."[96] From the text "Sargon in Foreign Lands" (ii:16–18): "'My heroes, the country of Mardaman I want to fight. Anything that you say to me, I will do.' His heroes answered him, the great oxen, who had met (in battle) with the Didnu-nomads, the exterminators (??), who had met (in battle) with…"[97] We see some contrast here between the predication of male and female bovines, with the bulls representing warriors and the cows representing people who are controlled and driven. Ephraim is portrayed only as a cow.

YHWH as Animal

YHWH, by contrast, is consistently portrayed as a predator. He is pictured as a lion in three passages, the third of which also includes other predatory animals. The first case in 5:14 uses the first person: "For I will be like a lion [כשחל] to Ephraim, like a young lion [וככפיר] to the house of Judah. I, I will tear and I will go and carry away, and there is no one who can deliver [אני אני אטרף ואלך אשא ואין מציל]." The second instance in 11:10 employs the third person: "Afterwards YHWH will go out roaring like a lion [כאריה ישאג] and when he roars, sons will tremble from the west." The third case in 13:7–8 parallels lion imagery with that of leopards, bears, and other wild animals: "I am like a lion [כמו־שחל] to them, like a leopard [כנמר] I stalk on the way. I encounter them like a bear bereft [אפגשם כדב שכול], and I will tear the enclosure of their heart. I will devour them there like a lioness [כלביא]; the beasts of the field [חית השדה] will rip them open."

Lion imagery is used to describe YHWH in several other places in the HB, mostly in the prophetic literature.[98] Twice YHWH is described as attacking an individual person, making him ill (Isa 38:13; Job 10:16). YHWH also acts as a lion in acts of vengeance against both his own people and those who fight against them (Jer 25:38, 49:19, 50:44; Lam 3:10). Isaiah 31:4, by contrast, shows YHWH as protecting Jerusalem like a lion guards its prey. This is a double-edged image, showing both protection and danger, since Jerusalem is portrayed as YHWH's prey.[99] Amos 3:8 likens the word of YHWH to the roaring of a lion in a series of rhetorical questions: "The lion has roared, who will not fear? My lord YHWH has spoken, who will not prophesy?"

The imagery of 5:14 and 13:7–8 fits closely with the most common category of the biblical lion imagery, that expressing YHWH's displeasure at the actions of, in this case, Israel/Ephraim/Judah, and picturing violent consequences. Verse 11:10 more closely resembles the situation in Isa 31, where the unpredictable power and protectiveness of YHWH are both factors, but the irresistible force of the lion's roaring, as expressed in Amos, also illuminates the passage.

Lion imagery is commonly used for gods and kings elsewhere in the ANE and shares characteristics with that in the biblical texts. One older example comes from the legend of "Sargon, the Lion" (tablet A reverse, ll. 6–16), which describes the awesome power and potential violence of the ruler:

> Was it not because of his frightening radiance, and his bellowing roar that no one dared to approach [him]? 'I, Sargon, am your raging lion [...]. No one will approach my sanctuary(?). When there is combat, invoke my name! They will not block (my way) before the Cedar (Forest)/Elam. As for you, beseech Šamaš! My gnashing panther, his heart is (filled with) fury. (But) seeking the evil one, he will not countenance (or: seek the evil one, his countenance is not...).[100]

A similar sense is conveyed in a hymn to Ninurta: "Ishkur, lion of heaven, noble bull, glorious, your name reaches heaven's zenith....Father Ishkur coming forth from the house is a howling wind, Coming forth from the house, from the city, is a young lion, Setting forth from the city he is a roaring storm."[101] The fierceness of the lion is often highlighted. The author of one prayer of lamentation describes Ištar as a "shining one, lioness of the Igigi, subduer of angry gods" and implores her "O exalted Irnini, fierce lion, let thy heart be at rest."[102] Similar examples come from Egyptian literature. A Hymn of Victory of Thut-Mose III reads: "I cause them to see thy majesty as a fierce lion, as thou makest them corpses throughout their valleys."[103] Likewise the Memphis and Karnak steles describe Amen-hotep II:

> His majesty proceeded to Retenu on his first victorious campaign to extend his frontiers…He hacked it up in a short moment, like a lion fierce of face, when he treads the foreign countries." (Karnak variant: "His majesty achieved a happy feat there, (for) his majesty himself took Booty. Now he was like a fierce lion, smit[ing the] foreign countries [of Ret]en[u]…[104]

The lion's fierceness, as well as that of some of the other big cats, like the panther, provides a fitting image for prowess in battle, unmatched by others. Amen-hotep II is again described in the Amada and Elephantine Steles: "Raging like a panther when he treads the field of battle. There is none who can fight in his vicinity."[105] The Sumerian king Šulgi in his self-laudatory poem proclaims that he is "the king, I, the Wild Bull of extraordinary vigour, I, the lion with the wide open mouth!…Vigour of a raging lion, hero in battle, I have no rival."[106]

Other Animal Imagery

While the imagery describing YHWH as predator and the people as prey is the most prevalent, there are a handful of other passages with animal imagery of a more general nature. Verse 8:1 has a rather enigmatic image of a bird of prey on the house of YHWH: "To your mouth a shofar: (one) like a raptor [כנשר] is over the house of YHWH." While the verse is difficult to translate, the sense is of impending doom, conveyed by an antagonistic predator.[107] Consumption by eagles and vultures is also found twice in Esarhaddon's succession treaty: "May Ninurta, the foremost among the gods, fell you with his fierce arrow; may he fill the plain with your blood and feed your flesh to the eagle and the vulture.…May Palil, the fore[most] lord, let eagles and vultures [eat your f]lesh."[108]

Wild animals are used as the agents of YHWH's punishment of the wife in 2:14, where the beasts of the field consume her vineyards. The turning over of civilized areas to wild animals and wilderness is a common image of devastation. Animals also serve to reflect the brokenness

(4:3) or wholeness (2:20) of the relationship of humans to YHWH, which ends up affecting the whole land.

Analysis of Animal Imagery

Several points emerge from these examples. First, YHWH is only portrayed as a predator, mostly as a lion or leopard/panther. These animals are commonly associated with gods and kings in the ANE, because they are powerful, violent, and at the top of the food chain. YHWH pictured thus is clearly active and powerful: tearing, carrying away, and able to prevent any rescue. As with most powerful creatures, goodness is harder to measure. Mauling people does not sound like a positive trait (13:8), but the context suggests that YHWH is justified in seeking to punish Ephraim.[109]

Ephraim/Israel/Judah, on the other hand, is only portrayed as a prey animal, either as birds or an herbivore. The predications are telling, especially if one considers what identities are noticeably absent. First, it is interesting to note that elsewhere in the Hebrew Bible, people and tribes are represented as lions. Judah is described such in Gen 49:9, Dan in Deut 33:20–22, Israel in Num 23:24 and 24:9. Micah 5:8 imagines the restoration of the remnant of Jacob, who will rend, with none to deliver, much like the language used of YHWH in Hosea. In addition, lions represent courage, so that the heart of a lion (2 Sam 17:10) or the faces of a lion (1 Chr 12:9) or the confidence of a lion (Pro 28:1) represent bravery and vigor in battle. In Hosea, the people are represented with no such traits. YHWH has all the lion traits, and Ephraim is left trembling like birds.

Second, when identified as a bird, Ephraim does not get to be a raptor with talons and a sharp eye. Instead he is a dove or a sparrow. The raptor in 8:1 hanging over the house of YHWH, representing an enemy, serves to emphasize this fact. Third, when Ephraim is a herbivore, he is not a virile bull, roaming around goring people. He is, rather, a cow, and not even an old, mean, herd-leading cow. Ephraim is a heifer, who had never previously been yoked, young and tender. Even as a wild ass, the emphasis is (contra many commentators) not on his free-spirited independence (although willfulness is certainly a strong factor), but rather on his location—wandering in the wilderness alone, as in the treaty curses.

A real wild ass may be perfectly happy wandering around in remote places, but for the ruling elite this represents exile.

Ephraim/Israel/Judah in all of these metaphoric predications falls toward the impotent end of the continuum. The activity axis is mixed. Most of the animals are active in some way. The birds fly hither (11:11) and yon (7:11, 9:11). The cow balks (4:16) and loves to thresh (10:11). Much of this action seems to be in the wrong direction, however, and thus scores poorly on the goodness axis. The text re-directs some of this action, at least in hypothetical situations. The birds that fly away in 7:11 are brought down by YHWH's net. In 11:11 they fly in the correct direction, back to YHWH.[110] The heifer loving to thresh (10:11) is harnessed and made to plow. The balky cow is transformed from a cow with an attitude into a lamb (4:16), which is definitely a demotion on the power scale.

One final feature of this imagery is the relation between the imagery used for YHWH and that used for Ephraim. Lions obviously eat herbivores, and are explicitly named as enemies of herds in some ANE literature.[111] Lions are frequently used to represent enemies in the Psalms, as those who attack and maul the singer.[112] Lions are also in curses used to enforce treaties. A treaty of Esarhaddon states: "May Bethel and Anath Bethel [deliver] you to the paws of a man-eating lion."[113] Similarly the Aramaic treaty threatens that "[if Mati'el should be un]faithful to Bar-Ga'yah…[and may] the mouth of a lion[אריה][eat] and the mouth of [a…] and the mouth of a panther [נמר]."[114] YHWH acts in opposition to Ephraim, through imagery often associated with enmity and treaty curses.

Agricultural Imagery

Hosea employs a substantial amount of agricultural imagery, as indicated by the above analysis of animal imagery. Agricultural imagery involves the raising of both plants and livestock, and applies both YHWH and humans. In addition, a few unassigned agricultural images are used to express judgment.

Ephraim as Farmer

Ephraim appears as a farmer in two contexts: as a herder and as a sower. The herding role is a small one. A personified Ephraim, Israel, and Jacob bring their flocks and herds to seek YHWH in 5:6, which may represent a literal action. Ephraim is a figurative herder in 12:2: "Ephraim herds the wind and pursues the east wind all day [אפרים רעה רוח ורדף קדים כל־היום]. He causes falsehood and violence to increase [ושד ירבה כזב]." A shepherd generally causes his flocks to increase, through care and protection. Ephraim likewise causes his herd to increase, but what he herds is inappropriate, producing destructive offspring: falsehood and violence.

Ephraim appears more frequently as a tiller of the fields. Just as he herded the wind in 12:2, so Israel sows the wind in 8:7: "For they sow the wind [כי רוח יזרעו] and they shall harvest the whirlwind [וסופתה יקצרו]. The standing grain has no sprout; it will not make flour. Even if it did, strangers would swallow it up." The image here shifts between more figurative and more literal language. The first half of the verse shows the failure, or worse, the success of Israel's sowing. The wind Israel sowed has grown into a whirlwind that threatens to sweep them away, in the form of a military assault.[115] The image moves into the real consequences of Israel's actions in the second half of the verse. Israel will not reap the benefit of the grain he has sown. Not only their food, but Israel himself will be consumed, as described in 8:8: "Israel will be swallowed up. Now he has been among the nations like a vessel in which there is no value [ככלי אין־חפץ בו]."[116] The people's inappropriate sowing has reaped a bad harvest, in which they themselves are harvested.

Ephraim sows badly in 10:12–13 as well: "Sow for yourselves righteousness [זרעו לכם לצדקה] and harvest according to faithfulness [קצרו לפי־חסד]. Till for yourselves fallow ground. It is time to seek YHWH until he comes and rains righteousness [ויֹרה צדק] for you. You have plowed wickedness and harvested injustice [חרשתם־רשע עולתה קצרתם]. You have eaten the fruit of lies [אכלתם פרי־כחש]." Ephraim is instructed in how to grow good crops, putting in the righteous seed, waiting for YHWH to provide the righteous rain, then reaping a good harvest with faithfulness.[117] Alas, Ephraim chooses to plant wickedness, which grows a crop of injustice, and bad fruit. This will lead to a loss of his "fruit," namely his offspring, when war comes and destroys Ephraim.

Verses 9:1–2 discuss the next step in the agricultural cycle, that of the threshing floor: "Do not rejoice, Israel, do not make a joyful cry like the peoples, for you have fornicated from upon your God [זנית מעל אלהיך].

You loved your hired fee upon the threshing floors of grain [אהבת אתנן
על כל־גרנות דגן]. Threshing floor and wine vat will not feed them, and
new wine will disappoint her [גרן ויקב לא ירעם ותירוש יכחש בה]. "

Because of the frequent connections scholars make between the references to fornication in the text and the Baal fertility/sex cult that they
imagine existed, this verse is often interpreted to mean that people were
having orgies on the threshing floor, appealing to Baal.[118] The possible
sexual connotations of the encounter between Ruth and Boaz on the
threshing floor (Ruth 3:6–13) have done nothing to discourage this viewpoint. The word threshing floor is used several other times in various
verses in the Hebrew Bible, however, and only in Ruth and here is it possibly associated with sexual activity.

Threshing floor in other HB citations has several major connotations,
most commonly as a symbol for food provisions (Deut 15:14; 1 Sam
23:1; 2 Kgs 6:27; Job 39:12; Joel 2:24; and probably Hos 9:3) and, in a
related sense, as the provision for the sacrificial tithe (Num 15:20, 18:27,
18:30; Deut 16:13). Within the prophetic literature, the threshing floor
often indicates judgment, stating the offending party will be threshed (Isa
21:10; Jer 51:33; Mic 4:12). The threshing floor is also an important place
for approaching YHWH. Gideon asks for a sign of the verity of YHWH's
command by placing a fleece on the threshing floor in Judg 6:37. In the
story of David in both 2 Samuel and 1 Chronicles, the threshing floor
plays an important role. The destroying angel, who is to wipe out the
people because David took a census against YHWH's command, stops at
the threshing floor (1 Chr 21:15). When the pestilence strikes the land as
punishment, David makes a sacrifice on the threshing floor (2 Sam
24:16–24; 1 Chr 21:18–28). Later Solomon builds the temple on that
threshing floor, because that is where YHWH met David (2 Chr 3:1).
The threshing floor also seems to be a place for prophecy, as that is
where Ahab listens to his prophets (1 Kgs 22:10; 2 Chr 18:9). Jacob's fu-
neral is also held on a threshing floor (Gen 50:10–11).

Threshing floor clearly appears as a metonym for agricultural produce in 9:2, but its use in 9:1 is less certain. Considering the fact that
grain, wine, and oil were the usual items of trade in Israel, and that
Egypt and Assyria are mentioned in 9:3, however, it seems likely that זנה
has the political implications discussed in ch. 3, in which Israel's lovers
are his allies.[119] Israel has sold out in its foreign policy and will suffer the

consequences, in that its grain and wine will be taken away as tribute, not feeding its own people. This continues the image from ch. 8 of Israel's grain being swallowed up by strangers. The image also invokes connotations of judgment as the subsequent verses discuss an impending exile.

YHWH as Farmer

The first instance of YHWH as farmer occurs in 2:24–2:25a: "The earth will attend to [תענה][120] the grain and the new wine and the fresh oil, and they will attend to Jezreel, and I will sow her for myself into the earth [וזרעתיה לי בארץ]." In this verse YHWH is the sower of seed, expecting a crop of obedient children. As noted in the last chapter, sowing seed is a common euphemism for human reproduction, with the male planting the seed into the soil of the female. Some ANE literature describes a god inseminating the earth to make it bear fruit and flourish.[121] The situation here is somewhat different, however. YHWH is not specifically inseminating the earth, but is, rather, planting an already born child into the earth with connotations of returning a people to their homeland, rather than of indicating fertility. The restoration of Lo-Ruhamah to pitied status, and Lo-ami to claimed people confirms the quasi-political interpretation. In addition, the sowing is the culmination of a series of images related to fertility, not the initiation. The earth takes care of making the grain, wine, and oil, which then take care of Jezreel, who is returned to the land, after representing the end of the monarchy in ch. 1.

The three other agricultural references show YHWH as a tender of animals. Verse 4:16, discussed above, predicates two domestic animal identities on Israel. YHWH is the farmer who, while not able to control the actions of his balky cow, can change her identity into a sheep, a dumber animal kept out on the range. YHWH shows better control of the heifer Ephraim, who loves to thresh in 10:11. Cattle were used to tread the cut grain on the threshing floor, in order to separate the grains from the heads.[122] Such work was relatively easy, and perhaps provided ready access to food.[123] YHWH will put the heifer to more difficult work, however: "I passed over her goodly neck [ואני עברתי על־טוב צוארה]. I will cause Ephraim to draw, Judah will plow, and Jacob will harrow for himself." Some have observed that YHWH finding the young heifer Ephraim is equivalent to finding the grapes in the wilderness in 9:10, or the boy in Egypt in 11:1. As a newly elect nation in the wilderness, Israel was pleased to serve. Once asked to do more difficult work of plowing, or settling into the land of Canaan, Israel balked.[124] The final reference to YHWH as farmer is in 13:5–6: "I knew you in the wilderness, in a land of drought. When they grazed, they became sated [כמרעיתם וישבעו]. They were sated and their heart lifted up, therefore they forgot me." Because they forgot YHWH, YHWH will turn from a shepherd to a lion, tearing them and devouring them (13:7–8). Once again the theme surfaces of Ephraim not acknowledging YHWH's care (2:10; 8:1; 10:3; 11:3).

Other Agricultural References

There are also a few images that refer to Ephraim/Judah as the crop. Judah faces harvest in 6:11, an image of judgment used elsewhere:[125] "Also Judah, a harvest is set for you [שת קציר לך]."[126] In addition, Ephraim is likened to chaff driven by a storm from the threshing floor in 13:3, perhaps by the whirlwind it grew in 8:7. The metaphor of chaff as a quick and total defeat is fairly common, and is often used to indicate the judgment of the wicked by YHWH.[127]

Analysis of Agricultural Imagery

Both YHWH and Ephraim/Israel/Judah are portrayed as farmers. The ways in which they act differ, however. YHWH is always the farmer and never the farmed, whereas Ephraim takes on both roles. When YHWH farms, Ephraim is always the object of his activity. In addition, YHWH is more frequently shown as a herder, whereas Ephraim more often sows. The two activities are by nature different. A sower plants seeds that offer little resistance. The seeds grow on their own, mostly beyond the farmer's control. A herder, on the other hand, takes a much more active role in caring for animals that have wills of their own and require much more daily attention. The distribution of roles indicates that YHWH occupies a more active, powerful space than does Ephraim.

YHWH is shown as sower only once in 2:25, which derives from a play with the child's name Jezreel [God sows]. The object of the sowing is a human and what s/he represents.[128] In this relationship, YHWH is active, while Jezreel is passive, although having more potential for activity than does a seed. YHWH has the power to plant Jezreel into the ground, while Jezreel cannot resist. The context of reconciliation in these final verses of the chapter indicates that the relationships shown between power and activity are good. Jezreel's passivity and powerlessness is its correct role, and the active care of YHWH is also good.

By contrast, when the human is the sower, the result is never good. Israel/Ephraim sows the wind (8:7) and wickedness (10:13). As a sower, Ephraim is active. Its potency rating is less clear, however. While Ephraim shows the power to sow, it seems to have little control over the harvest. A whirlwind, the crop of 8:7, is unpredictable and likely to overthrow the harvester who comes close to it. The fruit of lies (10:13) is poor nourishment and will lead to Ephraim's demise. Israel/Ephraim clearly scores poorly on the goodness axis, choosing the wrong crops to plant (10:12).

When YHWH appears as a herder, the object of his labors is Ephraim/Israel. The axes of activity and power show more ambiguity here than is usual for portrayal of YHWH. In the examples in Hosea, the actions of the herder are typically not discussed. The text instead focuses on the response of the herd animals. YHWH is unable to control all of the actions of the herd and must use extraordinary means to reassert his position at the top of the power chain. Israel as the balky cow in 4:16 cannot be moved, so YHWH changes the metaphoric predication, trans-forming Israel into a passive sheep. The flock of 13:5–6[129] eats its fill in the pasture, but forgets its shepherd. Because YHWH cannot control what the sheep remember, he changes his own predication, turning into a predator and devouring the ungrateful flock rather than protecting it as would a shepherd (13:7). In the case of the working heifer in 10:11, YHWH shows more success, making Israel, Ephraim, and Judah plow. So while YHWH ends up as the powerful figure, there is some slippage in power relations along the way. The goodness axis is somewhat more difficult to assess. YHWH shows care of the flock and appropriate train-ing of the working cow, but finally devours the flock when it disobeys.

Ephraim rarely acts as a herder. His role is implied when he brings his flocks and sheep (5:6), but it is not developed. The only other occur-rence is 12:2, in which he is obviously tending the wrong thing. As a herder, he is active, but seems to have little power. The objects of his herding, the wind and the east wind, are uncontrollable and produce un-wanted offspring. The image of Ephraim pursuing, or chasing after, his herd is the opposite of power. The results of his labor are clearly bad.

Plant Imagery

Plant imagery plays an important role in Hosea. Plant identities are pre-dominantly predicated upon Israel/Ephraim, but in one case is applied to YHWH. Both negative and positive plant images are associated with Israel. In addition, some plant imagery is used to indicate judgment of Israel.

Ephraim as Plant

Negative and Ambiguous Images
Several references to Ephraim focus particularly on his fruit. Ephraim is himself the fruit in 9:10: "Like grapes in the wilderness [כענבים במדבר] I found Israel. Like the first fruit of the fig tree in its first season [כבכורה בתאנה בראשיתה] I saw your fathers." The combination of vine and fig has several connotations. The two are frequently paired (Zech 3:10; Song 2:13; Deut 8:8; 1 Kgs 5:5; 2 Kgs 18:3; Mic 4:4) and often serve to symbol-ize a secure and prosperous life.[130] Eidevall suggests that grapes and figs are metaphors for upright acts and attitudes.[131] Their destruction is a sign of judgment (see Hos 2:14; Isa 34:4; Jer 5:17; 8:13; Joel 1:7, 12; Ps 105:33; Amos 4:9; Num 20:5). The location in the wilderness is highly unusual, as grapes and figs require intense care and cultivation.[132] Their presence there in this passage invokes Israel's wilderness tradition, simi-lar to the betrothal of the wife in 2:16 and the calling of the son in 11:1. Further, the image of the vine and fig may symbolize YHWH's long-planned election and careful cultivation of Israel, as grapevines and figs take several years to reach maturity and produce fruit, especially because Israel is portrayed as the fruit, not the vine.

Twice, rather than being the fruit, Ephraim is the plant that has po-tential to produce fruit. When the plant is unhealthy, however, it is un-fruitful. Such is the case in 9:16: "Ephraim is stricken, their root is dried up [שרשם יבש], they do not produce fruit [פרי בלי־יעשון]." The plant me-taphor clearly indicates human reproduction, as the verse continues with the threat that if they do bear children, YHWH will slay them.[133] The dried up root echoes the shriveled breasts of 9:14. It also suggests the normal fate of grapes in the wilderness, which would be to wither (9:10).

The question of fruit production is more ambiguous in 10:1: "Israel is a luxuriant/empty vine [גפן בוקק], he makes fruit like himself [פרי ישוה־לו]. When his fruit increases, he increases altars. When his land improves, he improves pillars." The translation of בוקק is disputed, with the majority of scholars interpreting it as "luxuriant" in light of the Arabic cognate *baqqa*, meaning "to grow profusely."[134] In other prophetic texts, however, it is used to indicate stripping bare a land, so some translate it as "empty."[135] The translations are not necessarily at odds. Plants that grow profuse foliage sometimes do not fruit, expending their energy on growth rather than reproduction. Alternatively, an ironic pun may be intended. Even if Israel as a luxuriant vine produces fruit, because of the way he uses his fruit, he will be stripped and empty, as when plundered by invaders (see Isa 24:1, 3; Jer 51:2; Nah 2:3). That בוקק has negative connotations here is supported by its proximity to the withered, unfruitful vine (9:16). In addition, the rest of the chapter describes how Ephraim's misguided foreign policy will lead to disaster. As on most occasions when Hosea mentions Ephraim increasing things, Ephraim's fruitfulness (note the play between אפרים and פרי) has ill effects.[136]

Positive Images

Hosea predicates Israel with much more positive plant imagery in ch. 14. A cluster of images in 14:6–8 compare him to various budding plants: "I will be like dew to Israel. He will bud like the lily [יפרח כשושנה] and strike his root like the lebanon [ויך שרשיו כלבנון]. His shoot will go out [ינקותיו ילכו], his vigor will be like the olive [ויהי כזית הודו], and his fragrance like the lebanon [וריח לו כלבנון]."

An interesting assortment of plants is mentioned here. The lily is a plant noted for its beauty. Lebanon probably refers to the cedar, the most famous tree grown in that country, which is highly prized as premium building material.[137] It has a strong fragrance, which, among other things, repels moths, and also is a tall and stately tree.[138] Trees symbolize stability and fertility in some biblical texts. Psalm 92:13–14 compares the righteous to flourishing trees: "The righteous sprout like a date palm [צדיק כתמר יפרח], like a cedar of Lebanon they thrive [כארז בלבנון ישגה]. Planted in the house of YHWH, in the courts of our God they come to bloom." The olive tree is economically valuable, producing oil as well as food. It is used as a symbol of well-being and favor in Ps 52:10 where the psalmist proclaims: "I am like a luxuriant olive tree in the house of God."

More plant imagery is found in 14:8, but the interpretation is unclear, in part because it mixes layers of metaphors: "Those who live in his shade will again grow grain.[139] They will sprout like a vine and his renown will be like the wine of Lebanon [ישבי בצלו יחיו דגן ויפרחו כגפן זכרו כיין לבנון]." The grain growing fits rather strangely in the context, which otherwise discusses Israel as a plant, although it continues the theme of restoration. Many emend to "they shall flourish as a garden" (NRSV).[140] While it can be argued that the referent of בצלו [his shade] is YHWH, the more likely antecedent is Israel, who is also the possessor of זכר in the second half of the verse. If this is so, then the shade producing tree is the nation of Israel, or the leaders of Israel, and the inhabitants of that shade are the people. The people then grow the grain, which reverses the cursed, withering grain of 8:7 and 9:2.[141]

The second half of the verse recalls the luxuriant/empty vine of 10:1. The vine's ambiguous nature is eliminated here, however, as the renown of the wine indicates that the vine has produced good fruit. Within these three verses, Israel is likened to the sources of the grain, the wine, and the oil, which were the three staples of importance in ch. 2.[142] YHWH as the dew nurtures all of this production.

9:13

One further reference to Ephraim as a plant possibly occurs in 9:13, the translation of which is highly disputed: "Just as I saw Ephraim as Tyre/a palm planted in a meadow [אפרים כאשר־ראיתי לצור שתולה בנוה], so Ephraim must send out his sons to the slayer [ואפרים להוציא אל־הרג בניו]."[143] צור is frequently rendered as "palm tree," based on an Arabic cognate.[144] For example, the NRSV translates the verse: "Once I saw Ephraim as a young palm planted in a lovely meadow, but now Ephraim must lead out his children for slaughter." Buss proposes translating: "Ephraim, as far as I can see, 'is planted on a rock as a (or: in the) meadow;' Ephraim must bring forth his children to the slayer." He sees the phrase planted on a rock as a proverb addressing barrenness.[145] Others read it as Tyre. For example, Jeffrey Kuan renders the verse: "Ephraim, just as I have seen Tyre planted in a pleasant place, so Ephraim must lead his children out to the slaughterer." He proposes that Hosea refers to the siege of Tyre by Shalmaneser V, after it revolted against Assyria in 727–726 B.C.E. As Samaria had also revolted, it must face the same consequences and send out its children to fight Assyrian forces.[146]

None of these translations is entirely satisfactory. The first fits well with the planting verb, but does little to explain the slaughtering of the children. The second solution has some appeal, reflecting the barrenness expressed in 9:12, but has some grammatical difficulties.[147] The latter makes sense of the military imagery of the children, but fails to address the plant imagery, or to explain the seemingly positive connotations of meadow. One would hardly expect a besieged city to be described as being in a pleasant place. Tyre was an island fortress, which was difficult to conquer through siege warfare. Even though Shalmaneser V cut off the water supply from the mainland, the city withstood the siege for five years.[148] Presumably a city in a meadow would be easier to besiege, as, perhaps, Samaria was. The translation, "I saw Ephraim as Tyre planted in a meadow," may indicate that Ephraim will suffer Tyre's fate, without having Tyre's natural protections.

A pun may be intended between Tyre and a palm tree. A palm transplanted in a meadow would be a solitary palm, standing above the grasses. Palms, however, are dioecious, with separate male and female trees, so that an isolated palm would bear no fruit, which fits into the theme of fruitfulness, or lack thereof, in the surrounding verses (9:10, 9:16, 10:1)[149] The fact that מָצוֹר means a siege entrenchment may make a three-way word play.

YHWH as Plant

YHWH is portrayed as a plant on only one occasion, v. 14:9: "I am like an evergreen cypress [אני כברוש רענן] and your fruit will be found from me." Tree imagery is often associated with idolatry in the biblical texts, so several commentators observe that this image of YHWH as a tree is somewhat radical.[150] The image of a fruit-providing evergreen, a symbol of fertility, places YHWH as the only source of life and fertility.[151] The image also suggests YHWH's authority, as forest trees are often used as symbols of kingship.[152] Oestreich argues that the tree imagery has two major components: the royal-tree image and the paradisiacal image.[153] This image thus conveys the idea that YHWH is both king and creator.

Other References to Plants

Plant imagery is used in a few more verses with an abstract subject or as personified plants to indicate the wickedness and judgment of Ephraim. Inappropriate political actions are likened to contaminated fields in 10:4: "Justice breaks out like poisonous weeds on the furrows of the field [ופרח

[כרוש משפט על תלמי שדי]." Such weeds not only interfere with the growth of the crop plant, but poison any cattle that might be grazing in the field. The conventional metaphor for disaster and abandonment, thorns and thistles,[154] is used in 9:6: "Nettles [קמוש] will possess their precious things of silver; brambles [חוח] will be in their tents." The image signifies that the people will abandon their homes, so that their children will not inherit, but rather the wild plants will take over the land. Likewise, in 10:8 their monarchy and cult will be carried away, leaving their altars unattended: "…thorns and thistles will grow up over their altars [יעלה על-מזבחותם קוץ ודרדר]."

Analysis of Plant Imagery

The plant imagery is heavily weighted towards use with Israel/Ephraim, which assumes the role of both the parent plant and the fruit. Plant imagery by nature is passive. Although plants grow, direct themselves toward light sources, reproduce, and wage chemical warfare with insects, they are, in most cases, rooted to one spot, and thus have limited activity. The image with the least activity is that of the grapes and figs in 9:10. Fruit does not produce itself, but is dependent on the parent plant for nourishment. It is also in a position of complete powerlessness, subject to, and in fact designed for, consumption. In this verse Ephraim is portrayed as potentially good, pleasing to YHWH, but that hope is quickly shattered.

In the next set of verses, Ephraim/Israel takes on the slightly more powerful role of the plant producing the fruit, at which task he shows varying success. His root dries up in 9:16, so that he cannot produce fruit. His fruitfulness is ambiguous in 10:1 where he is either a fruitful or an empty vine. He eventually produces fruit, but the fruit production is misguided, causing Ephraim to stray from YHWH.

Ephraim as plant takes on a relatively positive identity in ch. 14. The plants here are described as more active: budding, striking root, blooming, sending out shoots and fragrance, and sprouting. These are activities particularly characteristic of young plants, or at least, plants at the beginning of the growing season, when they are still vulnerable. There is some play along the activity and potency axes. On the one hand the plants are showing vigor and rapid growth, on the other, they are young and tender. New growth generally requires more water than old growth, as well as more protection from the sun and from herbivores. The water in this case is provided by YHWH, who acts as dew for them. All of the activity is thus under the control of YHWH, who can provide or withhold the moisture necessary for growth. Because YHWH is overseeing the growth, it moves in the right direction, towards goodness.

YHWH is identified as a cypress, a symbol of strength and majesty. While the cypress is not particularly active, it does represent strength. This tree also provides fruit for Ephraim, showing not only its power to sustain life, but also its positive care.

The references to plants not attributed to Ephraim or YHWH also show interesting features. They are relatively active and almost personified. The poison weeds break out, the thorns and thistles grow up over tents and altars. They appear powerful, in that neither the tents/altars, nor the people supposedly caring for them are able to stop them. Presumably the people have been taken away, but even so, they lack the ability to protect their homes, possessions, and religious sites. While the actions of these plants carry out YHWH's judgment on Ephraim, the images themselves are quite negative.

Natural Phenomena Imagery

Several images drawn from the inanimate natural world signify YHWH and Israel/Ephraim throughout Hosea. The most common is water and dew, which is quite understandable in a dry land. Other images are related to light and wind. Most of the images in this category apply to YHWH.

Water Imagery

Water appears as both positive and negative imagery. The negative aspect is used to signify YHWH's fury in 5:10: "on them I will pour out my fury like water [כמים]." The image is one of a continuous stream of fury, soaking the people and the land. In a similar manner, Ezek 13:13 describes how YHWH will release storms and hailstones in destructive fury. The use of rain or raining down as an image of judgment also appears in Esarhaddon's Succession Treaty, which curses the land with drought and the opposite of rain: "Just as rain does not fall from a brazen heaven so may rain and dew not come upon your fields and your meadows; instead of dew may burning coals rain on your land."[155]

A second negative use of water imagery is 10:7, where the monarchy of Samaria is swept away by a surge of water: "Samaria will be destroyed; its king will be like a splinter (foam) on the face of the water [כְּקֶצֶף עַל־פְּנֵי־מָיִם]."[156] The face of the water here is not identified here with YHWH, but does serve to fill out the concept of water as judgment.

Verse 10:12 expresses the idea of a rain shower as a positive attribute: "Until he comes and rains righteousness [וְיֹרֶה צֶדֶק] on you." It seems likely that a pun is intended here. The rare usage of the hiphil form of ירה to mean "rain" seems justified by the metaphorical agricultural context imploring Ephraim to sow righteousness. The hiphil form more commonly means "to teach," however, which would also fit in the context, as Israel is in need of instruction. Isaiah 45:8 uses very similar imagery, with YHWH telling the skies to rain righteousness from above, so that the earth may open and sprout righteousness and salvation. Amos also uses water imagery, though in 5:24 the water is bubbling up, not flowing down: "But let justice cascade like water, righteousness like an everflowing stream."

The same pun on ירה appears in 6:3: "Let us know and let us pursue the knowledge of YHWH [וְנֵדְעָה נִרְדְּפָה לָדַעַת אֶת־יְהוָה]." Like the dawn, his going forth is sure, and he will come like the rain to us, like the latter rain rains on (instructs) the earth [וְיָבוֹא כַגֶּשֶׁם לָנוּ כְּמַלְקוֹשׁ יוֹרֶה אָרֶץ]." Ephraim's pursuit of the knowledge of YHWH would result in instruction, equivalent to the life-giving rains that saturate the earth.

Gary Rendsburg suggests that there may be another allusion to rain, through the name Lo-Ruhamah.[157] He proposes that רחם can mean to rain upon, as well as to have mercy. He finds support for this in an Arabic cognate, some parallels in other HB passages, and the attestation of this meaning in some rabbinic texts.[158] Thus, when YHWH sows Jezreel into the land in 2:25, he also rains on Lo-ruhamah [וְרִחַמְתִּי אֶת־לֹא רֻחָמָה].[159] A final reference to YHWH as water is the promise to be like dew to Israel, which is pictured as a plant, in the reconciliation on 14:6: כַּטַּל לְיִשְׂרָאֵל אֶהְיֶה. Dew plays a crucial role in keeping vegetation alive in a Mediterranean climate that receives little or no summer precipitation, so the image is one of sustenance.[160]

The water metaphor is used twice with human subjects, in two nearly identical phrases in 6:4 and 13:3. The ephemeral nature of Ephraim and his faith are compared to quickly evaporating dew: "like the cloud of morning, like the dew than goes away early [כענן־בקר וכטל משכים הלך]." The first citation in 6:4 describes Ephraim's faithfulness [חסד], or lack thereof, as part of a more general complaint about his lack of commitment. The second citation applies the imagery directly to Ephraim, threatening that because of his actions, he will be like the dew evaporating at dawn, swept away like the chaff, like smoke from a window (13:3). Dew and clouds are normally positive images in a dry land, as when used with YHWH above. The image appears here in a clearly negative context, however, suggesting that the transitory nature of the image is the focus. The clouds and dew offer the promise of nourishment, but because they go away early, they do not fulfill this promise.[161]

Wind Imagery

As the antithesis of water imagery, YHWH is likened in 13:15 to desiccating wind that will dry up Ephraim: "the east wind [קדים] will come, the wind of YHWH will come up from the wilderness and dry out his fountain and dry up his spring [ויבוש מקורו ויחרב מעינו]." YHWH likewise turns the wife into a parched land in 2: "I will set her like a wilderness and place her like a land of drought [כארץ ציה]." The east wind [קדים] that comes from the desert and has the power to desiccate and to sweep things away is frequently used as a metaphor for YHWH's judgment on the land.[162]

Other References to Natural Phenomena

The earth itself is personified in 4:3: "...therefore the earth will mourn and all its inhabitants will languish, with the beasts of the field and the birds of the sky and also the fish of the sea will be gathered up." The languishing of the land is intimately related to the sin of the people. In a similar manner, the crops of the people fail as a result of their improper actions in 8:7 and 9:2. Katherine Hayes observes: "The agricultural metaphors and similes in such oracles, in which the acts of the Israelites are compared to agricultural phenomena and the state of Israel to the state of the earth, contribute to the theme of the organic connection between acts and their consequences (or the effects of punishment) throughout the book of Hosea."[163] In a very anthropocentric view of creation, the state of the earth and its inhabitants seems to depend on Israel's faithfulness to YHWH.[164]

Analysis of Natural Phenomena Imagery

With the nature imagery, YHWH is more frequently the subject than is Ephraim. The largest set of images in this category is water. YHWH appears as the one who causes rain in 5:10, 6:3, and 10:12, and possibly 2:25. As the one able to control the rain, YHWH shows ultimate power.[165] YHWH acts like the dew in 14:6, providing nourishment for the young plant Israel. Most of these references are positive, though 5:10 represents YHWH's presumably justified wrath. Israel/Ephraim is only pictured as clouds and dew, and not very good ones at that, because they dissipate early without giving much moisture. Their action and power disperses into the air without result. Their king is carried away by water in 10:7, shown thus as passive and powerless.

YHWH is also likened to the wind, exercising judgment on the people and the land and drying up and sweeping them away. This wind is powerful and active, unpredictable and unable to be controlled. The people are the objects of this wind, unable to resist. The imagery as a whole shows YHWH to be in control of nature, using it to enforce his judgment on the people, whereas the people are generally subject to the forces of nature, unable to stand up against their power. When humans are portrayed as natural substances, it is as transitory phenomena. The dew passively condenses out of the air, and the clouds are pushed around by the wind.

Conclusions

In this chapter I have looked at metaphors for YHWH and Israel or Ephraim drawn from seven image fields: parent-child, sickness and healing, hunting, animals, agriculture, plants, and natural phenomena. The metaphors serve to place YHWH and the humans at different points in social space, which can be analyzed by the axes of activity, potency, and goodness. In the next chapter I will lay out in more depth some of the trends that can be drawn from the imagery, but a few things can be noted here.

First, the text indicates that in Israelite society the axes are arranged so that high activity and high potency are correlated with greater goodness. Goodness is not necessarily moral goodness, although it can be, but is rather what is esteemed in the society. The axes are correlated with what are perceived as masculine traits, which are also those commonly ascribed to kings and gods in the ANE: activity, including the ability to lead and to make decisions for oneself and one's family or people; potency, including military, sexual, political, and economic; and goodness, including wisdom, honor, honesty, justice, and mercy. Because masculinity can be fairly well assessed by a social space defined by the three axes, there is a correlation between the placement of a pronoun within this space by any image and the degree of masculinity assessed to that pronoun by the image.

Second, YHWH is consistently placed in the optimal or most masculine octant, which seems to be high activity, high potency, and high goodness. While not always at the same point in the octant, he never leaves it entirely. Several of the images are identities directly related to masculinity: father, hunter, farmer, shepherd; others have strong masculine associations, and are often predicated on kings: lion, cypress, hurricane. In general the images serve to reinforce the perception of YHWH's power and masculinity.

Third, the humans are consistently placed in less optimal octants. The octants vary, however. Sometimes Ephraim is active and powerful and bad, sometimes passive, impotent and good. The octant that Ephraim does not reside in is that occupied by YHWH—powerful, active, and good. The masculinity of the humans always lacks some of the desired elements, although these differ according to the image. Thus the rhetoric of the prophet serves to undermine the audience's perception of its masculinity.

CHAPTER FIVE

Syntheses and Subversions

What is perhaps most fascinating about such reified spatial hierarchies…is their potential for inversion or ritual reversal, or "degradation" as Bakhtin puts it. This may be because vertical scales are inherently unstable—being after all continuous ladders going both ways—and because their antimonies, such as sky/soil, heaven/hell, better/worse, bear the unstable dialectical relationship of all binary oppositions.

David Gilmore, "Above and Below"

Summary

This study has explored the use of tropes as rhetoric in Hosea. Utilizing James Fernandez's concept of metaphor as that which situates and moves people in a social cultural space, I have examined the nature of the identities predicated on YHWH and on the human, male audience of Hosea and their arrangement in the social quality space. The elite males who make up the audience are those who have the most power in Israelite society, making the decisions in the political realm and controlling many aspects of the economy and religious practice. Within the social space, they are normally conceived as occupying the optimal positions. The rhetoric of Hosea reserves that position for YHWH, however, and moves the audience, represented by Ephraim, Israel, and Judah, to various lesser points in the space.

Three axes have proved particularly useful for analysis of the effects of the metaphoric predication: an axis ranking activity, one ranking potency, and a third assessing goodness. These axes not only account for much of the meaning of language, as Osgood determined, but also form an apt framework for the assessment of masculinity in the culture of the ANE. Some measures of masculinity that appear important in ANE society, including ancient Israel, are strength, power, independent action, sexual potency, the ability to provide for one's family, honor, honesty, leadership/political power, military prowess, hospitality, the upholding of justice, and the display of mercy to the helpless.[1] Many of these attributes can be correlated with the three axes. The action axis includes independence and leadership, as well as generally instigating an activity rather than being its object. The potency axis includes political, economic, social, military, and sexual power, as well as the ability to provide for and protect one's family and property. The goodness axis contains various elements of honor, which includes the honor of one's family, honesty, hospitality, justice, and mercy.

Hosea contains much gender imagery that clearly addresses the issue of the audience's masculinity, but it also contains other imagery that lends itself to analysis by the three axes. Because masculinity is closely associated with action, potency, and goodness in the culture of the ANE, the movement along these axes resulting from the non-gender imagery also affects the perception of the masculinity of the audience and of YHWH.

Female Imagery

The female imagery, which has drawn by far the most scholarly discussion, falls into two categories: female as subject and female as object. The female as subject appears only in chs. 1, 2, and 4. Other than the conceiving, bearing, and weaning performed by Gomer, the female subject is portrayed as promiscuous, actively pursuing her lovers. The female as object generally receives punishment for her straying. She is also, however, the recipient of forgiveness and betrothal, as the object of YHWH's restoration of a utopian relationship at the end of ch. 2.

While the female imagery has traditionally received attention for its portrayal of women, I examined its implications for masculinity. The actions of the leaders in Samaria have challenged YHWH's authority, and ch. 2 provides a defense of YHWH's masculinity. In particular, three areas of masculinity are called into question: his provisioning for his family, the fidelity of the women under his authority, and the existence and legitimacy of his children. The first area is clearly a concern in ch. 2. Grain, wine, and oil, along with clothing, are major points of contention. The wife's improper attribution of them to her lovers, rather than her husband, attacks the masculinity of her husband, who is supposed to provide for her. Fidelity is another issue of concern. The wife has been unfaithful and thus raises questions about the husband's authority and virility. The legitimacy of the children is also in doubt. The names of the latter two children indicate that the husband refuses to claim them, and the children are disowned in 2:6 because of their mother's infidelity. Yet they are reclaimed in 2:1–3 and 2:24–25. So while questions are raised in each of the above-mentioned areas, the husband responds to protect his masculinity. By removing the provisions, the husband shows that he had provided them. By stripping the wife in front of her lovers, the husband shows that he is stronger than they. As a father he chooses whether or not to acknowledge the children as his own.

Male Imagery

Outside of the first three chapters, instances of male imagery greatly outnumber those of female imagery and show greater diversity. I divided the male imagery into seven categories, which can be grouped into sexual relationships and potency images. The imagery of sexual relationships, expressed through the words זנה [fornication] and נאף [adultery], relates to political and religious fidelity and honesty. The former word occurs in a variety of contexts, with economic, political, and religious connotations. It indicates short-sightedness and a lack of loyalty. The fornication is futile and impure. Adultery occurs specifically in a political context, in a plot against the king. The more concrete situation of regicide matches the more concrete imagery of adultery, which refers to a specific crime one man commits against another.[2]

The imagery relating to potency divides into several aspects. Images of sticks and staffs are particularly phallic and are used to show Ephraim's lack of judgment. Other images are polyvalent. The word און incorporates general manly characteristics. It implies active vigor, youthful strength, and sexual potency. References to lifting up indicate excessive pride as well as sexual potency. Baking imagery is prominent in ch. 7. The metaphors take Ephraim from the early stages of kneading bread and letting it rise, symbolizing the rising of the traitors' rising hubris and treachery, to baking it, with poor result, leaving Ephraim half-baked and impotent, to the late stages when the bread molds, revealing Ephraim's final impotence. The oven used for baking is also a phallic image, and the heat it generates represents the passion of the illicit actions of the traitors.

They heat up and rise in their sense of masculine power and preeminence, attacking (and defeating) that of the king. The final category of bow imagery is well attested in the cognate literature. As a military symbol it represents masculinity *par excellence.* Drawn and wielded bows represent victorious warriors, and abandoned, cut, or slack bows indicate defeat and symbolic castration. In several ANE texts, bows are part of the stereotypical symbols of men, as spindles and distaffs represent women. Hoséa refers to bows twice, once in 1:5, where YHWH breaks the bow of Israel, and once in 7:16, where Ephraim is like a slack bow. In both of these cases the masculinity of the personified nation is seriously attacked.

In a relentless manner the male imagery chisels away at the masculinity of the audience. They are called impotent sexually and militarily. They are represented as dishonest and disloyal. Their actions are misdirected and futile. The assertion of their masculinity leads to iniquity and murder. Male imagery is never used positively to represent the male audience in Hosea.

Parent-Child Imagery

The most developed non-gender-based image field is the parent-child metaphor. The imagery can be divided into two major groups: Ephraim or humans-as-child and Ephraim or humans-as-parent. The Ephraim-as-child metaphor is the more extensively developed category.

The Ephraim/human-as-child metaphors appear mostly in chs. 1–2 and ch. 11. The children in 1–2 seem to be differentiated from the mother Samaria, probably being the common people. They are passive and undeveloped, and their status is dependent on that of their mother. At first they are disowned, but later reclaimed. The son in ch. 11 has a different identity, similar to the wife in ch. 2. YHWH establishes his relationship to Israel by using adoption language in 11:1. The son quickly rebels, however, not recognizing the source of his healing or support and inviting disownment, which is the fate of adoptees who rebel against their adoptive parents. Ephraim proves to be a poor child from the start, refusing to be born in 13:13. In the depictions of Ephraim/Israel as a child, it is improperly active, not accepting its role as a subordinate, subject to the authority of the father. Though the parent provides appropriate care, the child does not show proper respect and acknowledgment.

The leaders are generally pictured as bad parents. First, they bear alien children (5:7). Second, they fail to instruct their children properly, leading to their bad actions (4:5–6; 13–14). Finally, they fail to protect their children, and the bad deeds of the parents lead to the destruction of their children, mostly, it appears, through warfare.

The parent-child imagery serves two purposes. First, the Ephraim-as-child imagery serves to show that he has rejected his proper position under the authority of YHWH. The leaders think that they are adults capable of independent, powerful action, but Hosea predicates upon them the identity of a child, who, by ignoring parental guidance, makes bad decisions. Second, the Ephraim-as-parent imagery shows that he fails to execute properly his position of authority. He either does not act when he should or acts in the wrong way. Both the inactivity and misdirected activity display his impotency. Not only is Ephraim unable to protect his children, but actively contributes to their destruction.

Sickness and Healing Imagery

The roles in the sickness/healing metaphor field are well-established with only minimal overlap. Ephraim is the sick person, and YHWH is the healer. These roles are never inverted. Both YHWH and Ephraim can cause sickness, however. When Ephraim is sick, he is often shown as a bad patient. He does not recognize his illness and does not always go to the correct healer when he does. The one occasion on which Ephraim turns willingly to YHWH (6:1–2) raises doubts about the sincerity of the move. Ephraim is either the passive one, afflicted by the illness, or actively pursues the wrong cure. As a sick person, Ephraim is weak/impotent, especially because he is not self-aware. As the illness results from improper activities, Ephraim also scores poorly on the goodness axis. On one occasion humans make other humans ill, when the conspirators make the king and his princes sick with wine before killing them. While such activities are active and potent, they are obviously bad.

YHWH is able to inflict and cure disease, which shows he is active and powerful. The power is limited in some ways, however, because Ephraim seems to be able to resist healing. YHWH is also unable to make Ephraim properly attribute the healing. On the other hand, sickness from YHWH is irresistible. As the healer and as the one inflicting illness to punish misdeeds, YHWH scores fairly high on the goodness scale.

Hunting and Seeking Imagery

Both YHWH and Ephraim are cast as hunters. Ephraim engages in pursuit and ambush, as well as laying snares and traps. The latter imagery, often a descriptor of evil-doers in the psalms, automatically implicates Ephraim in negative activity. The specific objects of their snares (other cities and the prophet) confirm this assessment. The seeking imagery, loosely included in the hunting imagery, has a variety of objects, including the lovers and YHWH, but is never successful. Thus while the active pursuit is on occasion good, it is never potent. YHWH's actions are successful in bringing down the straying Ephraim. As prey Ephraim is trapped not only by YHWH, but by unspecified enemies. YHWH's trapping of Ephraim reflects Assyrian treaty curses, which claim that the treaty offenders will be hunted down like birds.

Animal Imagery

Animal imagery is predicated upon both YHWH and Ephraim, but the animals used are quite different. YHWH is represented as a predator, either a lion, a panther, or a bear. Lion imagery in particular occurs frequently in ANE literature as a symbol of gods and kings.[3] It represents power and dominance. Ephraim is always portrayed as prey animals, either birds or herbivores. As a bird it is brought down in a net and flutters to and fro. Language of birds fleeing or being caught in a trap is standard in the treaty curses to represent the result of the violator's rebellion. Fleeing is a particularly unmanly action, not only because it indicates cowardliness, but also because it leaves one's people unprotected. In addition, the fleeing will prove futile because the suzerain will capture them in a net or trap. The power differential between the hunter or the lion and the bird is represented by the tremendous difference in size between the two and by the fluttering nature of the birds.

Ephraim is also shown as a herbivore, most often as a cow, but also as a sheep. The cow Ephraim is an uncooperative farm animal, but YHWH eventually makes it submit. As a herbivore Ephraim is not very active—its resistance to YHWH is usually a refusal to work rather than an active rebellion. As this resistance proves futile, Ephraim is rendered impotent. In addition Ephraim is usually a female herbivore. The exception to this is the wild ass of 8:9, which symbolizes a (forced) retreat to the wilderness. The animal imagery thus shows YHWH as an active, potent, and just, if violent, enforcer, while Ephraim, despite sometimes being active, is misguided, impotent, and either blatantly bad or stupid.

Agricultural Imagery

Hosea draws extensively on the metaphor field of agriculture. Both YHWH and Ephraim/Israel are farmers, but only Ephraim is the seed or the farm animals. YHWH appears once as the sower (2:25) planting Jezreel in the land. Often YHWH tends animals. While not able to have complete control over the cow Ephraim, in the end YHWH prevails, either by forcing the animal to comply or by changing the predication, turning Ephraim from a cow into a sheep in 4:16.

When Ephraim sows, the action is futile, either because others will consume the produce or because Ephraim is planting the wrong thing (8:7, 10:12), which will become uncontrollable and destroy Ephraim. As a herder Ephraim fares no better. While active, Ephraim is ultimately impotent and not directed toward the good.

Plant Imagery

Plant imagery is predicated in all but one case on Ephraim/Israel. Several different types of plants appear. The first type is agricultural plants, especially grapes and figs. Sometimes Ephraim is the fruit and in 9:10 is unexpectedly found in the wilderness. Their promise quickly turns sour, however. At other times Ephraim is the vine, which generally does not produce its expected fruit. It is withered in 9:16 and makes fruit that leads it astray and may be stripped away in 10:1. The possible palm in 9:13 is also fruitless, and the implications of the second half of the verse are that what fruit it has (children) will be brought out to be destroyed. In these cases Ephraim the plant or fruit has great potential for goodness, but it is not realized.

Chapter 14 provides a different tone for the plant imagery. Nourished by YHWH, Ephraim/Israel grows vigorously and is finally responsive to him. The three major agricultural products, grain, olives, and grapes, grow bountifully in this chapter. Israel is also likened to a lily and a cedar. This chapter provides the only example of YHWH as plant, a green cypress that provides fruit for Israel. The plant imagery that is not predicated on either Ephraim or YHWH generally indicates the decay of human society, as thorns and thistles take over human habitations.

Because plants are rooted, the plant imagery is generally passive, although the thorns and thistles seem particularly active. The plant imagery locates the subject at different places along the potency axis, however. Withering fruitless plants are impotent, while flourishing vines producing much fruit are potent. YHWH as verdant cypress is a particularly strong image. The goodness of the imagery depends largely on the amount and type of fruit produced.

Natural Phenomena Imagery

While the plant imagery predominantly centers on Ephraim, the imagery of natural phenomena is more frequently used with YHWH. The most common image is that of water, which can be both positive and negative. YHWH's fury pours down in 5:10, and Samaria's king is swept away in 10:7.[4] Water as rain has positive connotations. YHWH will water the earth and cause it to be fruitful. In a play on the word ירה, the rain may symbolize instruction, causing righteousness to grow. YHWH acts as the dew in ch. 14, nourishing the newly loyal Israel. YHWH is also represented by the wind, an image directly opposed to the water imagery, as the east wind desiccates the land (13:15).

Ephraim is only represented twice by natural phenomena, and the two citations are virtually identical. Unlike the nurturing dew of YHWH in ch. 14, Ephraim is like a morning cloud, or dew that goes away early. Any positive hopes for Ephraim's usefulness quickly dissipate. Dew is a relatively passive image, but with YHWH it is potent, whereas with Ephraim it is impotent. YHWH's dew is good, nurturing the plants, but Ephraim's dew is ephemeral and useless. The other images used for YHWH, the rain and the wind, are much more active and potent. Rain is clearly good, but the wind is used to punish Ephraim for its misdeeds.

Trends in Metaphoric Predication

While the metaphorical fields noted above are diverse and show somewhat different movements along the axes of activity, potency, and goodness, some trends emerge. YHWH and Ephraim are clearly placed in different octants in the social space.

Trends for YHWH

The metaphors predicated upon YHWH generally establish and reinforce YHWH's position in the social space. They cause relatively little movement along the axes.

Activity Axis

YHWH is consistently portrayed as active. As a husband, he provides for the wife, but also blocks the wife's ways, punishes her, and reestablishes relationship. As a father he nurtures and raises the son. YHWH inflicts sickness and heals. YHWH hunts down Ephraim, both as a human hunter spreading nets and as a predator ripping and dragging away. The farmer YHWH sows Jezreel and tends the balky cattle, putting them to work. As a tree, YHWH provides fruit. YHWH as water pours out fury, but also provides moisture for the land, allowing for fruitfulness. Finally, YHWH as wind sweeps across the land drying up fountains. YHWH is the one who acts and is not acted upon.

Potency Axis

YHWH also occupies a high position on the potency axis. Within the marriage metaphor, the most telling line is 2:12: "Now I will uncover her nakedness before the eyes of her lovers, and no man can deliver her" [ועתה אגלה את־נבלתה לעיני מאהביה ואיש לא־יצילנה]. The language of ultimate power, stating that no man can deliver her from his grasp, is a common claim for Assyrian kings, asserting their authority and might over all others.[5] YHWH also shows the power to block her ways, to give and take provisions, to turn her into a desert, and to seduce her back into relationship. As a father YHWH is able to adopt and disown the children at will, and in the end to call them home. YHWH is the only one in the text with the power to heal. As a hunter YHWH captures the prey. YHWH the lion expresses a power similar to the husband in 5:14: "For I am like a lion to Ephraim, like a young lion to the house of Judah. I, I will tear, and I will go and carry away, and there is no one who can deliver" [כי אנכי כשחל לאפרים וככפיר לבית יהודה אני אני אטרף ואלך אשא ואין מציל]. As a farmer YHWH sows Jezreel in the earth and herds Ephraim. YHWH has the power to predicate a new identity on Israel, changing it from a balky cow into a sheep. The cypress tree, the one plant identity predicated on YHWH, is a symbol of kings and strength in the ANE. Finally, imaged as natural phenomena YHWH shows the power to nurture or desiccate Ephraim. YHWH consistently appears powerful. He exerts power over others, while never being overpowered by another.

Goodness Axis

The goodness axis shows more variability, but the goodness can be divided into two categories. The first contains the actions of protecting, provisioning, nurturing, and healing. The second contains the actions of upholding justice and punishing iniquity and disloyalty. It is this second category with its accompanying violence that gives present day readers pause, but the actions were probably considered justified and necessary for maintaining order, at least through the prophet's eyes. YHWH does not seem to act arbitrarily in the book. Provisioning and nourishment images are especially prominent in the parent-child, sickness and healing, agriculture and plant metaphor fields. Punishment of iniquity shows up especially in the marriage metaphor and in the hunting and animal metaphor fields, occurring a few times in other fields. YHWH also forgives the people and desires reconciliation, themes that appear throughout the text, but most systematically in ch. 14. Hope of reconciliation also emerges in 2:1–3 and 2:16–25, although 16–17 are somewhat ambiguous. If one considers the administration of justified punishment good, despite its violence, in order to uphold the proper order, YHWH is consistently portrayed as good.

Trends for Ephraim/Israel

YHWH occupies a rather stable position in the octant of positive action, potency, and goodness values, which is reinforced by metaphoric predication. The metaphors predicated on the human subjects, however, work to change their position in the social space rather than to reinforce it. The human leaders seem to perceive themselves as residing in the same octant as YHWH. Hosea seeks to disabuse them of this idea, moving them around in several different ways.

Activity Axis

The leaders, represented by Ephraim/Israel/Judah, seem to start from the position of valuing action that they initiate, which they presumably expect will provide them benefit. Hosea's rhetoric criticizes their actions, claiming that they are misdirected and will lead to disaster. In almost all of the metaphor fields Ephraim is active at some point. The men fornicate, act as adulterers, and consult their sticks and staffs. The wife pursues her lovers, and the son walks away from his adoptive father. The sick person goes to Assyria to be healed. The conspirators make the king sick and draw near in ambush. As an animal Ephraim flutters to and fro, wanders alone, and threshes. As a plant he makes fruit. Ephraim the farmer sows and herds.

Ephraim is also passive at times. As a flock of birds, he gets caught by the net and as a cow he refuses to work. Ephraim the vine often does not produce fruit. As a parent Ephraim fails to instruct his children and does not protect them.

Ephraim therefore shows different levels of activity. The rhetoric works to move Ephraim down the activity axis. In the idealized states put forth by the prophet, Ephraim takes a passive role. At the end of ch. 2 the wife passively submits to the husband. Likewise, the children of ch. 2 also submit to the father. The idealized role of Israel in ch. 14 is a plant, though it flourishes. Some activity has positive potential, however. The farmer does have the capacity to sow righteousness and seek YHWH (10:12), even though he has chosen otherwise in the text. Thus while the general trend of the rhetoric is toward passivity, some other possibilities are allowed, depending on movement along the other axes, especially up the goodness axis.

Potency Axis
Along this axis in particular there is conflict between where the leaders think they are and where Hosea tries to place them. Hosea tries to indicate that many of the activities the leaders undertake are futile and that they do not possess the power that they think they have. Within the marriage metaphor, the wife thinks she has power to act on her own volition and does pursue her lovers for awhile, but she is eventually overpowered by the husband, who proves more potent than the lovers. The children of ch. 2 have no power to determine whether or not their father claims them. They have no control over their status, because they inherited it from their mother, and their father has the sole capacity to change it. The son of ch. 11 has the power to leave the father, but is then subject to being disowned. Ephraim is vitiated by illness and often does not recognize this, and as such is deluded about his state of potency. As a farmer Ephraim shows little control over his crops or herds. Ephraim is predicated with identities of small birds and herbivores which are hunted

down or controlled by the (divine) farmer. The plant Ephraim is dependent on the rain. Sometimes he has the power to produce fruit, and sometimes he does not. As dew he does not have sufficient potency to withstand even the early morning sun.

The male imagery demonstrates the highest degree of conflict over potency. Ephraim takes great pride in his strength [אוֹן] but will be overpowered by the nations. He consults his "sticks and staffs" the symbols of his power, but is misled. He "lifts up" in Ephraim, but is brought down. His bow is slack and broken. The area in which Ephraim shows the most power is in his ability to ensnare and commit crimes against fellow humans. Ephraim shows various degrees of power within the text, but in general the rhetoric works to lower Ephraim's place on the potency axis.

Goodness Axis
Ephraim scores consistently poorly on the goodness axis. If he is active, those actions are usually either futile or misdirected. The wife goes away from her husband. The child rebels against the father. The conspirators make the king and princes sick, then kill them. The hunter leads others astray and entraps the prophet. The birds fly in the wrong direction, and the cow balks. The sower sows wind and injustice, and the herder herds the wind. The plants that show promise squander their fruit or dry up, fruitless. The men are led astray by their "sticks." Their actions are categorized as fornication and adultery. When Ephraim is passive, it is usually at the wrong time. He does not protect and educate the children. He refuses to be born. The dew evaporates too early.

The rhetoric thus works to move Ephraim down the goodness axis from his self-perceptions of goodness, which are evidenced in 12:8, where he denies any iniquity. It is only in wished-for activity that Ephraim is good. The wife will be newly betrothed and recognize her husband. The sons will come home. The most extended example of this is ch. 14, where Israel will grow vigorously in the correct place, at the correct time, under the correct supervision. Thus Ephraim has the potential for goodness and the prophet tries to move the audience in that direction.

Subversions

Within these general trends, however, there are exceptions and hints of subversions.[6] For the purposes of this study, subversions are those elements that serve to undercut the major trends or to hint at alternate ways of structuring or aligning people in social space. The rhetoric of Hosea seems to assume a prevailing hegemonic masculinity, which equates prowess on the battlefield, in the political and economic realms, and in the marital/reproductive realm with manliness. Both the audience, represented by Ephraim/Israel/Judah, and YHWH are compared with hegemonic norms. The conformity of the audience with the masculine ideal is continually challenged throughout the book, but the ideal itself is not questioned. Instead, YHWH is portrayed as the purest example of the hegemonic masculinity. YHWH is the hunter, the healer, and the provider.[7] Therefore, when the images used for YHWH show some play or subversion of the categories, then the whole system is subject to deconstruction, and not just the relative positions of people within it.

The metaphorical fields of gender are particularly susceptible to slippage. As Cornwall and Lindisfarne note: "We suggest that such attributions [of masculinity] are neither exclusive, nor permanent. Nowhere is there ever only a single system which defines people's success and failure as gendered subjects in absolute or enduring terms."[8] The ruling class has an interest in maintaining a particular hegemonic masculinity of its own definition, but it can never be absolute. Hosea's rhetoric works to change the position of the men in relation to this definition of masculinity, and at points to subvert and redefine this masculinity. Of course, as I have noted, the book of Hosea does not present a description of a complete society, so that much of the gender variation and subordinate masculinities one would see in an actual society are not represented. Because it is critiquing the hegemonic masculinity, however, or at least those who are occupying the hegemonic position, fissures start to appear.[9] The clear hierarchies of power, wealth, and prestige are shaken up. Gilmore notes the irony that even extremely hierarchical structures are in some sense unstable:

> The hierarchical model is both right-side-up and upside-down at the same time, suggesting that all behavior, no matter how seemingly monolithic, is ambivalent; all hierarchies are reversible; and men and women are both on top and at bottom at the same time, for there is no negative in the imagination.[10]

Bipolar categories almost by definition lend themselves to this kind of questioning, because in such as system one pole cannot exist without its opposite pole. Because most people are situated at some position on the continuum between the poles, there is tension between them. The amount of play in a system is increased even more if instead of focusing on particular dichotomous pairs, one considers the multidimensional social space represented by Fernandez's axes.[11] Relatively small movements up and down one or more of the axes can subvert rigid social understandings, perhaps even more than a movement from one pole to the other.[12]

To reiterate, my main concern is on the level of social understanding rather than on the level of lived experience. It is difficult to get at the latter from a text, especially a highly metaphorical text, because metaphors also work at the level of the social perception of an image and not at the level of facts. Social understanding is usually more static than experience. Hegemonic masculinities continue to exert influence because of this. Whether or not a given person's individual experience conforms to the model, he or she may profess that the hegemonic model is or should be in effect. Subversions of the hegemonic model, however, are almost inevitable.

I will address two types of subversions in this section. The first is subversion in the imagery itself, particularly in the gender imagery, which shows variation from the hegemonic norm. The second is subversion in the way the imagery makes movement in social space. Predication of unexpected identities on YHWH and the audience seems to allow some flexibility in fulfilling and subverting the force of the rhetoric.

Subversions in the Gender Imagery

Gender imagery shows the most potential for subversion. Both imagery applied to humans and to YHWH differs on some occasions from the expected norms.

Imagery Applied to Humans

Subversions in the Male Imagery. As shown in ch. 3, the gendered metaphors used for humans fall into two major groupings: male images and female images. The male imagery works primarily to portray the men as impotent and misdirected. They are less masculine, but still men.[13] The hegemonic masculinity apparent in the ANE values action, potency, and goodness, especially with regard to protecting one's own and displaying prowess in warfare. Military ruthlessness can be tempered by mercy, as long as the superiority of the merciful one is clear. Portraying the men in Hosea as weak and not very masculine has two opposite effects. On the one hand, because the language is clearly disparaging in its context, the rhetoric reinforces the prevailing hegemony, indeed often placing YHWH as the top of this particular standard. On the other hand, simply showing these less masculine men opens the door to thinking about subordinate masculinities. The latter effect is very small compared to the former, but does demonstrate some slippage in the prevailing rhetoric of the text. Perhaps because I am studying male imagery as well as female imagery, I prefer to make a distinction between images that feminize or emasculate men with their connotations of castration and those that "demasculate" men. This creates more semantic space for a range of masculinities. Much of the male imagery works to de-masculate.

Subversions in the Female Imagery. The female imagery, however, clearly feminizes the men. Portraying the male audience as a woman, the promiscuous wife of Hos 2, is the most obvious predication. Beyond the implications that I discussed in ch. 3, there are a few more subtle plays within the gender imagery and its implications for the audience.

The first indication of this play is the name of Hosea's wife. Gomer is used as a female name only in this book. It occurs two times, in Gen 10 and 1 Chr 1 in genealogical lists, as a male name. It occurs once more in Ezek 38 as the name of a nation or tribe. While three occurrences are hardly definitive about the customary uses of a name, it should be noted that the name Gomer is at least gender neutral. Using such a name starts to break down the boundaries between male and female, easing the male audience into the story and making it easier to portray them as the wife.

A second play occurs with the child Jezreel, first named in 1:4 and sowed into the land in 2:25. Somewhere between the beginning of ch. 1 and the end of ch. 2, Jezreel changes gender from the masculine son to the feminine "her" sowed in the land. The feminine object pronoun is somewhat unexpected [וזרעתיה] and many commentators emend to "him," but there is no textual support for this.[14] Those who prefer to let it stand ascribe the change to a variety of factors. Sweeney proposes that the verse refers to the valley of Jezreel, which like other features of the land is feminine.[15] Calvin notes the grammatical form and admonishes the reader that "the relative pronoun in the feminine gender ought not to embarrass us, for the Prophet ever speaks as of a woman: the people, we know, have been as yet described to us under the person of a woman."[16] Landy takes a substantially psychoanalytic approach to the issue, discussing it in terms of male fantasy of submission and gender inversion.[17] Whether or not the transformation symbolizes male submissive fantasies, it is noteworthy that it is the child Jezreel who is transformed, and not the other son, Lo-ami. Jezreel in ch. 1 stands for the violence and bloodshed of the monarchy and the usurping of power. YHWH promises to destroy the monarchy and break the bow of Israel in Jezreel. It is just such military and political contexts that produce the curses to turn men/warriors into women. By the end of ch. 2, this transgendering has occurred, and the passive, female Jezreel is sowed in the earth. YHWH has taken full control of the sowing process, with all of its masculine reproductive potential.[18]

Chapter 2 raises some interesting subversions. In his discussion of gender construction in Jeremiah, Herbert B. Huffmon observes that subversion is, by its nature, ambiguous and subtle: "As subversion, these subverting texts do not attack the gender categories in a frontal assault, they undermine them....Subversion involves, instead of specifically opposing the traditions of the 'real' world, problematizing reality, opening up alternative possibilities."[19] One of the alternative possibilities appears in 2:8, where the husband threatens to hedge up the wife's roads and raise walls against her. Stepping a bit outside of the metaphor, this sounds like language of siege. The city Samaria is under attack and its people unable to leave. Another layer of meaning, however, may rely on male, rather than female imagery, which in a manner similar to the name Gomer, would serve to link the audience more directly to the metaphor. Language about blocking ways and roads is used in the *ŠÀ.ZI.GA* potency incantations to symbolize impotence: "Who has blocked your ways like (those of) a traveler (And) like the son of Gubaba has burned your forests?"[20] "Who has blocked your [way] like a ro[ad]?"[21] "Who are you who have blocked up my way like a road, made my...fall limp like taut cords (when they are loosed), just like a merchant's leather bag for weights have drawn up and bound all my muscles tightly?"[22] The gender play opens a third way for the image of the barricaded wife to undermine the masculinity of the audience, in addition to identifying them as a woman, and suggesting military enclosure and defeat: by emphasizing the impotence of the audience as males.

A second instance of gender subversion in ch. 2 emerges from the re-lationship between the male audience, the adulterous wife, and the curses found in Assyrian treaties. As I noted above, some of the treaty curses specify that if the treaty partner should violate the treaty, his wife will be stripped as a harlot or will sit in the lap of another in his sight. Such im-agery exposes some interesting layers and ironies in the rhetoric. The treaty violators in this case would be the male audience, in particular the king, but perhaps also the top advisors who encourage the king to break the treaty. In ch. 2, however, they are not portrayed as the bereft, dishon-ored husbands, whose wives are with another, but rather as a straying wife. Perhaps the rhetoric could be summarized this way: Because you did not act as a faithful wife (metaphorically), therefore you will see your wife with another (literally).

Yet another possible slipperiness in the marriage metaphor occurs because the leaders are in effect challenging the masculinity of YHWH by breaking treaties overseen by YHWH and forming political alliances without divine approval. As noted above, adultery is often a contest be-tween men. YHWH responds to this challenge not only by asserting that he has fulfilled the masculine duties, but in a more extreme manner by portraying Israel not as his rival male, but as the woman.

The slipperiness of some of these images shows complexity in the metaphoric predication. The male audience is not portrayed as female in a strictly dichotomous way. Rather, there is a play between the male and female constructions. Images that seem exclusively female show some male possibilities (wife Gomer, hedged up wife), while those that seem exclusively male may end up as female (son Jezreel).

Some work has been done on this type of gender reversal in the prophets, looking at the relation between the male audience and the por-trayal of the female who represents them, mostly from a more psychoan-alytic perspective. In particular, S. Tamar Kamionkowski's work on Ezek 16 develops the portrayal of masculinized women and feminized men. She proposes that Ezekiel's rhetoric, or at least its subtext, starts from the point of the "cultural psychology of the male victims" who are experienc-ing extreme gender anxiety.[23] The anxiety stems from the threats of emasculation presented by the military conquest of Jerusalem and the exile. The chaos of social and cultural upheaval is represented in the text through gender reversals.[24] The woman in Ezek 16, she argues, differs from the ones in Ezek 23 and those in Jeremiah and Hosea, because she is the subject of most of the action in vv. 15–34 and seems to take the assertive masculine role in use of goods, violence, building, and sexual encounters.[25] The woman Jerusalem is, in effect, acting like a man, and this creates cultural chaos.[26] To restore some semblance of order, YHWH, through Ezekiel's interpretation, must punish the woman and make her submit, returning to her "natural" (or culturally mandated) position of dependence. In fact, as one who is overturning the natural order, the woman is taking over the role of YHWH and must be stopped.[27] The use of the Jerusalem-as-woman metaphor helps to resolve some of the male audience's own feelings of gender reversal: "[Ezekiel's] generation of male Judeans directly experienced what earlier prophets had predicted—that men would become like women....Ezekiel brilliantly shifts the experience of emasculation so that men are not objects of God's wrath, but victims of women."[28] Kamionkowski contends that because members of the male audience are able to transfer their anxieties onto this metaphor, they can better rationalize their own feelings of emasculation by recognizing that "it is all part of God's plan to set things back in order."[29] This interpretation suggests a lot of tension in the interaction between the audience and the text. The males project their anxieties onto the female and her misbehavior, yet the female really represents them.

The rhetoric of Hosea is not completely dissimilar, but there are important differences. First, the political and social situation is not as extreme. The context of most of Hosea's oracles seems to be before the final defeat and exile of Samaria. The later chapters, including ch. 3, probably describe the time during which Hoshea was under arrest and the cultic paraphernalia had been removed to Assyria, but even then there were still possibilities to save the nation.[30] In addition, even with the northern kingdom dispersed, Judah and the temple remained. The rhetoric, therefore, is not as shaped by trauma. Second, I argue that Hosea does not portray as sharp a gender dichotomy as does Ezekiel, at least in Kamionkowski's account. She works from the conceptual metaphors A WEAK MAN IS A WOMAN and the converse A STRONG WOMAN IS A MAN. I argue that these are indeed important, perhaps even predominant, concepts in the cultural context, but in the less chaotic situation in Hosea, there is room in the rhetoric for more play in the system. Both male and female imagery is used, along with a variety of other images. Much of the imagery serves to attack one aspect or another of the audience's masculinity, but to differing degrees. Because of the gender slippage in the wife metaphor discussed above, which links it to male concerns, it is less possible for the male audience to separate itself from the wife as "other" than in the Ezekiel text.

Imagery Applied to YHWH

Hosea shows gender slippage not only in the imagery predicated on the humans, but also with the divine imagery. YHWH is predominantly portrayed as the powerful husband, the patriarch of the family, the god who upholds justice and loyalty with fierce passion. Several images, however, subvert the picture of omnipotence. These subversions are particularly noticeable in the familial imagery.

Subversions in the Husband Metaphor. The first case is the husband metaphor. While in the end the husband shows the power to punish the wife and to create a new relationship, the first half of ch. 2 indicates a very different dynamic. The husband implores the children in 2:4 to intervene with their mother, who has gone after her lovers. The husband obviously does not have the power to control the actions of the wife.[31] YHWH is thus displayed as the cuckolded husband. Such a situation violates the norms expected of an ultra-masculine YHWH. As noted in ch. 3, when a man's wife is unfaithful, he loses status. The worst case, however, is if the man knows about the infidelity and tolerates it.

There is some play concerning the issue of the husband's toleration here. On the one hand, YHWH clearly told Hosea to marry an אשת זנונים. Laurie Braaten observes that the order for Hosea to marry is typical of the instruction that fathers give to sons. The order to marry a promiscuous woman, however, reverses the norm in which the father would want a high status wife and legitimate children for his son.[32] Insofar as the wife and children of ch. 1 relate to those in ch. 2, it would appear that the husband knew about the wife's promiscuity before marriage.[33] As Ken Stone observes: "With that decision Hosea/Yhwh actually transgresses in advance, or at least opens the door knowingly for a transgression of, the cultural protocols of masculinity according to which a man should insure the sexual purity before marriage and the sexual fidelity within marriage of the women of his household."[34] On the other hand, ch. 2 describes in detail the punishments the husband plans to inflict upon the wife for her unfaithfulness, suggesting that he will not tolerate her infidelity. At the end of the chapter, however, he reconciles with her. There is clearly tension within the chapter around the issue of whether or to what extent the husband tolerates the wife's actions.

In addition to the question of the husband's toleration is the issue of his activity. At the beginning of ch. 2, and presumably in the events leading up to it, the husband is passive. While the wife has been going off to her lovers, the husband has done nothing. As the chapter unfolds, the husband becomes more active, threatening to inflict the various punishments, and then to remake the relationship.[35] The activity and passivity of the husband and wife invert as the chapter progresses. In the role of YHWH as husband, therefore, we see slippage along two of the axes of analysis from the position where YHWH is generally placed. YHWH's position on the potency axis is ambiguous: while having the power to punish the wife, he did not have the power to prevent her straying. Likewise YHWH's position on the activity axis is mixed. YHWH in some ways subverts normal masculine and moral values in relations with the wife, while in other ways reinforcing them.

Subversions in the Parent Metaphor. Similar tensions appear in YHWH's role as parent in ch. 11. As with the wife, YHWH is unable to control the actions of the son after caring for him from his youth. In addition to ambiguity surrounding power, there is also some slippage in the gender of YHWH in this passage. As noted in ch. 4, the translation of 11:4 is in dispute. Those who choose to translate עֻל as infant often note that YHWH in many ways acts as a mother in this passage, lifting the infant to the cheek and bending down to feed.[36] They note that childcare is primarily a woman's task. Others argue that a father could just as easily perform these actions and that it seems unlikely that YHWH would be portrayed as female in a patriarchal text.[37] Subversive passages by definition, however, subvert the norm. The imagery is ambiguous, but as such opens up possibilities for the play of gender.

YHWH is clearly likened to a mother is 13:8, but in this case it is a mother bear whose cubs have been taken. Enraged, she will rip open the hearts of Ephraim. Perhaps because of the violence of the imagery and its animal origin, scholars have not really discussed the play of gender here, but it does provide a contrast to the more stereotypical female animal imagery applied to Ephraim: cow, dove, sheep.

Subversions in Other Imagery. A third gender subversion occurs in 11:9: "because I am God and not a man [כי אל אנכי ולא־איש]." The separation between God and man may be working on two levels: the separation of the divine from the human, and the separation of the divine specifically from the masculine. This phrase is particularly interesting in light of Chapman's work on the rhetoric and imagery of Assyrian kings. She notes that the titulary of every Assyrian king from Aššurnasirpal II to Aššurbanipal contained at least one epithet with a form of *zikaru* [man, male, manly one, warrior], implying the king's valiant and potent nature, especially on the battlefield.[38] The word in Hosea is איש and not the cognate זכר, but the rejection of the image of a man happens in the midst of the soliloquy about YHWH's compassion for Ephraim and the decision not to destroy it, thus in a section in which YHWH rejects a military response. Verse 1:7 also seems to separate YHWH from masculine battle imagery. YHWH states that he will deliver Judah, but not with the bow, the sword, battle, horses, or horseman.

In addition to the gender imagery, a few other images show some slippage from the general trends. One instance of this is the use of lion imagery in Hos 11:10–11. Elsewhere, both in Hosea and in other biblical texts, when YHWH is portrayed as a lion, it is as a negative image of destruction. In this verse, by contrast, YHWH calls home the children like birds from Assyria and Egypt. The fact that the children return trembling shows, however, that the danger implied in the image is still present.[39] Two other examples of subversive imagery appear in ch. 14, where YHWH is a tree in 14:9 and dew in 14:6. While in the context of this chapter these are strongly nurturing images, they are rather passive. The divine dew imagery appears stronger, more lasting, and better able to support plant life than the human dew imagery in 13:3, but it is still dew, which at some point during the day evaporates. The tree symbolizes strength and nobility and provides nurturing for Ephraim, but it is still passive. These images play with other possible ways to order social space, especially in the utopia that seems to be presented in ch. 14.

Movement in Social Space

The movement of the subjects within the social space shows some interesting features. Most notable is the fact that no one position in the social space is always optimal. As noted above, YHWH primarily occupies the octant of maximal activity, potency, and goodness. Yet the tree metaphor shows YHWH as passive, powerful, and good, and the image of YHWH as a maggot and putrefication have lesser values on all three of the axes, acting slowly (less active) and incrementally (less potent).[40] Even if used in the service of punishing iniquity, neither maggot nor putrescence has particularly positive connotations (less good). The social space thus allows for some flexibility for even the most powerful entity, which may indicate that YHWH should not be linked too closely to human norms.

The humans have even more possibilities. There does not seem to be one ideal position for the people to occupy. The space contains many points that balance different factors to create multiple acceptable or near-optimal positions. The problem that Hosea seems to address is that while there are many possible positions that humans could properly occupy, the leaders are not in any of them. In addition, they are self-deluded and perceive their own position quite differently from the way the prophet perceives it. It appears the elite males think they occupy a position similar to that of YHWH—active, potent, and good. Hosea claims that in almost every case, they are mistaken about their place along at least one of the axes. Hosea's rhetoric serves two purposes. One is to reveal the audience's true positions in the social space. The second is to indicate spaces that they could favorably occupy.

The rhetoric that addresses the first purpose generally moves the audience from the octant of activity, potency, and goodness to other octants. Nearly all of the rhetoric attributes negative goodness values to them. Within the bad half of the space, however, they occupy different points. They can be active, powerful, and bad, as are the conspirators in the ambush and regicide. They can be active, impotent, and bad, as are the sowers of the wind, and the wife futilely pursuing her lovers. As traps and pits they are passive, powerful, and bad. As an unfruitful plant, Ephraim is passive, powerless, and bad. Much of the gendered imagery concentrates on showing the impotence of the audience, while also frequently criticizing their actions. For a substantial part of this first type of rhetoric, the message seems to be that the leaders are impotent, and when they are not, they are bad. Both their action and inaction are bad, because neither comes at the right time.

Rhetoric fulfilling the second rhetorical purpose moves the audience into the good half of the space. The prophet's suggestions for proper identity are much less frequent than critiques of improper identities, but a few different possibilities are offered. They can be passive, powerless, and good, as the newly betrothed wife. They can be active, powerless and good, as the children fluttering home like birds. Israel will be like the cedar and the olive in ch. 14, which are like YHWH in this chapter, passive, powerful, and good. Finally, if Ephraim the farmer sows righteousness, he can be active, relatively powerful, and good.

Implications for Masculinity

The rhetoric in Hosea consistently works against the masculinity of the audience. With the gender imagery this is most obvious. The female imagery predicates the identity of an unfaithful woman on the men, a blatant attack on their masculinity, and one that is present as a curse and a taunt in both the HB and other ANE literature. By using an unfaithful woman, Hosea adds to this image the anxieties the men may have with regard to the fidelity of their own wives. The male imagery is more direct, mocking several important signs of the audience's masculinity, including sexual, economic, and military prowess. The non-gender imagery also raises challenges to masculinity. All of it serves to move the audience out of the active, powerful, and good octant of social space, the one most closely associated with hegemonic masculinity.

The rhetoric of the first type, which places the audience where Hosea perceives that they are, removes them from the good half of the space. Such a move is already a substantial blow to their masculinity. The value of goodness is sometimes overlooked, but honesty, hospitality, and mercy are important components of male honor. YHWH shows generosity, forgiveness, and upholds justice in the text, while the humans do not. Much of the rest of the imagery serves to disabuse them of ideas of potent or productive masculine activity.

Masculinity is sometimes challenged not only at the human level, but also at the divine level. Although YHWH is consistently portrayed as the über-male, there is some variation in his masculinity. YHWH is not always active, sometimes taking on a passive identity. YHWH is not even always powerful. In relation to humans, YHWH is not able to control their actions and must depend on their receptiveness in order to give gifts such as healing and forgiveness. Although in Hosea YHWH eventually proves most powerful, there is play in the system. YHWH's actions also seem morally questionable at times. The rhetoric often extends beyond what seems necessary to uphold justice into language of revenge. Finally, there are hints of feminine characteristics in YHWH. These hints subvert the overall tone of the text and suggest that the hegemonic masculinity functioning in society may not be the divine ideal.

The second type of rhetoric, which suggests acceptable positions for the humans in the social space, has even more interesting implications, because it does not provide a simple solution for a proper understanding of masculinity in relation to YHWH.[41] Several options open up for the men. They can choose a passive, feminized role, like the reformed wife. They can choose the relatively active and potent role of the good farmer. They can be a passive, strong tree, or an active, weak bird fluttering home. Hosea presents all of these options, and others at different places within these octants, as desirable places for the people, including the leaders.[42]

Hosea does not, in the end, require the audience to renounce completely its masculinity in order to be in proper relationship to YHWH. While much of the rhetoric of the first type in Hosea aims to emasculate the male audience, the rhetoric of the second type provides some options to merely de-masculate—the images lower the masculinity of the subject without necessarily feminizing him. A cedar may be less masculine than a warrior by certain measures, but it is not necessarily more feminine. The portrayal of the audience as a woman is prominent and powerful, but Hosea does not offer this as the only acceptable position in the social space. Rather, the imagery opens up possibilities for different subordinate types of masculinity. In this way, there is a subversive thread in Hosea that opens the door to redefine the concept of masculinity, especially in relation to YHWH. The general patriarchal nature of the text with its hegemonic definition of masculinity remains largely intact, but the variety of metaphors Hosea uses to create identity and relationships among the people and with YHWH create some play in the system.[43]

> The experience of hegemony lies in the repetition of similar, but never identical, interactions. This experience is never comprehensive; it changes over time and space. Multiple gendered (and other) identities, each of which depends on context and the specific and immediate relations between actors and audience, are fluid and they are often subversive of dominant forms.[44]

I do not want to overemphasize the subversive factor, because the text in general maintains the hegemonic masculinity, using its constructs to create rhetoric to which the elite male audience might be particularly sensitive. Nevertheless, it is important to note that even the thickest wall has cracks, which sometime in the eschatological or exegetical future may cause it to crumble.

CHAPTER SIX

Conclusion

The political arena in Israel during the 8th c. B.C.E. was dominated by the concerns and rhetoric of masculinity. Literature from the Bible and other Ancient Near Eastern sources is replete with language and images that both assume and shape certain norms of masculinity. Much of the rhetoric works on the basis that men want to be perceived as conforming to those norms, and thus threatening that they will fall short of those norms is an effective motivator. Treaty curses, victory inscriptions, and prophetic oracles all employ imagery that resonates with conceptions of masculinity. The prophetic oracles in Hosea show some variation in that they encourage the human leaders to accept a non-optimal masculinity with respect to YHWH.

Masculinity in the ANE included several elements: potency, which itself contains political, military, economic, and sexual components, the ability to provide protection and the necessities of life to one's dependents, and honor, which includes displaying honesty, upholding justice, and providing proper guidance to one's dependents and subjects. There are thus many different images that can be interpreted through the lens of masculinity. To aid in analyzing how the rhetoric of masculinity works in the various images in Hosea, both those that are clearly related to gender and those that are not, I utilized a model from cognitive anthropology that examines how metaphors position people in social space. This social space was defined by the axes of activity, potency, and goodness and showed how both kinds of imagery work rhetorically to relate YHWH and the audience, represented by Ephraim/Israel, to a particular conception of masculinity.

The study of masculinity in the rhetoric of Hosea has several implications. Two sets of implications are those relating to the purpose of Hosea and those relating to broader methodological issues.

The Function of Masculinity in Hosea

The rhetoric of masculinity in Hosea serves to manipulate the positions of YHWH and the audience in social space. Three elements are important to consider: the position of YHWH, the position of Ephraim, and the relationship between the two. Both gender and non-gender imagery serve to establish, to critique, and to re-conceive these relationships. Both types serve to emphasize different facets of YHWH's and Ephraim's identity.

The rhetoric first reinforces YHWH's position as the most masculine being in the relationship by consistently portraying YHWH as active, potent, and good. The gender imagery used to portray YHWH appears primarily in the marriage metaphor, where the husband imagery serves largely to defend YHWH against questions about his masculinity. The wife's misattribution of provisions, infidelity, and the possible illegitimacy of the children all attack important components of the male role. The imagery responds to these challenges, showing that YHWH controls the provisions, has no rival in the lovers, and has control over the legitimacy of the children. YHWH's masculinity is shown to be superior and it is reinforced by the non-gender imagery that follows.

Many elements of masculinity emerge even from the non-gender imagery. While YHWH is generally a figure who is in control and powerful, this persona takes different forms. Two aspects in particular are highlighted: those of nurturer and enforcer. Nurturing comes out in several of the image fields, including parent, farmer, plant, and natural phenomena. The more judgmental aspect of the enforcer is found especially in the hunting, animal, and natural phenomena imagery, but also occurs in the disownment of the son and the discipline of the farm animals. These roles encompass the characteristic positions of YHWH along the axes of activity, potency, and goodness. In both roles YHWH is active (providing care or punishment), powerful (showing, for the most part, the ability to carry out the care or punishment), and good (either directly as the caregiver, or as the enforcer of justice). The two roles also fulfill expected masculine norms. As a nurturer YHWH is able to provide for and protect his charges. As an enforcer, YHWH shows the will to carry out justice, with power that no one is able to thwart.

The second purpose of the rhetoric is to subordinate the audience to YHWH. Fulfillment of this purpose requires that the rhetoric move the audience in social space. The movement occurs primarily through an attack on the audience's masculinity, which is expressed through both gender and non-gender imagery. In the gender imagery, the audience's masculinity is attacked by portraying it as a promiscuous woman.[1] The male imagery uses terminology relating to several generally masculine characteristics, including strength, vigor, potency, and military might, to mock the audience, showing that they do not actually have the attributes they think they do. Hosea shows their bows as slack and broken, their vigor as iniquitous, and their actions as dishonest.

The non-gender imagery highlights other aspects of Ephraim/Israel. Two main roles emerge, those of object and misdirected actor. Ephraim is often shown as the object of YHWH's actions. This aspect is emphasized in the child imagery, the sickness and healing imagery, the hunting imagery, and the animal imagery. As an object, Ephraim is acted upon, relatively powerless, and often bad. Ephraim appears as a misdirected actor primarily in the parent-child and agricultural image fields, but also occasionally in the other categories. As a misdirected actor, Ephraim's pursuits are often futile and bad. In neither of these roles does Ephraim adequately fulfill masculine norms. Ephraim is frequently passive, is most often powerless, whether active or not, and is not honorable. He does not show the ability to provision or protect, sometimes even causing harm to those under its care. He does not uphold justice, but acts as an evildoer. Most of his opponents show the ability to thwart Ephraim's power. The rhetoric thus shows Ephraim as less masculine than YHWH.

In the interactions between YHWH and Ephraim, the hierarchical relationship is clear. Only YHWH is allowed to occupy the spot of highest masculinity. Ephraim can occupy several other places in the space, but should always be subordinate to YHWH. The prophet criticizes any action Ephraim takes, usually in the political realm, which seems to grow out of a high estimation of his masculinity either in relation to other humans or to YHWH.

The imagery of masculinity is integral to the rhetoric of the text. The prophet's concerns relate primarily to the public realm of international and domestic politics, trade, and the state cult, areas controlled by men. The political situation of Hosea's time was in large part driven by military issues, including the Syro-Ephraimitic War and rebellion against Assyria. Constructions of hegemonic masculinity are the most stable and influential in public realms, and the realm of warfare is perhaps the area most thoroughly pervaded by masculine rhetoric.[2] An assault on the audience's masculinity is thus particularly appropriate when discussing these areas of social leadership in which concerns of hegemonic masculinity are most prominent.[3]

The prophet criticizes the foreign and domestic policies of the leaders, which were largely intertwined in Israel in the last half of the 8th c. In addition to domestic political intrigue, Hosea finds the vacillation between Assyria and Egypt particularly odious. Ephraim is consistently portrayed as weak and misguided when these issues arise. Israel had made vassal treaties with Assyria, which it then broke by joining in rebellions led by Aram and by making overtures to Egypt. The images of judgment in Hosea's oracles reflect those found in Assyrian treaty curses. As Chapman observes, many of the treaty curses relate directly to issues of masculinity. Those who break the treaties are subject to reduction in masculine status, particularly in relation to the suzerain. Furthermore, the act of breaking the treaty challenges the masculinity of YHWH, who witnessed and guaranteed the treaty. In response, YHWH, through the prophet, threatens to fulfill the treaty curses, thus reasserting his dominance.

Hosea attacks the leaders' perception that they occupy a dominant position, but he offers several alternatives for them to be in appropriate relationship to YHWH. They do not need to renounce fully the values of masculinity, but can properly reside in multiple places in the social space. Ephraim is shown to have the potential for properly directed action, although he is not currently realizing it. If Ephraim recognizes that his proper position is subordinate to YHWH, he can act with power and goodness. Rebelling against YHWH, as Israel has done by breaking the treaty, however, leads to a crushing of the leaders' masculinity.

The imagery itself shows subversive elements, however, which, especially when used with YHWH, serve to destabilize the norms of hegemonic masculinity. The gender imagery shows some degree of slippage, blurring the boundaries of male and female. When used with humans, the slippage seems to serve the purpose of identifying the audience with the female character in the marriage metaphor. The identity of YHWH may also blend male and female images in the parent metaphor. The norms of activity and power are also occasionally violated. In the plant imagery, YHWH takes on a more passive identity. In the parent-child and agricultural imagery YHWH shows less power, being unable to control completely the actions of his charges. The violence of YHWH's responses sometimes seems to mitigate the goodness of YHWH as well. Such subversions begin to undermine the primary societal conceptions of masculinity and their usefulness as a descriptor of YHWH and of the relationship between YHWH and humans.

The subversive elements are only minor distractions from the main thrust of the rhetoric, however, which generally follows a hegemonic norm. Hosea's use of masculine rhetoric plays on the concerns of the male elite audience and addresses issues of politics with imagery commonly used in politics throughout the ANE.

Methodological Considerations

The second set of implications of this study concerns methodology. Masculinity theory has begun to make inroads into the study of biblical texts, but a systematic examination of masculine components of Hosea has been lacking. I have here attempted to demonstrate the usefulness of taking a masculinity-centered approach to Hosea.

I see three major contributions of masculinity theory to the study of Hosea. First, it provides a perspective into the way the oracles specifically address men and male concerns. Focusing on masculinity helps to uncover the kinds of resonance the rhetoric may have had within a particular construction of masculinity, especially for an audience familiar with the masculine implications of the imagery used. Second, a concentration on the constructions of masculinity present in Hosea helps to develop masculinity as a concept of its own, not simply defined as the opposite of femininity. Through this perspective a more complex understanding of masculinity emerges, which may have implications for its interactions with femininity. Because the biblical texts and Hosea in particular are heavily weighted toward male concerns and audiences, a more thorough understanding of the construction of the male gender can provide insights into the rhetoric of the texts. Third, the frame of masculinity provides a way to synthesize the variety of images in Hosea. The images serve a similar function, namely to move the audience away from the active, potent, and good octant of social quality space. Examining the implications of these different images for the perception of masculinity provides a way to organize these effects.

To examine the implications of the non-gender imagery for masculinity, I employed a model that provided a way to analyze how metaphors move people in social space. The model could also have wider application for study of other texts rich in metaphor. Such analysis shows particular potential for prophetic texts because it concentrates on how metaphoric language is used to create identity and change people's positions relative to one another, which is what Fernandez calls the persuasive use of metaphor. In this study, the axes chosen for analysis—activity, potency, and goodness—proved to be helpful in assessing the ways the imagery affected masculinity. They are, however, not the only possible choices. I chose to concentrate on these three in order to retain analytical power to detect broad rhetorical trends related to masculinity.[4] Other important factors determine the social space in Israel or Judah, which could also be used to analyze different aspects of rhetoric. In addition, because not all metaphors show movement along all axes, the model can also indicate different rhetorical strategies at work in a text.

Final Words

The metaphors in Hosea are rich and varied and have provided interpretive space for many readers and scholars. In this study I have focused on the ways that the metaphors play around the concept of masculinity, which has allowed me to elucidate connections between many of the images and to analyze their cumulative rhetorical effect. Hosea uses images of masculinity to critique effectively the actions of the male audience, especially in the political sphere, by using types of images with the same rhetorical forces found in other political material of the time. Rather than focusing strictly on the political actions themselves, however, Hosea addresses the ways in which they affect the relationship between Israel and YHWH. Hosea uses imagery to reinforce YHWH's masculinity and dominance, while undermining the masculinity of the audience. In this way the rhetoric of the text attempts to bring the audience into an appropriately subordinate position with respect to YHWH and thereby to shape their actions and attitudes accordingly.

❖NOTES❖

1 Introduction and History of Interpretation

1. Several Assyrian inscriptions mention Israelite kings in lists of those defeated or paying tribute. The Monolith Inscription describing the western campaign of Shalmaneser III in 853–852 mentions the defeat of Ahab the Israelite (Jeffrey Kah-jin Kuan, *Neo-Assyrian Historical Inscriptions and Syria-Palestine* [Jian Dao Diss. 1; Hong Kong: Alliance Bible Seminary, 1995], 31). Several other skirmishes are mentioned in the following years, and in an inscription dated 12 years later, a tribute from Jehu is recorded. Three years after that the Black Obelisk inscription records Jehu's tribute in greater detail: "The *maddattu* of Jehu, the (Bit)-Humrite. Silver, gold, a golden bowl, a golden vase, golden goblets, golden pitchers, tin, a *hutartu* for the hand of the king, and *puašhatu*, I received from him." It also displays a picture of Jehu prostrating himself before Shalmaneser (Kuan, *Neo-Assyrian Historical Inscriptions*, 63–64).

2. J. Maxwell Miller and John H. Hayes, *A History of Ancient Israel and Judah* (Philadelphia: Westminster, 1986), 289.

3. Kuan, *Neo-Assyrian Historical Inscriptions*, 65.

4. John H. Hayes and Paul K. Hooker, *A New Chronology for the Kings of Israel and Judah and Its Implications for Biblical History and Literature* (Atlanta: John Knox, 1988), 55.

5. My translation.

6. Kuan, *Neo-Assyrian Historical Inscriptions*, 147–48.

7. H. J. Cook, "Pekah," *VT* 14 (1964): 121–35; Hayes and Hooker, *A New Chronology*, 54.

8. Hayes and Hooker, *A New Chronology*, 60.

9. Miller and Hayes, *History of Ancient Israel*, 332; Hayes and Hooker, *A New Chronology*, 63. Syria may have already controlled most of the former Israelite territory.

10. Miller and Hayes, *History of Ancient Israel*, 334.

11. See, *e.g.*, John Day, "Pre-deuteronomic Allusions to the Covenant in Hosea and Psalm LXXVIII," *VT* 36 (1986): 1–12; James Luther Mays, *Hosea* (OTL; Philadelphia: Westminster, 1969), 112.

12. Similar rhetoric was employed by Assyrian kings, who claimed that their military campaigns against rebel vassal kings were manifestations of the treaty curses and ordained by the gods (Jeremy D. Smoak, "Assyrian Siege Warfare Imagery and the Background of a Biblical Curse," in *Writing and Reading War:*

Rhetoric, Gender, and Ethics in Biblical and Modern Contexts [ed. Brad E. Kelle and Frank Ritchel Ames; Symposium 42; Atlanta: SBL, 2008], 90).

13.   Throughout this study I will use the masculine pronoun with YHWH, who, I will argue, is clearly constructed as a masculine entity.

14.   Cynthia R. Chapman, *The Gendered Language of Warfare in the Israelite-Assyrian Encounter* (HSM 62; Winona Lake, IN: Eisenbrauns, 2004), 22–24.

15.   I will discuss further examples of masculine assertions in ANE and biblical texts in ch. 3.

16.   Chapman, *Gendered Language*, 59.

17.   See Chapman, *Gendered Language*; S. Tamar Kamionkowski, *Gender Reversal and Cosmic Chaos: A Study on the Book of Ezekiel* (JSOTSup 368; London: Sheffield Academic Press, 2003).

18.   See Ken Stone, "Lovers and Raisin Cakes: Food, Sex, and Divine Insecurity in Hosea," in *Queer Commentary and the Hebrew Bible* (ed. Ken Stone; Cleveland: Pilgrim, 2001), 116–39; John Goldingay, "Hosea 1–3, Genesis 1–4 and Masculist Interpretation," in *A Feminist Companion to the Latter Prophets* (ed. Athalya Brenner; FCB 8; Sheffield: Sheffield Academic Press, 1995), 161–68.

19.   A cogent summary of the major positions on the redaction of Hosea up through 1980 can be found in Gale A. Yee, *Composition and Tradition in the Book of Hosea: A Redaction Critical Investigation* (SBLDS 102; Atlanta: Scholars Press, 1987).

20.   Yehezkel Kaufmann proposes that chs. 1–3 are in such a different style from chs. 4–14 that they must have been written by different authors in different time periods (*The Religion of Israel* [trans. and abridg. Moshe Greenberg; Chicago: University of Chicago Press, 1960], 368). Karl Marti connects ch. 2 with 4–14, but claims 1 and 3 were added later (*Das Dodekapropheton: Hosea* [KHC 13; Tübingen: J. C. B. Mohr, 1904], 1–2, 8–10). William Rainey Harper tries to use poetic meter to separate redactional layers (*Amos and Hosea* [ICC 23; Edinburgh: T&T Clark, 1905], clix). Felix E. Peiser applies poetic features drawn from Babylonian epics to the poetry in Hosea to try to determine the original oracles (*Hosea* [Philologische Studien zum Alten Testament; Leipzig: J. C. Hinrichs'sche, 1914], VII–IX).

21.   See William J. Doorly, *Prophet of Love: Understanding the Book of Hosea* (New York: Paulist Press, 1991), 117. Rolland Emerson Wolfe posits that Gomer, in fact, was put to death, according to the community sanctions for adultery and that her restoration was an exilic addition to the text (*Meet Amos and Hosea* [New York: Harper, 1945], 84–87). See also Curt Kuhl, *The Prophets of Israel* (trans. Rudolf J. Ehrlich and J. P. Smith; Richmond: John Knox, 1960), 65, 67; G. I. Davies, *Hosea* (NCBC; Grand Rapids: Eerdmans, 1992), 36–37.

22.   See Duane A. Garrett, *Hosea, Joel* (NAC 19A; Nashville: Broadman & Holman, 1997); Douglas Stuart, *Hosea-Jonah* (WBC 31; Waco: Word Books, 1987); Eugen J. Pentiuc, *Long Suffering Love: A Commentary on Hosea with Patristic Annotations* (Brookline, MA: Holy Cross Orthodox Press, 2002); Leon J. Wood, "Hosea," in *The Expositor's Bible Commentary* (12 vols.; Grand Rapids:

Zondervan, 1985), 7:161–225; Francis Landy, *Hosea* (Readings; Sheffield: Sheffield Academic Press, 1995).

23.   See Karl Budde, "Eine folgenschwere Redaktion des Zwölfprophetenbuchs," *ZAW* 39 (1922): 218–26; Rolland Emerson Wolfe, "The Editing of the Book of the Twelve," *ZAW* 53 (1935): 90–129; Jörg Jeremias, "Die Anfänge des Dodekapropheton: Hosea und Amos," and "Hosea 4–7. Beobachtungen zur Komposition des Buches Hosea," in *Hosea und Amos: Studien zu den Anfängen des Dodekapropheton* (FZAT 13; Tübingen: J. C. B. Mohr, 1996), 34–66.

24.   Members of the Scandinavian school were the early promoters of this position, including H. S. Nyberg, *Studien zum Hoseabuch. Zugleich ein Beitrag zur Klärung des Problems der alttestamentlichen Textkritik* (Uppsala: A. B. Lundequistska, 1935); Thomas Naumann, *Hoseas Erben: Strukturen der Nachinterpretation im Buch Hosea* (BWANT 11[131]; Stuttgart: Kohlhammer, 1991); See also Good, "Composition of Hosea," 29–30. Martin J. Buss proposes that chs. 1–3 circulated orally, while 4–14 were written down fairly quickly, although they were joined together by catchwords, an oral technique (*The Prophetic Word of Hosea* [BZAW 111; Berlin: Alfred Töpelmann, 1969], 33–36).

25.   See Hans Walter Wolff, *Hosea* (trans. Gary Stansell; ed. Paul D. Hanson; Hermeneia; Philadelphia: Fortress, 1974), xxx–xxxii; Wilhelm Rudolph, *Hosea* (KAT 13; Gütersloh: Gütersloher Verlagshaus Gerd Mohn, 1966), 25–27; Mays, *Hosea*, 15–16; Ina Willi-Plein, *Vorformen der Schriftexegese innerhalb des Alten Testaments* (BZAW 123; Berlin: Walter de Gruyter, 1971); Francis I. Andersen and David Noel Freedman, *Hosea* (AB 24; New York: Doubleday, 1980); Grace I. Emmerson, *Hosea: An Israelite Prophet in Judean Perspective* (JSOTSup 28; Sheffield: Sheffield University Press, 1984); A. A. Macintosh, *A Critical and Exegetical Commentary on Hosea* (ICC; Edinburgh: T&T Clark, 1997).

26.   This is true even among some of the pre-modern commentators, who were more likely to seek unity. Matthew Henry calls the style "very concise and sententious...in some places it seems to be like the book of Proverbs, without connexion" (*An Exposition of the Old and New Testament. III. The Prophetical Books* [New York: Robert Carver, 1827], 739); T. K. Cheyne agrees, "nor is there any clear evidence of a designed logical connexion" (*Hosea* [CBSC; Cambridge: Cambridge University Press, 1889], 20).

27.   Kuhl, *Prophets of Israel*, 67.

28.   Morris understands poetry and rhetoric to be genres, drawing from Aristotle's four foundational genres—epic, drama, lyric, and rhetoric (Gerald Morris, *Prophecy, Poetry, and Hosea* [JSOTSup 219; Sheffield: Sheffield Academic Press, 1996], 18). Others may argue that rhetoric and poetry are not themselves genres, or at least are too broad to be useful.

29.   Morris, *Prophecy*, 42–44.

30.   Morris, *Prophecy*, 132–33.

31.   Morris, *Prophecy*, 146.

32.   Buss, *Prophetic Word*.

33.   Buss, *Prophetic Word*, 61–62.

34.   Buss, *Prophetic Word,* 119.

35.   Buss, *Prophetic Word,* 122.

36.   Buss, *Prophetic Word,* 127–28.

37.   Paul N. Franklyn, "Prophetic Cursing of Apostasy: The Text, Forms, and Traditions of Hosea 13" (Ph.D. diss., Vanderbilt University, 1986).

38.   Franklyn, "Prophetic Cursing," 232–33.

39.   R. L. Lewis, "The Persuasive Style and Appeals of the Minor Prophets Amos, Hosea, and Micah" (Ph.D. diss., University of Michigan, 1958).

40.   Richard D. Israel, "Prophecies of Judgment: A Study of the Protasis-Apodosis Text Structures in Hosea, Amos and Micah" (Ph.D. diss., Claremont Graduate School, 1989).

41.   Israel, "Prophecies," 400.

42.   Israel, "Prophecies," 401.

43.   Israel, "Prophecies," 408, 410.

44.   Israel, "Prophecies," 411–12.

45.   For a summary of the various interpretations of the marriage metaphor up to the mid-20th century, see H. H. Rowley, *Men of God: Studies in Old Testament History and Prophecy* (London: Thomas Nelson, 1963).

46.   Wood is typical: "It is quite unthinkable that God would have commanded anyone—much less a religious leader—to marry such a person" ("Hosea," 165).

47.   See Pentiuc, *Long-Suffering Love,* 22.

48.   Francis Sparling North argues that ch. 1 was originally in the first person and that the third person reference, "Yahveh said to Hosea, 'Go and get yourself a prostitute wife and illegitimate children," was added later to allegorize the marriage in analogy to ch. 3 ("Hosea's Introduction to His Book," *VT* 8 [1958]: 429–32). Doorly takes a similar view, placing the naming of Gomer in the hands of the collector of the oracles, which changes the way the reader views the allegory of the mother and the children (*Prophet of Love,* 51–54). Kaufmann views the actions of Gomer and the children as a sign act, representing the prophecy, rather than a description of reality (*Religion of Israel,* 370–71).

49.   See Pentiuc, *Long-Suffering Love,* 22; Abe Lipshitz, *The Commentary of Rabbi Abraham Ibn Ezra on Hosea* (New York: Sepher-Hermon, 1988), 20; John Calvin, *Commentaries on the Twelve Minor Prophets* (trans. John Owen; 5 vols.; Grand Rapids: Eerdmans, 1950), 1:44–45.

50.   Proponents include Harper, *Amos and Hosea,* cxliii. Andersen and Freedman hold that ch. 2 "portrays the actual situation of the prophet and his family" and that ch. 3 is "a brief statement about what really happened" after the events of ch. 2 (*Hosea,* 117–18). Beeby asserts that "the details of Hosea's life are unlikely to be imaginary" (*Grace Abounding,* 3). Though Cheyne thinks the marriage is real, he considers ch. 2 to be an allegorical expansion of ch. 1 (*Hosea,* 19). Wolff expresses a typical reasoning for this position: "The variations within the schematic framework—the alternation of son and daughter; the weaning of the daughter in v 8—together with the mention of the wife's name (v 3) suffice to eliminate any question of the narrative's historicity" (*Hosea,* 10). He

characterizes ch. 1 as a *memorabile* and not an allegory. See also Macintosh, *Hosea*, 9. R. L. Lewis claims that Hosea's speeches are based largely on his experiences with Gomer ("Persuasive Style," 78).

51.   As stated by Pentiuc, although he himself does not take this position (*Long-Suffering Love*, 13).

52.   Advocates include Harper, *Amos and Hosea*, cxliv; Cheyne, *Hosea*, 17; Sydney Lawrence Brown, *The Book of Hosea* (London: Methuen, 1932), xi; Wolfe, *Meet Amos and Hosea*, 81–83; Andersen and Freedman, *Hosea*, 116; Wood, "Hosea," 166. Macintosh states: "The author testifies that Hosea had eventually come to understand that the history of his marriage and of his children reflected the promiscuous idolatry of Israel and the disastrous consequences of it. The terms 'wife/children of promiscuity' are, therefore, in no sense contemporary descriptions of Gomer or of her family and they afford no evidence whatsoever as to her status or character at the time of her marriage to the prophet" (*Hosea*, 120). Yosef Green argues that the husband's anger in ch. 2 would make no sense if he knew she was promiscuous from the beginning ("Hosea and Gomer Revisited," *JBQ* 31[2003]: 84–89).

53.   Beeby, *Grace Abounding*, 14. Wolff argues that Gomer was not a professional or cultic prostitute, but was, rather, among the many young women "who had submitted to the bridal rites of initiation then current in Israel" (*Hosea*, 15). F. C. Fensham sees no reason to force the grammar from its normal meaning that Hosea married a woman who is already promiscuous ("The Marriage Metaphor in Hosea for the Covenant Relationship Between the Lord and His People," *JNSL* 12 [1984]: 71–78). He assumes she was engaged in occasional cultic prostitution. Ehud Ben Zvi argues that the Gomer's premarital promiscuity (not prostitution) was vital for the metaphor to work, because it implies that Hosea could have chosen a better wife, but did not, hence emphasizing that YHWH's love for Israel is inexplicable ("Observations on the Marital Metaphor of YHWH and Israel in its Ancient Israelite Context: General Considerations and Particular Images in Hosea 1:2," *JSOT* 28 [2004]: 379–82). See also Rowley, *Men of God*, 90.

54.   James M. Ward, *Hosea: A Theological Commentary* (New York: Harper and Row, 1966), 27; Eberhard Bons, *Das Buch Hosea* (NSKAT 23/1; Stuttgart: Katholisches Bibelwerk, 1996), 27–29.

55.   That is, when he was not identified solely as a prophet of doom. As mentioned in the composition history section, many early redaction critics thought all of the salvation passages were secondary. Those who interpret the book as it stands now, however, have tended toward the love angle, at least with respect to the marriage metaphor. See, *e.g.,* Lewis, "Persuasive Style," 105; Doorly, *Prophet of Love*, although he understands the theme of love to be an addition of the final exilic redactor; Beeby argues against a simplistic understanding of Hosea as the prophet of love, but remarks: "But God is God and therefore gracious. God's last word is a word of compassion and restoration" (*Grace Abounding*, 4).

56. Cheyne remarks: "Hosea was to learn what no prophet had learned before, and what no prophet ever could have learned by a mechanical revelation from without—viz. that the essence of the divine nature was not justice but love" (*Hosea*, 21). Brown concurs: "His [Hosea's] sole interest is in Israel the nation as the object of Jahveh's love" (*Hosea*, xxii).

57. Harper concludes: "The fundamental point to be noted is that the principal contribution of the domestic experience was not the message concerning the destruction of Israel, but that concerning the great love of Yahweh in spite of faithlessness" (*Amos and Hosea*, cxliv).

58. Several commentators express this "tough love" sentiment: Kuhl: "The intention of the telling of the story of Hosea's marriage (which is so essentially bound up with his message) is not to give a motive for rejection and judgment but rather to illustrate, through Hosea's dealings with this faithless wife, the love of Yahweh for His People....His heart is full of love and compassion" (*Prophets of Israel*, 70). Wolff: "Impelled by his suffering and love for his people, God seeks a variety of paths by which to lead her back" (*Hosea*, 44). Macintosh: "Again, where attempts to mend the marriage are concerned, the author shows the whole gamut of tactics which a husband adopts in his quest: appeal to the children of the marriage to join their father in an attempt to save it (v. 4); the desire physically to isolate the wayward wife from temptation (vv. 8, 16) and above all to reason with her, to make a fresh start in trust and love (vv. 16ff)" (*Hosea*, 114). Brown: "He represents the relationship between Jahveh and the nation as a marriage, as a relationship of love, and as such he reverts to it again and again, even in his later prophecies. Love for Israel is an ineradicable trait of the Divine Being, and that love is shown by the fact that, while Jahveh can punish, and even hate, He cannot entirely destroy the people of His choice" (*Hosea*, xxix).

59. Macintosh: "All of this is an expression of Hosea's caring love and is a reflection of Yahweh's love for Israel, a love which expresses itself in correction and discipline" (*Hosea*, 104).

60. Rut Törnkvist, *The Use and Abuse of Female Sexual Imagery in the Book of Hosea: A Feminist Critical Approach to Hosea 1–3* (Uppsala Women's Studies A: Women in Religion 7; Stockholm: Gotab 1998), 15–16. Fokkelien van Dijk-Hemmes also notes how use of this metaphor acts as propaganda "extolling the ideal patriarchal marriage" ("The Metaphorization of Woman in Prophetic Speech: An Analysis of Ezekiel 23," in *A Feminist Companion to the Latter Prophets* [ed. Athalya Brenner; FCB 8; Sheffield: Sheffield Academic Press, 1995], 246).

61. Athalya Brenner, "Pornoprophetics Revisited," *JSOT* 70 (1996): 63–86. See also Susan Brooks Thistlethwaite, "Every Two Minutes: Battered Women and Feminist Interpretation," in *Feminist Interpretation of the Bible* (ed. Letty M. Russell; Philadelphia: Westminster, 1985), 96–107. Naomi Graetz discusses the problems of having these verses read in the Haftora, which tends to propagate its patriarchalism into the modern day. She does observe, however, that the men recite these verses when putting on their tefillin, placing themselves in the

woman's role with respect to God ("God is to Israel as Husband is to Wife: The Metaphoric Battering of Hosea's Wife," in *A Feminist Companion to the Latter Prophets* [ed. Athalya Brenner; FCB 8; Sheffield: Sheffield Academic Press, 1995], 126–45).

62. Athalya Brenner, "On Prophetic Propaganda and the Politics of 'Love': The Case of Jeremiah," in *A Feminist Companion to the Latter Prophets* (ed. Athalya Brenner; FCB 8; Sheffield: Sheffield Academic Press, 1995), 256–74.

63. T. Drorah Setel, "Prophets and Pornography: Female Sexual Imagery in Hosea," in *Feminist Interpretation of the Bible* (ed. Letty M. Russell; Philadelphia: Westminster, 1985), 87.

64. Setel, "Prophets," 86–95.

65. Alice A. Keefe, *Woman's Body and the Social Body in Hosea* (JSOT 338; GCT 10; Sheffield: Sheffield Academic Press, 2001), 143. Athalya Brenner expresses a similar view, stating that in the marriage metaphor the marriage contract is always broken by an adulterous wife, never the husband. This reinforces a negative view of female sexuality vs. a neutral or positive view of male sexuality ("Introduction," in *A Feminist Companion to the Latter Prophets* [ed. Athalya Brenner; FCB 8; Sheffield: Sheffield Academic Press, 1995], 26).

66. Yvonne Sherwood, "Boxing Gomer: Controlling the Deviant Woman in Hosea 1–3," in *A Feminist Companion to the Latter Prophets* (ed. Athalya Brenner; FCB 8; Sheffield: Sheffield Academic Press, 1995), 120.

67. Teresa J. Hornsby, "Israel Has Become a Worthless Thing: Rereading Gomer in Hosea 1–3," *JSOT* 82 (1999): 115–28.

68. To name just a few: Green, "Hosea," 86; Fensham, "Marriage Metaphor," 73; Gerlinde Baumann, *Love and Violence: Marriage as Metaphor for the Relationship between YHWH and Israel in the Prophetic Books* (trans. Linda M. Maloney; Collegeville, MN: Liturgical Press, 2003), 90. See also Macintosh, *Hosea*, 42, 49; Rudolph, *Hosea*, 64–68; Pentiuc, *Long-Suffering Love*, 36–39; Harper, *Hosea*; Andersen and Freedman, *Hosea*, 220–32; R. Abma, *Bonds of Love: Methodic Studies of Prophetic Texts with Marriage Imagery* (SSN; Assen: Van Gorcum, 1999), 257; Renita J. Weems, "Gomer: Victim of Violence or Victim of Metaphor?" *Semeia* 47 (1989): 87; Kaufmann, *Religion*, 369, though he dates this chapter to the reign of Ahab. Paul Kruger argues that 2:7 describes the cultic rites Israel performs in order to continue receiving the gifts from the foreign god lovers ("Israel, the Harlot [Hos. 2:4–9]," *JNSL* 11 [1983]: 114).

69. A secondary reason why so many commentators support the "Gomer chaste at marriage" hypothesis is that they imagine the hope for restoration in 2:16–25 returns Israel to the time of ideal faithfulness when the covenant was first given. Nelly Stienstra's comment is typical: "In terms of the marriage metaphor YHWH had a period of marital happiness with His people, just after the Exodus, when the Covenant of the Sinai had been concluded. True, it did not last very long, but there is no reason to assume that the people had already committed 'fornication' before the Covenant," (*YHWH is the Husband of His People: Analysis of a Biblical Metaphor with Special Reference to Translation* [Kampen:

Kok Pharos, 1993], 102). The Pentateuch preserves a different tradition, however, in which Israel murmurs and rebels every step of the way. Carole Fontaine is one of the few who make this observation: "Hosea's use of national traditions makes it clear that, from the outset, faithlessness had marked Israel's response to Yahweh's redemptive labors on the people's behalf" ("Hosea," in *A Feminist Companion to the Latter Prophets* [ed. Athalya Brenner; FCB 8; Sheffield: Sheffield Academic Press], 48). It is not possible to know what exact exodus tradition Hosea employed, but the rhetoric in general seems to indicate trouble from the beginning.

70.   Herbert Marks, "The Twelve Prophets," in *The Literary Guide to the Bible* (ed. Robert Alter and Frank Kermode; Cambridge: Belknap of Harvard University Press, 1987), 214. Hans Jurgens Hendriks proposes that Hosea used the adultery metaphor because Israel was so caught up in Baalism, that the marriage metaphor with its fertility connotations was one of the only ways to reach them ("Juridical Aspects of the Marriage Metaphor in Hosea and Jeremiah" [Ph.D. diss., University of Stellenbosch, 1982], 93–94).

71.   Marks, "The Twelve," 212. He sees 4:2 as an early form of the Decalogue.

72.   Stienstra, *YHWH is the Husband,* 106.

73.   Mary Joan Winn Leith, "Verse and Reverse: The Transformation of the Woman, Israel, in Hosea 1–3," in *Gender and Difference in Ancient Israel* (ed. Peggy L. Day; Minneapolis: Fortress, 1989), 95–108.

74.   Else Kragelund Holt, *Prophesying the Past: The Use of Israel's History in the Book of Hosea* (JSOTSup 194; Sheffield: Sheffield Academic Press, 1995).

75.   Gale Yee, *Poor Banished Children of Eve* (Minneapolis: Fortress, 2003).

76.   Törnkvist, *Use and Abuse,* 17.

77.   Törnkvist, *Use and Abuse,* 17–18.

78.   Margaret S. Odell, "I Will Destroy Your Mother: The Obliteration of a Cultic Role in Hosea 4:4–6," in *A Feminist Companion to the Latter Prophets* (ed. Athalya Brenner; FCB 8; Sheffield: Sheffield Academic Press, 1995), 192. Few others have postulated that Hosea was inveighing against an official role for women in the cult, but some, including Marie-Theres Wacker, have speculated that the condemnation includes more popular religion, which may have included goddesses, noting the prevalence of female figurines found in Israel during that time ("Traces of the Goddess in the Book of Hosea," in *A Feminist Companion to the Latter Prophets* [ed. Athalya Brenner; FCB 8; Sheffield: Sheffield Academic Press, 1995], 232). She sees shadows of goddess language and symbols throughout Hosea. If Hosea is actively criticizing goddess worship, however, it seems unlikely that it would be suppressed in the text.

79.   Odell, "I Will Destroy," 181.

80.   Odell, "I Will Destroy," 182.

81.   Stephen L. Cook, "The Lineage Roots of Hosea's Yahwism," *Semeia* 87 (1999): 145.

82. He argues that as resources, including agricultural production, become concentrated, risk is also concentrated, so that crop failures are of greater concern (Cook, "Lineage Roots," 158).

83. The cultic language is particularly obvious in 6:1–3 (Cook, "Lineage Roots," 155).

84. Hornsby, "Worthless Thing," 115–28.

85. Doorly proposes that the original prophet was concerned with history and foreign relations, not Baalism. The religious references were added later by a Josianic (7th c.) redactor (*Prophet of Love*, 116, 120). Ward thinks Jezreel has political implications, and though El and sowing are associated with Canaanite religion, the cultic elements are not highlighted here (*Hosea*, 13).

86. Julie Galambush, *Jerusalem in the Book of Ezekiel: The City as Yahweh's Wife* (SBLDS 130; Atlanta: Scholars Press, 1992).

87. Galambush, *Jerusalem*, 45.

88. For a thorough discussion of the issues, see Brad E. Kelle, *Hosea 2: Metaphor and Rhetoric in Historical Perspective* (Atlanta: SBL, 2005), 82–94.

89. See John J. Schmitt, "The Gender of Ancient Israel," *JSOT* 26 (1983):115–25; idem, "Gender Correctness and Biblical Metaphors: The Case of God's Relation to Israel," *BTB* 26 (1996): 96–106.

90. Andrew Dearman, "YHWH's House: Gender Roles and Metaphors for Israel in Hosea," *JNSL* 25 (1999), 99–101.

91. Hendriks cites texts from Hana and Nuzi as evidence of stripping upon divorce, including stripping by the sons. He also claims that stripping was a punishment to humiliate harlots as well as defeated enemies ("Juridical Aspects," 47–48.)

92. Peggy L. Day observes: "The only text which *may* depict an adulteress stripped naked and publicly humiliated (IM 28051) is Sumerian, admits of radically different interpretations, is badly broken in the relevant section, ambiguous as to who is being punished, and dates, according to Greengus, to the early Old Babylonian period" ("Adulterous Jerusalem's Imagined Demise: Death of a Metaphor in Ezekiel XVI," *VT* 50 [2000]: 298).

93. The issue is discussed thoroughly by Kelle in *Hosea 2*, 60–63. Theodore W. Jennings, Jr., in fact, notes that in the biblical texts, stripping is used to humiliate only men, not women (*Jacob's Wound: Homoerotic Narrative in the Literature of Ancient Israel* [New York: Continuum, 2005], 153).

94. Day, "Adulterous Jerusalem," 298.

95. Kelle, *Hosea 2*, ch. 3.

96. Schmitt, "Gender," 100. Kelle, *Hosea 2*, 91. Others who concur that sexual violence and rape are metaphors for the conquering of a city, as well as real results of warfare, are Pamela Gordon and Harold C. Washington, "Rape as a Military Metaphor in the Hebrew Bible," 308–25, and F. Rachel Magdalene, "Ancient Near Eastern Treaty-Curses and the Ultimate Texts of Terror: A Study of the Language of Divine Sexual Abuse in the Prophetic Corpus," 326–52, both in *A Feminist Companion to the Latter Prophets* (ed. Athalya Brenner; FCB 8; Sheffield: Sheffield Academic Press, 1995).

97. Kelle, *Hosea 2*, ch. 4. See also Hendriks, "Juridical Aspects," 48.

98. William L. Moran, "The Ancient Near Eastern Background of the Love of God in Deuteronomy," *CBQ* 25 (1963): 77–87.

99. El Amarna 138:71–73, quoted in Moran, "Love of God," 80.

100. Moran, "Love of God," 80.

101. J.A. Thompson, "Israel's Lovers," *VT* 27 (1977): 475–81.

102. Galambush, *Jerusalem*, 49–50.

103. For an extensive discussion of the possible political meanings of lovers and baalim, see Kelle, *Hosea 2*, ch. 5.

104. Kelle, *Hosea 2*, ch. 5.

105. See Macintosh, *Hosea*, 238.

106. Galambush, *Jerusalem*, 34.

107. Quoted in Moran, "Love of God," 83–84.

108. See also Assurbanipal's annals during his campaign against the Arabian tribes, "[the gods inflicted upon them] as many curses as are written in their loyalty oaths" (Maximilian Strek, *Assurbanipal und die letzten assyrischen Könige bis zum Untergange Ninevehs* [Leipzig: Hinrichs, 1916], 76:60).

109. "The name Berith, however, does not occur in the old prophets, not even in Hosea, who certainly presents us as clearly as possible with the thing, in his figure of the marriage of Jehovah and Israel....The use of the phrase Berith (*i.e.* treaty) for law, fitted very well with the great idea of the prophets, and received from it in turn an interpretation, according to which the relation of Jehovah to Israel was conditioned by the demands of His righteousness, as set forth in His word and instruction" (Julius Wellhausen, *Prolegomena to the History of Israel* [repr. of 1885 ed.; Atlanta: Scholars Press, 1994], 418).

110. A. Malamat observes that foreign policy is frequently discussed in the prophets, and the running back and forth between Egypt and Assyria is particularly condemned: "In a situation of bipolarity there may occur a double breach of covenant: 1) the breach of covenant with God; 2) the breach of covenant with one of the countries in the bipolar system. Thus, the phenomenon of bipolarity may create a more intense mode of unfaithfulness, which in terms of the Biblical metaphor is likened to committing adultery" ("The Politics of Bipolarity in the Guise of Sexual Relations: The Case of Ezekiel 16 and 23," in *Sex and Gender in the Ancient Near East* [ed. Simo Parpola and R.M. Whiting; Helsinki: The Neo-Assyrian Text Corpus Project, 2002], 357).

111. Max Weber, *Ancient Judaism* (trans. Hans H. Gerth and Don Martindal; New York: Free Press, 1952), 130.

112. Yee, *Banished Children*, 10.

113. Yee, *Banished Children*, 10.

114. Yee, *Banished Children*, 23.

115. Yee, *Banished Children*, 20.

116. Yee, *Banished Children*, 83.

117. Yee, *Banished Children*, 83.

118. Yee, *Banished Children*, 85.

119. Yee, *Banished Children*, 91.

120. Yee, *Banished Children*, 86.

121. Yee, *Banished Children*, 96. A side effect of this policy, however, was the suppression of women's popular religion.

122. Rainer Albertz, *From the Beginnings to the End of the Monarchy* (vol. 1 of *A History of Israelite Religion in the Old Testament Period;* trans. John Bowden; OTL; Louisville: Westminster John Knox, 1994), 64, quoted in Yee, *Banished Children*, 95.

123. Alice A. Keefe, "The Female Body, the Body Politic, and the Land: A Sociopolitical Reading of Hosea 1–2," in *A Feminist Companion to the Latter Prophets* (ed. Athalya Brenner; FCB 8; Sheffield: Sheffield Academic Press, 1995), 75.

124. Keefe notes that the items mentioned in 2:10a that YHWH threatens to take back are the grain, the wine, and the oil, three chief cash crops (*Woman's Body*, 197).

125. Keefe, "Female Body," 93.

126. Abma, *Bonds of Love*, 12.

127. Robert P. Carroll, "Desire Under the Terebinths: On Pornographic Representation in the Prophets—A Response," in *A Feminist Companion to the Latter Prophets* (ed. Athalya Brenner; FCB 8; Sheffield: Sheffield Academic Press, 1995), 288.

128. Carroll, "Desire," 304.

129. Renita J. Weems, *Battered Love: Marriage, Sex, and Violence in the Hebrew Prophets* (OBT; Minneapolis: Fortress Press, 1995), 41–42, 80.

130. *E.g.*, Graetz, "Metaphoric Battering," 135.

131. Baumann, *Love and Violence*, 97; see also Weems, "Gomer," 97. Weems observes that "the image of the promiscuous wife played upon a range of ideas that tapped into some of the deepest, most subliminal social codes within a culture" (*Battered Love*, 29).

132. Weems, "Gomer," 97.

133. Weems, "Gomer," 98.

134. Baumann, *Love and Violence*, 103–4; see also Weems, "Gomer," 99–101.

135. Bernard Oestreich, *Metaphors and Similes for Yahweh in Hosea 14:2–9 (1–8): A Study of Hoseanic Pictorial Language* (Friedensauer Schriftenreihe; Frankfurt: Peter Lang, 1998).

136. Oestreich, *Metaphors*, 228.

137. For a thorough study of the root metaphor "God is King" in biblical texts, see Marc Zvi Brettler, *God is King: Understanding an Israelite Metaphor* (JSOTSup 76; Sheffield: Sheffield Academic Press, 1989).

138. Oestreich, *Metaphors*, 229.

139. Oestreich, *Metaphors*, 230.

140. Oestreich, *Metaphors*, 232–34.

141. Gören Eidevall, *Grapes in the Desert: Metaphors, Models, and Themes in Hosea 4–14* (ConBOT 43; Stockholm: Almqvist & Wiksell, 1996).

142.   Eidevall, *Grapes in the Desert*, 47–48.

143.   Eidevall, *Grapes in the Desert*, 1.

144.   Eidevall, *Grapes in the Desert*, 7–8. Martin Buss explores the elements of tragedy and comedy in Hosea in "Tragedy and Comedy in Hosea," *Semeia* 32 (1984): 71–82.

145.   Eidevall, *Grapes in the Desert*, 40.

146.   Eidevall, *Grapes in the Desert*, 229.

147.   Eidevall, *Grapes in the Desert*, 229.

148.   Eidevall, *Grapes in the Desert*, 230.

149.   Eidevall, *Grapes in the Desert*, 231.

150.   Eidevall, *Grapes in the Desert*, 233.

151.   Eidevall, *Grapes in the Desert*, 240. He takes his terminology from Michael Lee Catlett, "Reversals in Hosea" (Ph.D. diss., Emory University, 1988).

152.   Eidevall, *Grapes in the Desert*, 241.

153.   Eidevall, *Grapes in the Desert*, 243–52.

154.   Emmanuel O. Nwaoru, *Imagery in the Prophecy of Hosea* (Ägypten und Altes Testament 41; Wiesbaden: Harrassowitz, 1999).

155.   Nwaoru, *Imagery*, 50.

156.   Nwaoru, *Imagery*, 66.

157.   Nwaoru, *Imagery*, 93.

2 Masculinity and Metaphor: An Approach to Analysis

1.   See James W. Fernandez, *Persuasions and Performances* (Bloomington: Indiana University Press, 1986).

2.   The exact nature of this entity is the subject of great debate. See the discussion in ch. 1. I follow Galambush, Kelle, and others who identify the wife with Samaria, but the exact nature of the wife's identity is not of great importance to my thesis. Nearly all of the commentators agree that the wife represents some political entity (city, land, country, people of Israel/Ephraim, etc.) of which males are the leaders and are thus the main focus of the oracles. While feminist scholars often focus on the text's impact on female readers, their concern is with contemporary readers and those in the history of the religious tradition, more than with Hosea's original audience. My working assumption is that the oracles were not originally intended to address women, as women were not in political or public social power. The effect of the oracles on women in later times and situations is beyond the scope of this study.

3.   Among others emphasizing this point are Christina Bucher, "The Origin and Meaning of *ZNH* Terminology in the Book of Hosea" (Ph.D. diss., Claremont Graduate School, 1988), 162–63; Carroll, "Desire," 285; Yee, *Banished Children*, 98; Weems, *Battered Love*, 41–42; Leith, "Verse and Reverse," 97–98; Stone, "Lovers and Raisin Cakes," 137; Francis Landy, "Fantasy and the Displacement of Pleasure: Hosea 2:4–17," in *A Feminist Companion to the Latter Prophets* (ed. Athalya Brenner; FCB 8; Sheffield: Sheffield Academic Press,

1995), 155; Brad E. Kelle, "Wartime Rhetoric: Prophetic Metaphorization of Cities as Female," in *Writing and Reading War: Rhetoric, Gender, and Ethics in Biblical and Modern Contexts* (ed. Brad E. Kelle and Frank Ritchel Ames; Symposium 42; Atlanta: SBL, 2008), 107.

4. The term gender usually implies a social construction, rather than a biological marker, of sex. Marilyn Strathern provides a typical definition: "By 'gender' I mean those categorizations of persons, artifacts, events, sequences, and so on which draw upon sexual imagery—upon the ways in which the distinctiveness of male and female characteristics make concrete people's ideas about the nature of social relationships" (*The Gender of the Gift: Problems with Women and Problems with Society in Melanesia* [Studies in Melanesian Anthropology 6; Berkeley: University of California Press, 1988], ix).

5. See, *e.g.*, Harry Brod, "Introduction and Theses of Men's Studies," in *The Making of Masculinities: The New Men's Studies* (ed. Harry Brod; Boston: Allen & Unwin, 1987), 2.

6. Eve Kosofsky Sedgwick, "'Gosh, Boy George, You Must Be Awfully Secure in Your Masculinity,'" in *Constructing Masculinity* (ed. Maurice Berger et al.; New York: Routledge, 1995), 12. Masculinity studies should also be differentiated from the mythopoeic "men's movement." This movement, popularized by Robert Bly and others, tries to help men regain their "true" masculinity, which has been repressed in contemporary society (see Bly, *Iron John: A Book About Men* [Reading, MA: Addison-Wesley, 1990]; Sam Keen, *Fire in the Belly: On Being a Man* [New York: Bantam, 1991]; Warren Farrell, *The Myth of Male Power* [New York: Simon & Schuster, 1993]). Often the feminist movement is blamed for creating a culture in which masculinity is stigmatized and suppressed. Sometimes in organizations such as the Promise Keepers, the efforts to help men regain a sense of identity and responsibility slide into reinforcing hierarchical gender relationships. Such a view polarizes gender relationships. The men's movement can also tend to promote an essentialist view of masculinity and femininity.

7. Andrea Cornwall and Nancy Lindisfarne, "Introduction," in *Dislocating Masculinity: Comparative Ethnographies* (ed. Andrea Cornwall and Nancy Lindisfarne; Male Orders; New York: Routledge, 1994), 10. Even when women act in power structures traditionally dominated by men, they are sometimes described by male characteristics. In Andalusia, a powerful female entrepreneur is sometimes described as a *cojonuda*, a "big-balled woman." Such women are said to "have balls inside" and "should have been born as men" (Stanley Brandes, *Metaphors of Masculinity: Sex and Status in Andalusian Folklore* [Publications of the American Folklore Society New Series 1; Philadelphia: University of Pennsylvania Press, 1980], 93). Philo, known for his denigration of women, argues in his commentary on Gen 18:11 that the verse "and it had ceased to be for Sarah according to the ways of women," refers to the "ways of women" as irrational passions. Sarah now is in the place of men "where properly dwell the masculine thoughts (that are) wise, sound, just, prudent,

pious, filled with freedom and boldness, and kin to wisdom" (*QG.* 4.15, trans. Lincoln E. Galloway in *Freedom in the Gospel: Paul's Exemplum in 1 Cor 9 in Conversation with the Discourses of Epictetus and Philo* [CBET 38; Leuven: Peeters, 2004], 128). Similarly, Philo praises a prominent woman, temple patron Julia Augusta, for overcoming her natural female judgments: "The purity of the training she received supplementing nature and practice gave virility to her reasoning power (ἀρρενοθεῖσα τῶν λωγισμῶν), which gained such clearness of vision that it apprehended the things of the mind better than the things of sense" (Galloway, *Freedom*, 127). The verb ἀρρενοθεῖσα "give virility to" means "to make masculine" or "to make male children," so that her positive attributes are described with masculine terms.

8.   Andrea Cornwall and Nancy Lindisfarne, "Dislocating Masculinity: Gender, Power, and Anthropology," in *Dislocating Masculinity: Comparative Ethnographies* (ed. Andrea Cornwall and Nancy Lindisfarne; Male Orders; New York: Routledge, 1994), 20. A similar view that examination of power must include a careful study of the various elements of masculinity is expressed in Maurice Berger, "Introduction," in *Constructing Masculinity* (ed. Maurice Berger et al.; New York: Routledge, 1995), 7.

9.   Tim Carrigan, Bob Connell, and John Lee, "Toward a New Sociology of Masculinity," in *The Making of Masculinities: The New Men's Studies* (ed. Harry Brod; Boston: Allen & Unwin, 1987), 92. Carrigan introduced the term "hegemonic masculinity."

10.   Carrigan et al., "New Sociology," 94.

11.   R.W. Connell, *Masculinities* (2d ed.; Berkeley: UC Press, 2005), 76.

12.   Strathern, *Gender of Gift*, 77.

13.   Conversely, Geoffrey P. Miller in his study of the Song of Deborah proposes that claiming that a society's women were acting like men was an insult and associated with uncouth hill people. He argues that as a riposte, the song accepts the truth of part of the insult and turns it around as a virtue. In this way, the manly women dominate not their own men, but Sisera and the Canaanites ("A Riposte Form in The Song of Deborah," in *Gender and Law in the Hebrew Bible and the Ancient Near East* [ed. Victor H. Matthews, Bernard M. Levinson, and Tikva Frymer-Kensky; JSOTSup 262; Sheffield: Sheffield Academic Press, 1998], 114). Thus it appears that while women acting as men were generally looked down upon, there were occasions on which they could be celebrated. One should note, however, that the insult in Judges was not solely that the women were manly, but that they dominated their men, who were thus feminized.

14.   Brandes, *Metaphors of Masculinity*, 6, 12, 25, 31, 63, 212.

15.   David D. Gilmore, "Above and Below: Toward A Social Geometry of Gender," *American Anthropologist* 98 (1996), 56.

16.   Gilmore, "Above and Below," 60.

17. Peter Loizos, "A Broken Mirror: Masculine Sexuality in Greek Ethnography," in *Dislocating Masculinity: Comparative Ethnographies* (ed. Andrea Cornwall and Nancy Lindisfarne; Male Orders; New York: Routledge, 1994), 72.

18. The other main approach to masculinity studies is a psychoanalytic perspective. The most prominent source for such work is Michel Foucault's *Histoire de la sexualité* (3 vols.; Paris: Gallimard, 1976).

19. Gale Yee also notes the problems of the relationship between actual and inscribed gender relationships. "In the biblical text, one does not encounter 'real' gender relationships firsthand. Rather, one encounters them as a double absence: as already encoded in particular socially determined significations, in ideological formations that real situations of gender relations in the biblical world have actually produced" (*Banished Children*, 20).

20. Anthropologists have long noted the discrepancy between how people say society functions, especially with regard to such elements as gender relations, and their actual practices (see John K. Chance, "The Anthropology of Honor and Shame: Culture, Values, and Practice," *Semeia* 68 [1994]: 145–46).

21. Hence, when one describes a woman as eating like a bird, one does not mean that she is eating three times her body weight per day, but rather that she picks at her food, or eats what seems to be a small amount at any given sitting.

22. This is not to say that social perceptions are fixed, nor that the text encodes them exclusively. I will examine the slipperiness of both the conception of gender in the text and the ways that the text seems to play with established norms in ch. 5.

23. A large percentage of the literature on Hosea centers on Gomer and the "wife" in chs. 1–3, but women are barely mentioned in the remainder of the book. I argue for the masculine focus of the female imagery in the next chapter.

24. I do not mean to imply that I can reconstruct the thoughts of the assumed audience. Rather, I am drawing from the rhetoric of the oracles that they are making a strong critique of the status quo.

25. Sedgwick, "'Gosh, Boy George,'" 15.

26. It is not unusual to find in the gender literature a definition of masculinity as not feminine. One example come from David D. Gilmore: "Frequently the construction of male gender role begins with a definition of manhood on the basis of a polaric separation of what is considered male from what is considered female....That is, masculinity is, first, often defined as the complementary obverse of femininity; and second, this differentiation encourages a male role which is problematic, controvertible, or 'elusive'" ("Introduction," in *Honor and Shame and the Unity of the Mediterranean* [ed. David D. Gilmore; Special Publication of the American Anthropological Association 22; Washington, DC: American Anthropological Association, 1987)], 9). Such an opposition of gender is only the beginning of a definition of masculinity, however, and as noted, causes problems in finding a stable definition. It is less common to see femininity defined first and foremost as that which is not masculine.

27. Many of the studies mentioned in ch. 1 have considered the conception/perception of women to a greater or lesser extent.

28. *E.g.*, Eva Feder Kittay, *Metaphor: Its Cognitive Force and Linguistic Structure* (Oxford: Clarendon, 1987); Earl R. Mac Cormac, *A Cognitive Theory of Metaphor* (Cambridge, MA: MIT Press, 1985); Paul Ricoeur, *The Rule of Metaphor* (trans. Robert Czerny et al.; Toronto: University of Toronto Press, 1977); Sabine Maasen and Peter Weingart, *Metaphors and the Dynamics of Knowledge* (New York: Routledge, 2000); Andrew Ortony, ed., *Metaphor and Thought* (2d ed.; Cambridge: Cambridge University Press, 1993); Kuang-Ming Wu, *On Metaphoring: A Cultural Hermeneutic* (Leiden: Brill, 2001); Lynne Cameron and Graham Low, eds. *Researching and Applying Metaphor* (Cambridge: Cambridge University Press, 1999); A. E. Denham, *Metaphor and Moral Experience* (Oxford: Clarendon, 2000); Roger M. White, *The Structure of Metaphor* (Oxford: Blackwell, 1996).

29. Claude Lévi-Strauss, *The Savage Mind* (Chicago: University of Chicago Press, 1962). One example of this is among the Mota in the Banks Islands where a pregnant woman sometimes discovers, or divines, a particular fruit or animal which is then associated with the child, who will share characteristics with that entity. The child is prohibited from eating this kind of food, as it would be a type of self-cannibalism (77–78). Lévi-Strauss also notes that some types of totemism have persisted in western societies, such as the plant emblem systems of the Greeks and Romans, who used wreaths of olive, oak, laurel and others to represent different achievements (42). The names and mascots of contemporary sports teams also serve the purpose of predicating an identity, often of a predatory animal, on the team.

30. Lévi-Strauss, *Savage Mind*, 75–76.

31. In particular he considers plant classification systems.

32. Paul Friedrich, "Polytropy," in *Beyond Metaphor: The Theory of Tropes in Anthropology* (ed. James W. Fernandez; Stanford, CA: Stanford University Press, 1991), 55.

33. Works in the philosophical approach to metaphor theory include I. A. Richards, *The Philosophy of Rhetoric* (New York: Oxford University Press, 1936); Max Black, *Models and Metaphors* (Ithaca, NY: Cornell University Press, 1962); Paul Henle, ed., *Language, Thought, and Culture* (Ann Arbor: University of Michigan Press, 1958). Several important essays are reprinted in Mark Johnson, ed., *Philosophical Perspectives on Metaphor* (Minneapolis: University of Minnesota Press, 1981), including Monroe C. Beardsley, "The Metaphorical Twist," 105–21; Timothy Binkley, "On the Truth and Probity of Metaphor," 136–53; Ina Loewenberg, "Identifying Metaphors," 154–81; Donald Davidson, "What Metaphors Mean," 200–220; Paul Ricoeur, "The Metaphorical Process as Cognition, Imagination, and Feeling," 228–47.

34. The most prominent proponents of cognitive metaphor theory are George Lakoff and Mark Johnson, *Metaphors We Live By* (Chicago: University of Chicago Press, 1980). See also Lakoff and Johnson, *More Than Cool Reason: A*

Field Guide to Poetic Metaphor (Chicago: University of Chicago Press, 1989), and Mark Turner, *Death is the Mother of Beauty: Mind, Metaphor, Criticism* (Chicago: University of Chicago Press, 1987). Naomi Quinn provides a critique of this approach in "The Cultural Basis of Metaphor," in *Beyond Metaphor* (ed. James W. Fernandez; Stanford, CA: Stanford University Press, 1991), 56–93.

35. Metaphor and rhetoric have long been of interest to scholars, however, going back to Aristotle. See in particular *The Poetics* and *The "Art" of Rhetoric*. For a cogent analysis of Aristotle's position see Lynn R. Huber, *Like a Bride Adorned: Reading Metaphor in John's Apocalypse* (Emory Studies in Early Christianity; New York: T&T Clark, 2007), 46–49. For a more contemporary approach to rhetoric, see Wayne Booth, "Metaphor as Rhetoric: The Problem of Evaluation," in *On Metaphor* (ed. Sheldon Sacks; Chicago: University of Chicago Press, 1978), 47–70.

36. Fernandez, *Persuasions*, xi.

37. James Fernandez's ethnographic work has been primarily in Africa, especially among the Fang, and in Asturian mountain villages in southern Spain. He has written extensively about the interaction of language, identity, and social change in these cultures.

38. Fernandez does not claim that his definition addresses every use of metaphor. He is interested solely in its use in formation of human social identity.

39. Fernandez, *Persuasions*, 8.

40. Janet Martin Soskice, *Metaphor and Religious Language* (Oxford: Oxford University Press, 1985), 15. Her definition is purposely rather general and vague, seeking to provide a purely linguistic rather than functional account.

41. Lakoff and Johnson, *Metaphors*, 5.

42. The terminology used to identify parts of a metaphor is somewhat variable, but many have adopted that of I. A. Richards, calling what is here Ephraim the "tenor," and the cake the "vehicle" (*Philosophy of Rhetoric*, 96).

43. Fernandez, *Persuasions*, ix–x.

44. Paul Sherwen describes Jan Ullrich in this way, sometimes going on to explain his point of reference—it takes awhile to get moving, but once it is in gear, it keeps going indefinitely with great power.

45. Fernandez, *Persuasions*, 14.

46. W. T. Jones sets up seven more abstract axes, which represent pairs of contrasting values (*The Romantic Syndrome* [The Hague: Martinus Nijhoff, 1961], 35–36). The seven are order/disorder, static/dynamic, continuity/discreteness, inner/outer, sharp-focus/soft-focus, this-world/other-world, and spontaneity/process. In a given society, and for given subjects, one position or another along these axes may be considered normative or "good."

47. Polarizing models that either group people in discrete categories, such as male/female, or those that only consider one factor as most important for assessing people's places in society are unable to take into account more complex relations, including the idea that discrete categories often do not describe specific people well.

48. The criteria for determining optimal placement may differ depending on the context. Young, beautiful, and poor may win in getting cast for movie roles, but old, ugly, and rich will triumph in most other arenas in our society. For the purposes of illustrating the concept of social space, I have purposely chosen relatively concrete categories that apply predominantly to humans. More abstract categories may be more useful for analyzing movement through language. Language can, however, be used to change the perception of the position someone may seem to occupy objectively. For example, politicians often try to downplay the fact that they are rich, highly educated, and powerful, by employing images that identify them with the "common people."

49. Fernandez, *Persuasions,* 41.

50. Fernandez, *Persuasions,* 7.

51. Fernandez, *Persuasions,* 21–22.

52. The idea that the meaning of a metaphor arises from the interaction between the tenor and the vehicle is a hallmark of most contemporary metaphor theory.

53. Kenneth Burke also discusses literary forms, particularly proverbs, in terms of "*strategies* for dealing with *situations.*" He notes that while strategy may not be the perfect term, it is the best he can come up with. "The only one [alternative term] I can think of is 'method.' But if 'strategy' errs in suggesting to some people an overly *conscious* procedure, 'method' errs in suggesting an overly '*methodical*' one" (*The Philosophy of Literary Form: Studies in Symbolic Action* [3d ed.; Berkeley: University of California Press, 1973], 296–97). The same may be true of metaphorical strategies—some may be more consciously strategic than others.

54. Fernandez, *Persuasions,* 13–14.

55. Aristotle, *Rhet,* 3.2.10 (Freese, LCL).

56. John Eldredge, *Wild at Heart* (Nashville: Thomas Nelson, 2001), 63–64. The "men's movement," as articulated by the authors in n. 7 above, also frequently uses the metaphors of "soft" and "hard" men.

57. These first three missions relate more to persuasive metaphors. Fernandez gives four more missions, which relate more to performative metaphors and will not factor significantly into my analysis. They are to provide a means of ritual movement through cultural space, to help the subject fill in the frame or the links in the causality of existence, to allow the individual subject to "return to the whole," and to draw attention away from the parts to the whole of society (*Persuasions,* 62). Obviously not all metaphors fulfill all of these missions.

58. Not to mention the fact that with the evolution of vocabulary few have any idea what it actually means. They are stuck trying to figure out why Yankee Doodle wants pasta on his hat, but they sing it proudly.

59. Charles E. Osgood, George Suci, and Percy H. Tannenbaum, *The Measurement of Meaning* (Urbana: University of Illinois Press, 1967), 36–38.

60. Osgood et al., *Measurement of Meaning,* 38. Analysis of variance (ANOVA) is a statistical assessment of data that shows the probability that a change in one variable results in a change in another measure. For example, the method can

determine whether the data indicate that a certain amount of damage to the leaf of a sapling significantly decreases its shoot elongation rate. In a controlled experiment in which only one factor (in this case leaf damage) is allowed to change (clones are used to control genetic variation; light, water, temperature, etc. are identical for each subject plant), ANOVA must show that the variable accounts for 95% of the variance for the result to be statistically significant. In Osgood's analysis, the percentages are much lower: the three factors of potency, activity, and evaluation together only account for 70% of the variance. Considering the fact that language usage is by no means controlled and is influenced by many variables, as well as the fact that as in other soft sciences, much of the data depends on individual human assessment and responses, the percentages are quite high. These are the three factors that showed the most influence on determination of meaning. Lest one dismiss this method as a relict from the modern/positivist age, it should be noted that computational linguistics is still an active field, one that is becoming increasingly useful, especially for computer language programs.

61. While these concepts were elucidated from studies of American subjects, the metaphors in Hosea are quite amenable to analysis with these factors. Even if they do not account for the same percentages of variance in meaning in Hebrew of the 8th century as they do in contemporary American English, issues of action, power, and goodness are prominent in the biblical texts.

62. Fernandez, *Persuasions*, 13.

63. Black, *Models*, 35.

64. Black, *Models*, 37.

65. Nelson Goodman, "Languages of Art," in *Philosophical Perspectives on Metaphor* (ed. Mark Johnson; Minneapolis: University of Minnesota Press, 1981), 128–29.

66. Soskice, *Metaphor*, 59–60.

67. Soskice, *Metaphor*, 59.

68. Aristotle, *Rhet.* 3.4.1–2 (Freese, LCL).

69. Aristotle, *Rhet.* 3.10.3–4 (Freese, LCL).

70. Booth, "Metaphor as Rhetoric," 53.

71. See René Dirven and Ralf Pörings, eds., *Metaphor and Metonymy in Comparison and Contrast* (CLR 20; Berlin: de Gruyter, 2002).

72. Roman Jakobson studied aphasia, or the loss of particular language abilities, and determined that different areas of the brain control comprehension of these two types of tropes. Damage to one area will affect the ability to recognize contiguity relationships, while damage to another will affect recognition of similarity relationships ("The Metaphoric and Metonymic Poles," in *Metaphor and Metonym* [ed. René Dirven and Ralf Pörings; CLR 20; Berlin: de Gruyter, 2002], 41–47).

73. Soskice, *Metaphor*, 57.

74. Soskice, *Metaphor*, 58.

75. Lakoff and Johnson, *Metaphors*, 36.

76. Fernandez, *Persuasions*, 46.

77. Renate Bartsch, "Generating Polysemy: Metaphor and Metonymy," in *Metaphor and Metonymy in Comparison and Contrast* (ed. René Dirven and Ralf Pörings; CLR 20; Berlin: de Gruyter, 2002), 49–71.

78. Fernandez, *Persuasions,* xii. Terence Turner argues that to understand what may be broadly categorized as performative metaphors, such as the statement "we are araras [a type of parrot]" among the Bororo of Brazil, one has to look at the interaction or play of tropes that shapes relationships and cultural understanding and to recognize that both tropic and non-tropic elements "converge in a dialectical conception of the construction of meaning" ("'We are Parrots,' 'Twins are Birds': Play of Tropes as Operational Structure," in *Beyond Metaphor* [ed. James W. Fernandez; Stanford, CA: Stanford University Press, 1991], 150–51).

79. Fernandez, *Persuasions,* 12. David H. Aaron also recognizes the relations between understanding language and other realms of cognition. Particularly for the study of religion, expanding one's theory of interpretation beyond language is important for two reasons, he claims: to keep the theorist methodologically honest and in recognition of the fact that religion encompasses a variety of domains of human experience (*Biblical Ambiguities: Metaphor, Semantics and Divine Imagery* [BRLAJ 4; Leiden: Brill, 2001], 69–70).

80. Fernandez defines the inchoate as "the underlying (psychophysiological) and overlying (sociocultural) sense of entity (entirely of being or wholeness) which we reach for to express (by predication) and act out (by performance) but can never grasp" (*Persuasions,* 235).

81. Fernandez, *Persuasions,* 236.

82. For masculinity as an unstable concept, see Gilmore, "Introduction," 9; Maureen J. Giovannini, "Female Chastity Codes in the Circum-Mediterranean: Comparative Perspectives," in *Honor and Shame and the Unity of the Mediterranean* (ed. David D. Gilmore; Special Publication of the American Anthropological Association 22; Washington, DC: American Anthropological Association, 1987), 68; Connell, *Masculinities,* 71–81.

83. Cornwall and Lindisfarne, "Introduction," 10.

84. Gilmore, "Above and Below," 54. Gilmore acknowledges his use of Fernandez's concept of social space. His three axes, though phrased slightly differently, correspond to those of Osgood/Fernandez. Spatial separation in terms of gender relates to activity, because of the different spheres of action in which men and women operate in that culture. The normative axis is the equivalent of the goodness axis.

85. Gilmore, "Above and Below," 62.

3 Predications of Gender-Based Imagery

1. *Men and Masculinity in the Hebrew Bible and Beyond* (ed. Ovidiu Creangă; The Bible in the Modern World 33; Sheffield: Sheffield Phoenix, 2010) contains several essays relating to masculinity in various parts of the Hebrew canon.

Much work has also been done on the New Testament, but I will not explore these studies here. For an anthology with an excellent bibliography of masculinity studies in general, in ANE sources, the Hebrew Bible, and the New Testament, see Stephen D. Moore and Janice Capel Anderson, eds., *New Testament Masculinities* (SemeiaSt 45; Atlanta: SBL, 2003).

2. Howard Eilberg-Schwarz, *God's Phallus: And Other Problems for Men and Monotheism* (Boston: Beacon, 1994).

3. Eilberg-Schwarz, *God's Phallus*, 148. See also Stephen D. Moore, *God's Beauty Parlor: And Other Queer Spaces Around the Bible* (Contraversions; Stanford, CA: Stanford University Press, 2001). Yee also notes homoerotic implications for the relationships of males to YHWH, noting that males are "Other" with respect to God. Thus male tensions are often placed on and symbolized by women (*Banished Children*, 100).

4. Deborah W. Rooke proposes that the priestly undergarments in Exod 28:42 may serve to feminize the men and prepare them for their role as the wives of God. She notes that the language about "covering nakedness" in that passage is similar to that used in Hos 2 to describe the uncovering of the wife ("Breeches of the Covenant: Gender, Garments, and the Priesthood," in *Embroidered Garments: Priests and Gender in Biblical Israel* (ed. Deborah W. Rooke; Sheffield: Sheffield Phoenix, 2009), 29–30.

5. Eilberg-Schwartz, *God's Phallus*, 148.

6. Cultic texts from the Old Babylonian period have examples of both complementary and non-complementary gender assignments. The *en* priests could be either male or female and served gods of the opposite gender. *Ēntu* priests, on the other hand, were always female and served gods of both genders (Bucher, "Meaning of *ZNH*,"47).

7. Eilberg-Schwartz, *God's Phallus*, 160.

8. This position is also taken by S. H. Smith, "'Heel' and 'Thigh': The Concept of Sexuality in the Jacob-Esau Narratives," *VT* 40 (1990): 464–73.

9. Eilberg-Schwartz, *God's Phallus*, 156.

10. Jan William Tarlin, "Utopia and Pornography in Ezekiel: Violence, Hope, and the Shattered Male Subject," in *Reading Bibles, Writing Bodies: Identity and The Book* (ed. Timothy K. Beal and David M. Gunn; Biblical Limits; New York: Routledge, 1997), 182.

11. The idea that religious belief/activity results in a loss of masculinity affects religious practices in some cultures. Brandes has observed that Andalusian men only rarely take communion because it requires kneeling in front of another man, the priest, which lowers their masculine status (*Metaphors of Masculinity*, 187–88). Prostrating oneself before another man is somewhat different than prostrating oneself before God, however. My colleague Juan Hernández Jr. noted that in Hispanic Pentecostal churches, while the men have a great concern with masculinity in other areas of their lives, they have no difficulty calling themselves the bride of Christ in church. Hetty Zock explores the implications of Erik Erikson's theories of the feminine mode, understood as

passivity, possessed by both men and women, as the primary mode of religious experience in "The Predominance of the Feminine Sexual Mode in Religion: Erikson's Contribution to the Sex and Gender Debate in the Psychology of Religion," *International Journal for the Psychology of Religion* 7 (1997): 187–198.

12.   David J. A. Clines, *Interested Parties: The Ideology of Writers and Readers of the Hebrew Bible* (JSOTSup 205; GCT 1; Sheffield: Sheffield Academic Press, 1995), 212–33.

13.   Apparently his powers of persuasion have waned by the time of the incident with Uriah, whom he cannot persuade to go visit Bathsheba, even with multiple tries.

14.   Clines tries to point to differences between contemporary and biblical conceptions of masculinity in this essay. While differences are certainly necessary to consider, at a few points he seems to overstate his case. He emphasizes how modern readers reject beauty as masculine. In terms of terminology this is true, but while ugly men fare better than ugly women, handsomeness is still part of the male ideal, even though this handsomeness may be supposed to be maintenance free, at least in the pre-metrosexual era. Stuart Macwilliam also notes that males are not unproblematically considered beautiful in the biblical texts. Rather than being a simple sign of divine favor, it often represents vulnerability ("Ideologies of Male Beauty and the Hebrew Bible," *BibInt* 17 [2009]: 265–287).

15.   Clines's assessment of the importance of sex is another issue which I find problematic. He contrasts the heavy emphasis and expectation of sex as part of masculinity today with the seeming lack of interest in the David story. He glosses over some important episodes, however, including the incident with Bathsheba, which seems primarily sexually motivated, as well as the negative portrayal of David's impotence in I Kgs 1. Instead he focuses on David's love of Jonathan, noting that it seems much more important than that of women. Love and sex are two different concepts, however, and as even contemporary masculine expectations greatly privilege the latter, it seems insufficient to equate the lack of discussion of the love of women with a lack of emphasis on sex and sexuality. The latter is a somewhat anachronistic term, but I use it here to refer to a public dimension of sex. See the discussion of Ken Stone's work below.

16.   Clines, *Interested Parties*, 228.

17.   Clines, *Interested Parties*, 228–31.

18.   David J. A. Clines, "He-Prophets: Masculinity as a Problem for the Hebrew Prophets and their Interpreters," in *Sense and Sensitivity: Essays on Reading the Bible in Memory of Robert Carroll* (ed. David J. A. Clines and Philip R. Davies; JSOTSup 348; Sheffield: Sheffield Academic Press, 2002), 311–28.

19.   The violence of the prophecies is obvious, but such episodes as 1 Sam 15:33, in which Samuel hacks up Agag, and 2 Kgs 2:23–24, in which Elisha sends the she-bears to attack the boys who taunt him, show that the prophets themselves were not averse to using their power in violent ways.

20. Clines may be interested in looking at particular masculinities or the variety of masculinities in the text, rather than at a normative masculinity, which is my concern. Especially in the essay on David, however, he interacts with normative masculinity in contemporary America. Clines also does not, in general, address the issue of whether these traits are primarily masculine or if they are general human traits in ancient Israel. It is not necessary, however, for the traits to be absent in females for them to form an important part of the masculine ideal.

21. These points seem to be where his actions provoke surprise or rebuke (death of Absalom, death of Bathsheba's child). It is difficult to pinpoint exactly which elements of his response are atypical, however, and whether they oppose masculine or some other norms.

22. Susan E. Haddox, "Favoured Sons and Subordinate Masculinites," in *Men and Masculinity in the Hebrew Bible and Beyond* (ed. Ovidiu Creangǎ; The Bible in the Modern World 33; Sheffield: Sheffield Phoenix, 2010), 2–19.

23. Ken Stone, *Sex, Honor, and Power in the Deuteronomistic History* (JSOTSup 234; Sheffield: Sheffield Academic Press, 1996).

24. Stone, *Sex, Honor, and Power,* 11.

25. It is not unusual for coerced sex to express a conflict between men. As Susan Brownmiller observes: "Rape by a conquering soldier destroys all remaining illusions of power and property for men of the defeated side. The body of a raped woman becomes a ceremonial battlefield, a parade ground for the victor's trooping of the colors. The act that is played out upon her is a message passed between men—vivid proof of victory for one and loss and defeat for the other" (*Against Our Will: Men, Women and Rape* [New York: Simon & Schuster, 1975], 38). The same type of dynamic occurs in the rape of Dinah in Gen 34, which pits Dinah's brothers against the rulers and men of Shechem.

26. That these situations were conflicts between men is evidenced by the fact that the women disappear from the scene soon after the unfortunate event, doomed to live as a desolate woman in her brother's house (2 Sam 13:20b) or to be shut up like widows by David for the rest of their lives (2 Sam 20:3). Their violation, however, gives motivation for the larger struggles between the men, leading to Absalom's revolt and Joab's defection.

27. Stone, *Sex, Honor, and Power,* 112.

28. Harold C. Washington, "Violence and the Construction of Gender in the Hebrew Bible: A New Historicist Approach," *BibInt* 5 (1997): 324–63.

29. Washington, "Violence," 330.

30. Carole R. Fontaine, "'Be Men, O Philistines!' (1 Samuel 4:9): Iconographic Representations and Reflections on Female Gender as Disability in the Ancient World," in *This Abled Body: Rethinking Disabilities in Biblical Studies* (ed. Hector Avalos et al.; Semeia 55; Atlanta: SBL, 2007), 67.

31. Washington, "Violence," 361; Mieke Bal, *Death and Dissymmetry: The Politics of Coherence in the Book of Judges* (Chicago: University of Chicago Press, 1988), 215; Susan Niditch, "Eroticism and Death in the Tale of Jael," in *Gender and Difference in Ancient Israel* (ed. Peggy L. Day; Minneapolis: Fortress, 1989), 46;

Robert Alter, "From Line to Story in Biblical Verse," *Poetics Today* 4 (1983): 615–37.

32. Barak refuses to go into battle unless Deborah comes with him. She agrees, but tells him that he will not get the glory of victory, but that Sisera will fall by the hand of a woman (Judg 4:8–9).

33. Ken Stone notes that in addition to the shame of being killed by a woman, the episode reverses the normal position of men and women, with the woman penetrating Abimelech from above ("Gender Criticism: The Un-Manning of Abimelech," in *Judges and Method: New Approaches in Biblical Studies* [2d ed.; Gale A. Yee, ed; Minneapolis: Fortress Press, 2007], 195–196).

34. The story of Eglon in Judg 3 also implies the feminization of the defeated man. Ehud, while alone in the chamber with him, thrusts his sword into Eglon's belly, after "going to him" (ויבא אליך), both sexually tinged actions (Robert Alter, *The Art of Biblical Narrative* [New York: Basic Books, 1981], 39).

35. Chapman, *Gendered Language*.

36. Chapman, *Gendered Language*, 26.

37. Chapman, *Gendered Language*, 39.

38. I will discuss the specifics of these threats below.

39. I treat many of these same issues in "(E)Masculinity in Hosea's Political Rhetoric," in *Israel's Prophets and Israel's Past* (ed. Brad E. Kelle and Megan Bishop Moore; New York: T&T Clark, 2006), 174–200.

40. As noted in ch. 1, Kelle treats the marriage and sexual imagery separately (*Hosea 2*).

41. Beeby, *Grace Abounding*, 2. Similar views are expressed by Brown: "Too often at these 'high places' there was loose conduct and unbridled lust. This was encouraged by the priests, who drew their income from the cult, and by intercourse with the sacred prostitutes, who could be hired by anyone on payment of a love-gift. This worship, described so vividly by Hosea, is the old local cult of Baal which the children of Israel had learnt from the Canaanites. In the popular religion Jahveh has come to be regarded as Baal, the god of fruitfulness, to whom the gifts of nature and the sacrifice of virginity are offered" (*Hosea*, xxiii).

42. Kaufmann, however, observes that the only time when the Baal cult had official state status was under Ahab and Jezebel's reign, which Jehu destroyed upon usurping power. Thus he argues that the references to Baal in chs. 1–3 must have been written at that earlier time (*Religion of Israel*, 369–70). He supports his case by emending 1:4 to read "blood of Jezreel" rather than "blood of Jehu" which seems to contradict the approval of the destruction of Ahab and the Baal cult. The former reading would refer to Naboth. Few have followed his emendation, however, which has no textual support. Wood agrees that the official Baal cult had been destroyed by Jehu, but thinks that it still lingered in popular religion, whose practices Hosea condemns (*Hosea*, 162).

43. Thus Kuhl, who says Hosea is concerned that though people think they are worshipping Yahweh, they are really doing it in the form of the Baal nature

religion cult (*Prophets of Israel*, 69). Macintosh observes that "in all this (and here is the root of the matter) it is his people's faulty perceptions which are the real cause of the national malaise. Their minds in times of plenty had been infected by a promiscuous impulse (4.12; 5.4) and this manifested itself most directly in their addiction to cultic exuberance, to the sensual pleasures of endless (8.13) feasting and drinking which were more typical of the worship of Baal than that of Yahweh (4.10–19). On the tops of the hills, under the shade of the trees, their consciences eased by sanctions of religious observance, they indulged in sexual orgies with prostitutes and cult-women who were wont to associate themselves with the sanctuaries. For Hosea such indulgence robbed men of their reason (4.11); they failed to see that it was their own society which suffered the resulting damage (4.13) and their own nation whose moral perception was disastrously atrophied" (*Hosea*, xc–xci). Ward links the perversion of the cult not with Baal, explicitly, but with licentious practices that distract from true worship of YHWH, which seemingly encompasses proper family values: "The chief perversion of which the cult is accused in this poem is the idolatrous preoccupation with economic goals and sensual experiences, to the exclusion of other aspects of life....In the popular worship of ancient Palestine, however, the use of sexual energies was deliberate and culminated in the sanctification of fornication and in sensual ecstasy....Needless to say, the cult led to the deterioration of Israelite sexual mores and thus contributed to the dissolution of normative family bonds. Another, even more basic evil was the dehumanization of all life by a cult preoccupied in a peculiarly narrow way with physical and sensual needs" (*Hosea*, 28–29).

44. Cheyne, *Hosea*, 15.
45. Kuhl, *Prophets of Israel*, 68.
46. Cheyne (*Hosea*, 15) quotes Edward H. Plumptre: "The two sins of idolatry and sensual licence were closely intertwined....It would not be too much to say that every harlot in Israel was probably a votary of the goddess" (*Lazarus and Other Poems* [4th ed; London: Griffith and Farran, 1884], 223).
47. Wolff states: "This was a fertility rite in which the women had sexual relations with strangers to bring new vitality to the clan" (*Hosea*, 14). Such a rite seems highly out of place with the usual assertions about Israel's strong honor/shame culture concerned with control of female sexuality.
48. Phyllis Bird, "Play the Harlot," 86.
49. See Bucher, "Meaning of *ZNH*," 41–42.
50. In fact in the epic Gilgamesh's assertion of this right is seen as an abuse of his power, leading to actions by the gods to contain him.
51. See Edwin M. Yamauchi, "Cultic Prostitution: A Case Study in Cultural Diffusion," in *Orient and Occident* (ed. Harry A. Hoffner Jr.; AOAT 22; Neukirchen-Vluyn: Neukirchener Verlag, 1973), 216.
52. See Keefe, *Woman's Body*, 55–56. Note also that Herodotus discussed Babylon and not Canaan.

53. See Randall Bailey, "They're Nothing but Incestuous Bastards," in *Social Location and Biblical Interpretation in the United States* (ed. Fernando F. Segovia and Mary Ann Tolbert; vol. 1 of *Reading from This Place*; Minneapolis: Fortress, 1995), 121–38. Gale Yee makes a similar point about groups defining themselves against a sexually licentious, immoral "other" (*Banished Children*, 89). See also Alice Keefe, "Female Body," 79. Lev 18 is also framed by warnings about not engaging in the degenerate practices of the people who formerly occupied the land.

54. See Keefe for a discussion of this issue (*Woman's Body*, 119). Note that Amos make no mention of widespread apostasy, as one might expect if Baalism was practiced extensively in Israel.

55. Baruch Margalit, "On Canaanite Fertility and Debauchery," in *"He Unfurrowed His Brow and Laughed" Essays in Honour of Professor Nicolas Wyatt* (ed. Wilfred G.E. Watson; AOAT 299; Münster: Ugarit-Verlag, 2007), 177–78, 184.

56. Susan J. Sanders, "Baal au Foudre: The Iconography of Baal of Ugarit," in *He Unfurrowed His Brow and Laughed" Essays in Honour of Professor Nicolas Wyatt* (ed. Wilfred G.E. Watson; AOAT 299; Münster: Ugarit-Verlag, 2007), 263.

57. Keefe, *Woman's Body*, 52. Chapters 2–3 of her book give a detailed analysis of the popularity and problems of the fertility cult hypothesis.

58. See Bucher, "Meaning of *ZNH*," 64–66. She observes that it is only by taking the myth and ritual approach, which assumes myth is derived from ritual, that one can use these texts to support the idea of ritual intercourse.

59. Dirk Kinet, *Ba'al and Jahwe: Ein Beitrag zur Theologie des Hoseabuches* (Europäische Hochschulschriften 23/87; Frankfurt: Peter Lang, 1977), 79–80. See also Tikva Frymer-Kensky, *In the Wake of the Goddesses: Women, Culture, and the Biblical Transformation of Pagan Myth* (New York: Free Press, 1992), 199–202.

60. Alice A. Keefe, "Family Metaphors and Social Conflict in Hosea," in *Writing and Reading War: Rhetoric, Gender, and Ethics in Biblical and Modern Contexts* [ed. Brad E. Kelle and Frank Ritchel Ames; Symposium 42; Atlanta: SBL, 2008], 115.

61. Several commentators have explained the grammatically unusual construction as indicating that Gomer was not a one time offender, but that harlotry was in her nature. See Nwaoru, *Imagery*, 146.

62. Galambush notes that "whoring after" is used as a dead metaphor in extra-prophetic texts (*Jerusalem*, 37).

63. Bird observes that this construction appears only in Hosea and in Ps 73:27 ("Play the Harlot," 81).

64. The fact that Hosea puts more emphasis on the men's actions than on the women's is unusual in most discourse about fornication or adultery in any context. Andersen and Freedman express incredulity at this situation: "It is inconceivable that the women could be exculpated, even if the men were primarily responsible" (*Hosea*, 369). The (male) lovers in ch. 2, as well as those in Ezek 16 and 23, while mentioned, seem to be removed from responsibility, with the blame falling on the wanton women. Such one-sided attention on illicit

relations is widespread, as noted by Angie Hart: "Textual and popular discourses of prostitution are generally negative discourses; not surprisingly, they are mostly discourses about women prostitutes. Precisely because of the hegemony of male/maleness discourses, (male) clientness is often given a privileged back seat, leaving prostitutes up front with only the faintest whiff of an idea that clients exist as well" ("Missing Masculinity? Prostitutes' Clients in Alicante, Spain," in *Dislocating Masculinity: Comparative Ethnographies* [ed. Andrea Cornwall and Nancy Lindisfarne; Male Orders; New York: Routledge, 1994], 48). The fact that in ch. 4 Hosea lets the odor of the clients linger strongly underscores the fact that they are his target audience.

65. For example, JPS translates the verse: "Assuredly, I will speak coaxingly to her and lead her through the wilderness and speak to her tenderly."

66. Gordon and Washington, "Rape as Military Metaphor," 314. They translate 2:17as "There she will submit," rather than "There she will respond/answer."

67. Susan Ackerman, "The Personal is Political: Covenantal and Affectionate Love (אהבה, אהב) in the Hebrew Bible," *VT* 52 (2002): 437–58.

68. Ackerman, "Personal is Political," 447.

69. Buss, *Prophetic Word*, 88. See also Kelle, *Hosea 2*, 67-69; Hendriks, *Juridical Aspects*, 67.

70. MAL A 36: "If a woman is still living in her father's house or her husband made her live apart and her husband has gone off to the fields, without leaving her either oil or wool or clothing or food or anything at all (and) without having even an ear of grain brought to her from the field, that woman shall remain true to her husband for five years...on the advent of the sixth year she may go to live with the man that chooses her; her husband upon coming back may not claim her" (*ANET*, 183).

71. Chapman, *Gendered Language*, 42–43.

72. Simo Parpola and Kazuko Watanabe, *Neo-Assyrian Treaties and Loyalty Oaths* (SAA 2; Helsinki: Helsinki University Press, 1988), 11.

73. Parpola and Watanabe, *Neo-Assyrian Treaties*, 46.

74. Stone, "Lovers and Raisin Cakes," 128–30.

75. A discussion of the concept can be found in Gilmore, "Introduction," 3–4. See also Dianne Bergant, "When honor and shame are gender-based, they have different meanings for men and for women. Honor is seen as a male attribute, and shame as a female aspect. For men, shame is a loss of honor; for women it is the defense of honor. Because such honor is thought to belong to men, a shameless woman dishonors the men of her family" ("'My Beloved is Mine and I am His' (Song 2:16): The Song of Songs and Honor and Shame," *Semeia* 68 [1994]: 33–34).

76. See a similar list of characteristics of an honor/shame model in John K. Chance, "The Anthropology of Honor and Shame: Culture, Values, and Practice," *Semeia* 68 (1994): 142.

77. See Jean G. Peristiany, ed., *Honour and Shame: The Values of Mediterranean Society* (London: Weidenfeld and Nicolson, 1965), especially Julian Pitt-Rivers,

"Honour and Social Status" pp. 19–78 in that volume. Peristiany and Pitt-Rivers introduced the honor/shame model into Mediterranean studies. See also Julian Pitt-Rivers, *The Fate of Shechem, or, The Politics of Sex: Essays in the Anthropology of the Mediterranean* (CSSA 19; Cambridge: Cambridge University Press, 1977), which applies the concept of honor/shame to Gen 34. See further David D. Gilmore, ed., *Honor and Shame and the Unity of the Mediterranean* (Special Publication of the American Anthropological Association 22; Washington, DC: American Anthropological Association, 1987). Sherry Ortner and Harriet Whitehead expand the concept to prestige studies which are applicable to more cultures (Ortner studies Polynesia). They note that prestige systems, which include honor/shame systems, rely considerably on sexual imagery and sex roles. See Sherry B. Ortner and Harriet Whitehead, eds., *Sexual Meanings: The Cultural Construction of Gender and Sexuality* (Cambridge: Cambridge University Press, 1981). That ancient Israel worked under an honor/shame system has become a commonplace assumption in biblical studies. See Victor H. Matthews and Don C. Benjamin, eds., *Honor and Shame in the World of the Bible, Semeia* 68 (1994); Victor H. Matthews, "Honor and Shame in Gender-Related Legal Situations in the Hebrew Bible," in *Gender and Law in the Hebrew Bible and the Ancient Near East* (ed. Victor H. Matthews, Bernard M. Levinson, and Tikva Frymer-Kensky; JSOTSup 262; Sheffield: Sheffield Academic Press, 1998), 97–112; also in the same volume: Tikva Frymer-Kensky, "Virginity in the Bible," 79–96; Miller, "Riposte Form," 113–27. For a focus on the shame aspect, see Lyn M. Bechtel, "Shame as a Sanction of Social Control in Biblical Israel: Judicial, Political, and Social Shaming," *JSOT* 49 (1991): 47–76. Jacqueline E. Lapsley examines both social and personal shame in Ezekiel ("Shame and Self-Knowledge: The Positive Role of Shame in Ezekiel's View of the Moral Self," in *The Book of Ezekiel: Theological and Anthropological Perspectives* [ed. Margaret S. Odell and John T. Strong; SBLSym 9; Atlanta: SBL, 2000], 143–73. While the concept should not be applied in an unreflective manner, several of the biblical narratives and certain ideologies present in the text indicate that at least some of the principles are applicable.

78.   See Stanley Brandes, who discusses aspects of male shame ("Reflections on Honor and Shame in the Mediterranean," in *Honor and Shame and the Unity of the Mediterranean* [ed. David D. Gilmore; Special Publication of the American Anthropological Association 22; Washington, DC: American Anthropological Association, 1987], 123).

79.   David D. Gilmore, "Honor, Honesty, Shame: Male Status in Contemporary Andalusia," in *Honor and Shame and the Unity of the Mediterranean* (ed. David D. Gilmore; Special Publication of the American Anthropological Association 22; Washington, DC: American Anthropological Association, 1987), 101. See also Michael Herzfeld who concentrates on male hospitality, an aspect of honor not usually related to female sexuality. Relationships of dominance and subordination factor significantly into host-guest relations ("'As in Your Own

House': Hospitality, Ethnography, and the Stereotype of Mediterranean Society," in *Honor and Shame and the Unity of the Mediterranean* [ed. David D. Gilmore; Special Publication of the American Anthropological Association 22; Washington, DC: American Anthropological Association, 1987], 75–89).

80. See Gary Stansell, who analyzes several of David's encounters in terms of honor and shame, including those with Jonathon, Nabal and Abigail, Absalom, Michal, and Amnon's rape of Tamar ("Honor and Shame in the David Narratives," *Semeia* 68 [1994]: 55–79). Saul M. Olyan examines David's more political encounters, with a focus on honor and shame in terms of covenant expectations, as also seen in ANE suzerainty treaties and records ("Honor, Shame, and Covenant Relations in Ancient Israel and Its Environment," *JBL* 115 [1996]: 201–18).

81. Galambush, *Jerusalem*, 34. That the shame of the cuckolded husband, in this case the man Hosea, has occurred to readers is expressed in the poem cited above by E. H. Plumptre: "Thy sin hath laid my honour in the dust. Men throw the blame on me, they mock my grief; They wondered at my choice, and whispered words—'The prophet woo the harlot!'—told their scorn. They saw in me the poor, weak victim-fool" (*Lazarus*, 86).

82. David Gilmore cites a case in which the wife of a childless couple ran off with another man. Villagers suspected that the husband was impotent, so in this case the blame and shame fell on the husband rather than on the wife ("Honor, Honesty, Shame," 96–97). Lindisfarne has observed that Durrani men in Afghanistan whose daughters elope or who are cuckolded are often labeled as dishonorable or feminized as "soft" or "weak" ("Variant Masculinities, Variant Virginities: Rethinking Honor and Shame," in *Dislocating Masculinities* [ed. Andrea Cornwall and Nancy Lindisfarne; Male Order; London, New York: Routledge, 1994], 85).

83. See Gilmore, *Honor and Shame*, 4–5; Stone, *Sex, Honor, and Power*, 48. The challenge to the man's protection and provision do not have to be true to negatively affect his social status as a man. See Lindisfarne, "Variant Masculinities," 87.

84. Parpola and Watanabe, *Neo-Assyrian Treaties*, 46.

85. Joseph A. Fitzmyer, *The Aramaic Inscriptions of Sefire* (Rev. ed.; BibOr 19/A; Rome: Pontifical Bible Institute, 1995), 47.

86. I will discuss this further in ch. 5.

87. זרע is the most common way to discuss progeny in the biblical texts. See, *e.g.*, Gen 12:7, Gen 35:12, Gen 38:9, 2 Sam 7:12. It was also used to refer to semen, see, *e.g.*, Lev 15:16. Likewise treaty curses often include the threat to destroy the king's seed from the land, meaning his progeny. See Parpola and Watanabe, *Neo-Assyrian Treaties*, 46, 51.

88. This imagery is discussed thoroughly by Carol Delaney, "Seeds of Honor, Fields of Shame," in *Honor and Shame and the Unity of the Mediterranean* (ed. David D. Gilmore; Special Publication of the American Anthropological

Association 22; Washington, DC: American Anthropological Association, 1987), 35-48.

89. For procreation as expected evidence of virility see Gilmore, "Honor, Honesty, Shame," 96; Gilmore, *Honor and Shame*, 10; Lindisfarne, "Variant Masculinities," 88.

90. In a combination of these two features of paternity, Brandes notes that in the town of Monteros in Spain, people will not say that a baby looks like its mother, which might raise the question of its paternity. Instead they will nearly always say that it looks like its legal father (*Metaphors of Masculinity*, 89).

91. Cornwall and Lindisfarne note that this sort of backhanded power has not been sufficiently studied from the viewpoint of the subordinate: "The hidden transcripts of subordinates [the subordinate response to hegemonic masculinity] are poorly documented....More dramatically, they may choose to engage in sexual liaisons which may diminish publicly men's masculine credentials" (Cornwall and Lindisfarne, "Dislocating Masculinity," 25).

92. Maureen J. Giovannini described how a six-year old boy she interviewed did not want a baby sister, because he and his brothers would have to keep her from being called a whore, which would make people laugh at them, whereas if they had a brother, they could call other people's sisters whores ("Female Chastity Codes in the Circum-Mediterranean: Comparative Perspectives," in *Honor and Shame and the Unity of the Mediterranean* [ed. David D. Gilmore; Special Publication of the American Anthropological Association 22; Washington, DC: American Anthropological Association, 1987], 67). That a similar sensibility operated in ancient Israel may be indicated by Gen 34:31, in which Dinah's brothers justify their massacre of the Shechemites saying: "Shall our sister be treated like a whore?"

93. Brandes, *Metaphors of Masculinity*, 88.

94. The effect of the punishment on the perception of the husband's masculinity is undercut, however, by the desire to reconcile expressed in the second half of ch. 2 and in ch. 3. I will discuss the implications of these actions below in ch. 5.

95. Weems, "Gomer," 97.

96. Gale A. Yee, "The Book of Hosea," *NIB* 7: 208.

97. Stone, *Sex, Honor, and Power*, 121.

98. Stone, *Sex, Honor, and Power*, 121. See also Ken Stone, *Practicing Safer Texts* (New York: T&T Clark/Continnum, 2005), 71–72.

99. Stone, *Sex, Honor, and Power*, 121–22.

100. The use of literature from Mesopotamia and other nearby regions in the interpretation of biblical texts has become increasingly common. One of the seminal works is Delbert Hillers, *Treaty-Curses and the Old Testament Prophets* (BibOr 16; Rome: Pontifical Bible Institute, 1964). He examines several Assyrian treaties from the 9th through the 7th c. B.C.E. and compares them to the curse lists in Deut 28 and Lev 26, as well as to the threats in the prophetic literature. Wilfred G. E. Watson has used Akkadian incantations to illuminate several biblical passages including Hosea 13:12 ("Reflexes of Akkadian

Incantations in Hosea," *VT* 34 [1984]: 242–47). He notes the high number of similes and simile clusters in the two literatures, as well as common images. Meir Malul discusses proper and improper use of ANE materials for comparative work in biblical studies (*The Comparative Method in Ancient Near Eastern and Biblical Legal Studies* [AOAT 227; Neukirchen-Vluyn: Neukirchener Verlag, 1990]). Some factors that require consideration are the nature of the connection: written or social context/tradition or both; the type of connection: direct (dependence of one source on another), mediated (borrowed from an intermediate source), common source, or common tradition, and whether similarity is a result of dependence or coincidence. I propose that the area under Assyrian domination shared a common image base, because of the dominance of Assyria, its repeated use of particular imagery in treaties with the nations under its control, and the similarity of imagery found in many of the biblical texts. This does not require that the biblical material is dependent on the Assyrian material, but rather suggests that the imagery could be mutually understood and was relatively common in the region.

101.   Robert D. Biggs, *ŠÀ.ZI.GA: Ancient Mesopotamian Potency Incantations* (TCS 2; Locust Valley, NY: J. J. Augustin, 1967). The *ŠÀ.ZI.GA* texts probably were standardized in the 14th c. B.C.E., as shown by texts found at Boghazköy, but the most of the texts in this volume come from the 7th c. B.C.E.

102.   Marvin Chaney, of San Francisco Theological Seminary, introduced me to the relevance of *ŠÀ.ZI.GA* literature to the text at hand in a seminar on Hosea.

103.   Bird, "Play the Harlot," nn. 33 and 50.

104.   Bucher analyzes the uses of זנה with male subjects in ch. 4, but immediately puts them into the realm of cultic apostasy, through comparison with the use of the hiphil in non-Hosean passages (Exod 24:16, 2 Chr 21:11, 13). The hiphil also occurs in Lev 19:29 when fathers are told not to make their daughters fornicate ("Meaning of *ZNH*," 146). She does not examine the cases after ch 4. John J. Schmitt highlights the multiple instances of זנה with a male subject, but his main point is that Israel always takes the masculine gender ("The Gender of Ancient Israel," *JSOT* 26 [1983], 121).

105.   A dead metaphor is one that ceases to be considered a metaphor in typical speech, such as the leg of a table.

106.   JPS translates the verb here and 4:18 as to drink, but as fornicate in 5:3. I translate זנה as fornicate to emphasize the illicit nature of the sexual activity. While not all male extra-marital activity may have been considered illicit, that with women under the supervision of other men would have been. I further understand the hiphil to refer to male role in fornication.

107.   Parpola and Watanabe, *Neo-Assyrian Treaties*, 12.

108.   Parpola and Watanabe, *Neo-Assyrian Treaties*, 46.

109.   Parpola and Watanabe, *Neo-Assyrian Treaties*, 51.

110.   Landy links sexual and sacred boundaries, interpreting the audience as the priests, who in this verse are "threatened with unremitting frustration" (*Hosea*, 58–59).

111.   Chapman, *Gendered Language*, 88, 110.

112.   Note that this verse uses both hiphil perfect and infinitive absolute forms.

113.   The translation of this phrase is far from certain, containing two hapex legomena, but for my purposes it is enough to get the idea that something is shameful about their love.

114.   Bird remarks that this preposition heightens the sexual connotations of the phrase ("Play the Harlot," 84).

115.   The other occasion in which זנה is associated with מעל is in Ezek 6:9 which reads, in part: את־לבם הזונה אשר־סר מעלי ואת עיניהם הזנות אחרי גלוליהם [their fornicating heart which turns from upon me and their eyes fornicating after their idols]. In this case, however, the subject is not directly fornicating from over God, but the heart is turning from upon God.

116.   Keefe understands the references to male fornication as a symbol of the economic misdeeds of the elite, including agricultural intensification and cash cropping, which might be linked to a lack of food for the common people ("Family Metaphors," 122).

117.   There is some debate about whether פרד indicates utilizing a prostitute's services, since the verb most naturally means "divide." Keefe suggests that "dividing" with the prostitutes in parallel with sacrificing with the holy women, may indicate that the זנות here are figures for the (male) priests, who have, in effect, prostituted the cult to the interests of the state (*Woman's Body*, 101–2). This is in opposition to most commentators, who assume the pairing means that the קדשות are prostitutes. Bucher agrees that זנות may refer to apostates rather than cult prostitutes, and that no literal sexual activities are being described ("Meaning of *ZNH*," 150–51). Galambush notes that פרד has no sexual connotations elsewhere (Gen 10:5, 25:23, Prob 18:1; 19:2, 2 Sam 1:23) but refers to fractures in familial or political relations, and in this case "splitting off with prostitutes" may refer to domestic political fracturing (*Jerusalem*, 50–51, n. 76).

118.   Some commentators see a situation in which the whore is paying her clients, as pictured in Ezek 16:33–34 (Wolff, *Hosea*, 143; Mays, *Hosea*, 121; Marvin A. Sweeney, *The Twelve Prophets* [Berit Olam 1; Collegeville, MN: Liturgical Press, 2000], 90). Macintosh sees it as an adulterous relationship, with Ephraim as the wife (*Hosea*, 218). The context more easily supports a male subject, however, as male clients soliciting services (cf. Eidevall, *Grapes in the Desert*, 135–36; Andersen and Freedman, *Hosea*, 505).

119.   I will return to this issue in ch. 5.

120.   A few commentators emend this to a form of אנף "to burn" in the sense of consuming rage. See, *e.g.*, Shalom M. Paul, "The Image of the Oven and the Cake in Hosea VII 4–10," *VT* 18 (1968): 115. Rudolph emends similarly, but more severely to "Ihr Herz hält ihren Zorn zurück"[Their heart repressed their rage] (*Hosea*, 146).

121.   Hendriks sees Hosea as an innovator in the figurative use of נאף. He notes that the context clearly suggests the word is a figure for political, not cultic nor marital situations ("Juridical Aspects," 89).

122.   The verb נאף occurs in the HB 14 times in a masculine form, 3 times in the infinitive absolute in a masculine context, and 13 times in a feminine form. Outside the prophetic literature נאף is used only twice in a feminine form, once in Lev 20:10, a verse in which the root appears 4 times: twice in a masculine finite form discussing the crime of adultery, and twice in the participial form, calling for the punishment of both the male and female parties to the crime. The other case is Prov 30:20, where a piel participle is used to describe the ways of an adulteress. Within the prophets the feminine form occurs 11 times. Seven of these are clearly figurative (Jer 3:8, 3:9, Ezek 16:32, 23:37 [2x], 23:45 [2x]). Hos 3:1 uses a piel participle to describe the woman Hosea is supposed to marry, which is probably figurative as a whole image, although it is developed as if it were literal. Ezek 16:38 also occurs within a larger figurative context describing the adulteries of Jerusalem, but the verse itself states that the woman Jerusalem will receive the punishment of adulterous women. The final two instances occur in Hos 4:13–14, which while in a context in which most if not all of the sexual imagery is figurative, does not have an immediate figurative reference. In the masculine form the verb occurs 9 times in a literal context (Exod 20:14, Lev 20:10 [3x], Deut 5:18, Job 24:15, Prov 6:32, Isa 57:3, and Mal 3:5) and 5 times in what are probably figurative contexts (Jer 5:7, 9:1, 23:10, 29:23, Hos 7:4), in which adultery seems to be a symbol for lying and deception in general, and perhaps also of apostasy.

123.   Andersen and Freedman also equate adultery with treachery (*Hosea*, 455).

124.   NRSV; See also Mays, *Hosea*, 73; Wolff, *Hosea*, 84; Sweeney, *Twelve Prophets*, 48; Macintosh acknowledges that others have seen these as phallic symbols, but finds this interpretation unlikely (*Hosea*, 151–52). Landy likewise sees these as idols even though he interprets nearly everything else with sexual connotations (*Hosea*, 61). Anderson and Freedman mention the possibility, but then equate this with either phallic shaped idols or with a derogatory reference to the idols (*Hosea*, 366).

125.   Followers of this view include JPS; Bird, "Play the Harlot," 83; H.L. Ginsberg, "Lexigraphical Notes," in *Hebräische Wortforschung* (ed. James Barr; VTSup 16; Leiden: Brill, 1967), 74. Note also the line from the Akkadian potency incantation no. 22, line 28: "May the penis of NN son of NN be a stick of *martû*-wood!"

126.   Fitting in with the masculine context of this oracle, רוח is masculine here, a less common, but not unique occurrence.

127.   Brandes observes that in Andalusia the male genitals are referred to as the source of the will. If a man does something because he wants to, and does not really care what other people (especially his wife) think, he says he is doing it "because it comes to me from the balls" or "because it comes out of my prick" (*Metaphors of Masculinity*, 92). A related expression with more pejorative

connotations is present in American slang. "Thinking with one's dick" indicates that lust is overriding rational thought, and often leads the man into undesirable situations.

128. Translation by G. R. Driver, *Canaanite Myths and Legends* (OTS 3; Edinburgh: T & T Clark, 1956), 123. Smith translates the phrase as "Your staff is going down; weakened is the rod of your hand" ("'Heel' and 'Thigh,'" 467). The wives, burning with passion, have to repeat this refrain three times before El can come over to kiss and embrace them.

129. Multiple connotations of the term are evident in Gen 49:3: ראובן בכרי אתה כחי וראשית אוני יתר שאת ויתר עז [Reuben you are my first born, my strength and the beginning of my vigor, exceeding in rank and exceeding in strength]. See also Deut 21:17 and Ps 78:51.

130. Eilberg-Schwarz, *God's Phallus*, 156. He also asserts that in the Genesis version, Jacob's "hip" injury is really a genital injury, thus making Jacob submit his potency to God's power. Whether this is correct is not relevant here, as the link between "manhood" and hubris does not require actual anatomical verification. With regard to the Hosea version, he writes: "Although Hosea does not explicitly allude to Jacob's injury, Jacob's weeping may be an oblique reference to that event. In his manhood, he has been made to cry."

131. Robert B. Coote asserts that אוֹן and אָוֶן meaning "iniquity," cf. 12:12, were "of course" pronounced identically in northern Israel, though without providing evidence. Thus the mention of the former in this verse brings up the connotations of the latter ("Hosea 12," *VT* 21 [1971]: 393). While this may be the case, and would add more support to my interpretation, the linkage and wordplay between אוֹן and עוֹן, supplied through the verb מצא, already links virility and iniquity. Buss also notes the play between the two meanings of אוֹן and connects the weeping of Jacob's struggle in 12:5 with the weeping associated with the cult center Bethel/Beth-awen (*Prophetic Word*, 112).

132. In Hos 7, a chapter full of potency images the word לב appears several times (2, 6, 11).

133. Jan Joosten notes that rabbinic circles and Aquila, Theodition, and Symmachus translate על as "yoke," and that word used for this in the targumic translations paraphrases this מרועא as "oppression, servitude" ("Targumic Aramaic מְרוֹעָא – 'Oppression' [Isa. LXVII 2, Hos. XI 7, Mic. VI 3]," *VT* 51 [2001]: 552).

134. For an exploration of several of these images in the biblical texts, see Ken Stone, *Practicing Safer Texts: Food, Sex and Bible in Queer Perspective* (New York: T&T Clark, 2005).

135. Stone develops this connection ("Lovers and Raisin Cakes"). See above discussion under Female Imagery-Provisioning.

136. J. F. Ross, "Bread," *IDB* 1:462.

137. KB notes that the verb אפה is mostly used for men, and lists only one instance of female bakers אפות in 1 Sam 8:13.

138. A very clear example of the symbolization of sexual superiority as political superiority is given by Loizos in his study of a Greek village: "The Old Man

should have fucked his two lads, and *then* they would have listened to him."
[Village saying describing a political sect leader whose adjutants rebelled.]
Loizos explains: "It appears from this that to discipline is to feminize; to have
penetrative sex with someone is to discipline him, and thus to feminize him"
("Broken Mirrors," 72).

139.   Shalom M. Paul notes that the root בלל is used in the qal form to describe the
process of mixing sacrificial cakes, *e.g.*, in Exod 29:2; Lev 2:5; Num 7:13. He
suggests it may be related to the Akkadian cognate for "kneading," *balālu*
("Image of the Oven," 117).

140.   Paul, "Image of the Oven," 118. See Hayim Tadmor, "The Campaigns of
Sargon II of Assur: A Chronological-Historical Study," *JCS* 12 (1958): 34: "The
Assyrians and the Egyptians I mingled together and made them trade with each
other."

141.   Macintosh, *Hosea*, 268; Mays, *Hosea*, 108; Rudolph, *Hosea*, 153.

142.   While Emmanuel O. Nwaoru does not discuss the sexual imagery in this
chapter, his assessment of the imagery used here is telling: "The prophet's
verdict is that Ephraim is totally worthless in his international contacts, for his
failed political outing results in a total *emasculation* [emphasis added] as
expressed in the subsequent verbal metaphors" ("The Role of Images in the
Literary Structure of Hosea VII 8 –VIII 14," *VT* 54 [2004]: 219).

143.   Nwaoru notes that the imagery recurs in 8:8 where Israel is נבלע "swallowed
up" ("Role of Images," 221).

144.   Paul, "Image of the Oven," 119. The meaning of mold is clearly intended
because the story describes the level of decay a cake of bread shows after a
particular number of days.

145.   Andersen and Freedman, *Hosea*, 467; Eidevall, *Grapes in the Desert*, 117.

146.   Choon Leong Seow notes that motifs from wisdom literature, particularly
relating to the foolish person, show up several times in Hosea, including this
verse ("Hosea 14:10 and the Foolish People Motif," *CBQ* 44 [1982]: 212–24).

147.   After all, not all old men are wise. Rivkah Harris, *Gender and Aging in
Mesopotamia: The Gilgamesh Epic and Other Ancient Literature* (Norman: University
of Oklahoma Press, 2000): 80. She also observes that the older gods in *Enuma
Elish* are portrayed as ineffectual, weak, depressed, and uninvolved, while the
younger gods take care of matters (82). Note also that Solomon is shown as
wise in his prime years, but "in Solomon's old age, his wives turned away his
heart after other gods" (1Kgs 11:4). See also Sirach 47:14a: "How wise you
were when you were young," in contrast to how Solomon went astray in his old
age.

148.   Harry A. Hoffner Jr. observes that since "the ancients" assessed masculinity
through prowess in battle and the ability to sire children, the image fields often
overlapped, so that, in particular, weapons took on sexual symbolism
("Symbols of Masculinity and Femininity: Their Use in Ancient Near Eastern
Sympathetic Magic Rituals," *JBL* 85 [1966]: 327). While the construction of
masculinity in Israel and the ANE is more complex than this, these two factors

are certainly prominent. Gordon and Washington also link military and sexual imagery, but concentrate on the representation of military defeat and violence as sexual violence ("Rape as Military Metaphor," 313).

149.   See Chapman for several plates of Assyrian palace reliefs showing the contrast between the victors' drawn bows and the losers' abandoned or surrendered bows (*Gendered Language*, 173–79).

150.   Earlier Jonathon had given David his cloak, tunic, sword, bow, and belt to ratify his pact with him (1 Sam 18:4), apparently a sign of total commitment.

151.   Chapman, *Gendered Language*, 176.

152.   Fitzmyer, *Aramaic Inscriptions*, 47.

153.   Parpola and Watanabe, *Neo-Assyrian Treaties*, 12. This treaty seems to involve the same person as Sefire treaty, as Mati'ilu and Mati'el are equivalent. The mysterious king of KTK has not been identified, however, so one cannot say that these are versions of the same treaty. It does show, however, that one would not have to know Akkadian to become familiar with the language and imagery of the treaty curses. For reference, Aššur-nerari V was in power 754– 745 B.C.E.

154.   Note that crouching puts the man in a submissive, feminized position. An idea also observed by Kelle, "Wartime Rhetoric," 105 and Fontaine, "'Be Men, O Philistines!'" 65–66.

155.   Parpola and Watanabe, *Neo-Assyrian Treaties*, 23.

156.   Parpola and Watanabe, *Neo-Assyrian Treaties*, 27. Note here the additional humiliation that the man will not be able to protect his possessions. In fact, the line is preceded by this curse: "May Melqarth and Eshmun deliver your land to destruction and your people to deportation; may they [uproot] you from your land and take away the food from your mouth, the clothes from your body, and the oil for your anointing." We have here the fuller spectrum of the inability to protect and provision the people or himself.

157.   Parpola and Watanabe, *Neo-Assyrian Treaties*, 48.

158.   Frank Moore Cross, *Canaanite Myth and Hebrew Epic* (Cambridge, Mass.: Harvard University Press, 1973), 35.

159.   Biggs, *ŠÀ.ZI.GA*, 19.

160.   Biggs, *ŠÀ.ZI.GA*, 37.

161.   Hoffner, "Symbols of Masculinity," 331.

162.   Wolff, *Hosea*, 108; Landy, *Hosea*, 99; Macintosh, with the meaning of "higher things" rather than YHWH specifically (*Hosea*, 284).

163.   For the former: Sweeney, *Twelve Prophets*, 83; Andersen and Freedman, *Hosea*, 477; for the latter: Beeby, *Grace Abounding*, 92; Harper, *Amos and Hosea*, 307; BHS.

164.   Mays, *Hosea*, 110; Rudolph, *Hosea*, 151; Ibn Ezra, with the nuance "to no purpose" (Abe Lipshitz, *The Commentary of Rabbi Abraham Ibn Ezra on Hosea* [New York: Sepher-Hermon, 1988], 75).

165.   עָל is a rare term. A similar construction occurs in 2 Sam 23:1: וּנְאֻם הַגֶּבֶר הֻקַם עָל [The utterance of the man who has been raised up]. Of course, this

interpretation is also controversial. 4Qsam[a] reads "God raised up." The word is usually understood as a noun, rather than an objectless preposition. The other occasions עָל is used, it occurs with the inseparable preposition as מֵעַל (*e.g.*, Gen 49:25).

166. Chapman (*Gendered Language*, 54) notes that Harold Dressler rejects the idea that the bow is a phallic symbol ("Is the Bow of Aqhat a Symbol of Virility?" *UF* 7[1975]: 217–25). He does admit that it is a symbol of masculinity, but because there is no evidence of castration as a condition of defeat, he argues that bow breaking does not symbolize emasculation. Chapman (and Hoffner and I) examines the metaphorical dimensions of these images, however, and while certain aspects correspond with reality, other aspects, as metaphors do, create extensions and juxtapositions.

167. See Prov 6:20–35.

168. In ch. 5 I will discuss some possible subversions of the power structure.

169. Landy, "Fantasy," 155.

170. As Gilmore observes: "As a result of the uncertainty of masculinity, men often feel themselves under continual pressure to avoid appearing feminine in speech, dress, comportment, or affect" (*Honor and Shame*, 9).

171. The polyvalent effect of feminization may partly account for the laws against sex between males in Lev 18:22 and 20:13. Saul M. Olyan's careful study of the texts examined their position in the holiness code, and compared the attitudes towards male-male sex in both ANE and classical sources. He observes that the subject of the law is the insertive, rather than the receptive partner. He also suspects that at an earlier stage in the development of the laws, only the insertive partner was punished, perhaps for assault or for feminizing the receptive partner. In their final form, as redacted by H, however, both parties are punished, probably out of a concern for mixing two defiling agents—semen and excrement ("'And with a Male You Shall Not Lie the Lying Down of a Woman': On the Meaning and Significance of Leviticus 18:22 and 20:13," in *Que(e)rying Religion: A Critical Anthology* (ed. Gary David Comstock and Susan E. Henking; New York: Continuum, 1997], 398–414); repr. from *JHS* 5 [1994]).

172. Yee, *Banished Children*, 98, emphasis original.

173. Yee, *Banished Children*, 99.

174. Claudia D. Bergmann examines several biblical, Hittite, Assyrian and Greek texts in which soldiers are cast as women. The assumption is usually that women are quite, passive, and weak ("'We Have Seen the Enemy, and He is Only a "She"': The Portrayal of Warriors as Women," in *Writing and Reading War: Rhetoric, Gender, and Ethics in Biblical and Modern Contexts* [ed. Brad E. Kelle and Frank Ritchel Ames; Symposium 42; Atlanta: SBL, 2008], 129–142).

175. Parpola and Watanabe, *Neo-Assyrian Treaties*, 56. Spindles are instruments used to signify women in many Akkadian texts, as bows often symbolize men. The transformation of men into women (and vice versa) is especially attributed to Inanna, a goddess associated with love and war. From the *Inninšagurra Hymn*: "To turn a man into a woman and a woman into a man are yours, Inanna"

(Kathleen McCaffrey, "Reconsidering Gender Ambiguity in Mesopotamia: Is a Beard just a Beard?" in *Sex and Gender in the Ancient Near East* (ed. Simo Parpola and R.M. Whiting; Helsinki: The Neo-Assyrian Text Corpus Project, 2002), 380.

176. Parpola and Watanabe, *Neo-Assyrian Treaties*, 12.

177. Ellen Goldstein notes that portraying men as sexually promiscuous women is particularly detrimental to their social status (Elizabeth W. Goldstein, "Genealogy, Gynecology, and Gender: The Priestly Writer's Portrait of a Woman," in *Embroidered Garments: Priests and Gender in Biblical Israel* (Deborah W. Rooke, ed.; Sheffield: Sheffield Phoenix, 2009), 82.

178. I prefer not to use the term emasculate in this case, because I am not suggesting a complete castration. Rather the text whittles away at the components of the audience's masculinity. In addition, I want to make a distinction between feminization and a reduction in masculinity.

179. I am referring here specifically to the figure of the woman in Hosea. Women in other biblical texts show greater degrees of positively portrayed activity.

4 Predications of Non-Gender-Based Imagery

1. The categories I employ are mostly a matter of convenience and do not have fixed boundaries. Some of them overlap considerably, and many of the images I discuss could fit into more than one. To avoid excessive repetition I will generally treat them in only one category. The most important caveat is that by separating what I call gender imagery and other imagery into two separate chapters, I do not mean to imply that gender is not important in the latter categories. Particularly in the parent-child imagery gender has been a significant subject of discussion. The governing metaphor, however, comes from a different image base.

2. The human-as-parent language is usually more literal, although it also contains figurative elements.

3. Most commentators who care to take a position on the issue of the legitimacy of the children claim that all three were fathered by Hosea. See Wolff, *Hosea*, 17, 20; Macintosh, *Hosea*, 13–14, 27; Andersen and Freedman, *Hosea*, 172, 187.

4. Most commentators do not find the sex of the child relevant (*e.g.*, Andersen and Freedman, *Hosea*, 127), except for possibly supporting the idea that the narrative preserves real events (*e.g.*, Wolff, *Hosea*, 27), but ibn Ezra thought that the female child indicated the weakness of the Israelite kings after Jehu (Lipschitz, *Ibn Ezra*, 23).

5. See Andersen and Freedman, *Hosea*, 168; Mays, *Hosea*, 26; Sweeney, *Twelve Prophets*, 15. Wolff, who proposes that the nature of Gomer's harlotry is that she participated in the so-called virgin bridal rites at the temple of Baal, suggests that her children were called children of harlotries because they owe their existence to a pagan god (*Hosea*, 15). This argument seems a bit strange,

however, because it implies that the rites really did lead to fertility, which seems to contradict Hosea's general argument.

6. Andersen and Freedman see the ריב that the children are asked to bring as "a dialogue going on within the covenant community" (*Hosea*, 219).

7. Mays, *Hosea*, 37; Laurie Braaten, "Parent-Child Imagery in Hosea" (Ph.D. diss., Boston University, 1987), 282; Harper, *Hosea*, 226.

8. *E.g.*, Wolff suggests perhaps youth vs. elders, morally superior vs. corrupt, or new repentance vs. "complacent transgression" (*Hosea*, 33).

9. For a more detailed discussion of the issue, see Kelle, who argues that the mother represents the capital city Samaria and stands for the royal house, whereas the children are the non-ruling inhabitants of Samaria and those Israelites living outside Samaria (*Hosea* 2, 231). Similarly, Marvin Chaney suggests that the children may be outlying rural/ agricultural villages, satellites of the mother Samaria (personal communication). Support for the idea that the children are the people of the mother city can be found in Jer 50:11–16, which inveighs against the inhabitants of Babylon who have plundered Judah. In particular, v. 12 reads: "Your mother will be very shamed, the one who bore you will be disgraced. She will be last of the nations, a wilderness, a dry land a desert." V. 15: "Raise a shout against her all around. She has surrendered, her bulwarks have fallen, her walls are thrown down."

10. Landy, *Hosea*, 33.

11. Macintosh, *Hosea*, 42. For those who understand ריב as a technical legal term, the children are asked to intervene in the divorce proceedings between their mother and her husband. See Sweeney, *Twelve Prophets*, 29.

12. Braaten, "Parent-Child Imagery," 8.

13. Braaten, "Parent-Child Imagery," 18–19.

14. Braaten, "Parent-Child Imagery," 12, 244–45. Braaten argues that 2:1–3 is a later addition to the text, and thus side-steps the problem that the children seem to be legitimated there without a remarriage or payment of a bridewealth (46–49). The legitimation theme is continued by the redactor, however, and even emphasized further, because Not-My-People is not only called My-People, but is more actively called Children of the Living God (245).

15. Braaten, "Parent-Child Imagery," 268–69.

16. Braaten, "Parent-Child Imagery," 278.

17. See Macintosh, *Hosea*, 438; Eidevall, *Grapes in the Desert*, 168; Mays, *Hosea*, 153; Sweeney, *Twelve Prophets*, 113; Beeby, *Grace Abounding*, 141. Wolff does not explicitly say it is adoption language, focusing instead on the idea of election, but he does assiduously argue against any kind of procreative relationship (*Hosea*, 198). Nwaoru also prefers election language (*Imagery*, 148). Andersen and Freedman note similarities to adoption language (observing, however, that נער commonly refers to a servant), but think the relationship has more quasi-political connotations (*Hosea*, 576). I do not find these concepts mutually exclusive.

18. Braaten, "Parent-Child Imagery," 11. Cf. Janet L. R. Melnyk, "When Israel Was a Child," in *History and Interpretation* (ed. M. Patrick Graham, William P. Brown, and Jeffrey K. Kuan; JSOTSup 173; Sheffield: Sheffield Academic Press, 1993), 245–59.

19. Braaten, "Parent-Child Imagery," 296.

20. Braaten, "Parent-child Imagery," 318–27.

21. For this translation, see, among others, Mays, *Hosea*, 154; Wolff, *Hosea*, 199.

22. *E.g.,* Andersen and Freedman, *Hosea*, 579; Eidevall, *Grapes in the Desert*, 171. Landy (*Hosea*, 137–38) and Sweeney (*Twelve Prophets*, 114) do not make a strong distinction between teaching to walk or guiding, suggesting that both indicate a parent's care of a child. Macintosh proposes that the root is related to an Arabic cognate with a more general sense of rearing children (*Hosea*, 442).

23. Eidevall thinks the metaphor changes from parent-child in v. 1 to that of a shepherd in v. 3, who guides the sheep, then carries a lamb in his arms (*Grapes in the Desert*, 171). No animals are actually mentioned in that verse, however, and although Hosea often switches quickly from one metaphor to the next, a shepherd metaphor in this verse would be particularly poorly defined.

24. Sweeney provides one of the most interesting solutions, translating חבל from its meaning of "labor pains": "with human labor pains I drew them out" (*Twelve Prophets*, 114). The "bonds of love" are then parental bonds. Duane Andre Smith, following Augustine, who mentions a Punic cognate, thinks אדם has a prothetic א and is thus related to דם. He translates the phrase "bonds of blood," or kinship ties ("Kinship and Covenant in Hosea 11:1–4," *HBT* 16 [1994]: 47).

25. Macintosh, *Hosea*, 447; Andersen and Freedman, *Hosea*, 581; Eidevall, *Grapes in the Desert*, 173; NRSV.

26. Mays, *Hosea*, 154–55; Wolff, *Hosea*, 199; Sweeney, *Twelve Prophets*, 114; Gale A. Yee, "Hosea," in *The Women's Bible Commentary* (exp. ed.; ed. Carol A. Newsom and Sharon H. Ringe; Louisville: Westminster John Knox, 1998), 213; Jopie Siebert-Hommes, "'With Bands of Love': Hosea 11 as Recapitulation of the Basic Themes in the Book of Hosea," in *Unless some one guide me...*(ed. J. W. Dyk et al.; ACEBTSup 2; Maastricht: Shaker, 2001), 169; Nwaoru, *Imagery*, 149.

27. An objection to the infant translation, in addition to requiring repointing, is that switch between singular and plural forms does not seem to make much sense. The "lifters" are plural, the infant is singular, the cheeks belong to "them" and "I" bent down [or gently—another ambiguity in the translation] to feed. Macintosh thinks that one would expect a singular parent to lift a singular child, and that it is odd that one would lift an infant to a cheek anyway, rather than a breast (*Hosea*, 447). I do not see that the singular/plural problem is solved with the yoke translation. Having observed parents, I also do not find it odd that mothers or fathers would lift a baby to their cheeks. Another objection is that the נער of v. 1 is already old enough to walk, certainly no longer called a nursling (see Eberhard Bons, "Zwei überlegungen zum Verständnis von Hosea XI," *VT* 45 [1995]: 286). The age of weaning could be two or three years,

however, well beyond the time a child learned to walk. An objection to the yoke translation is that yokes do not sit on cheeks, and thus requires an understanding that some sort of bridle is associated with the yoke. A more important objection is that the verse would read more logically, "I was for them like ones who lift a yoke upon their cheeks," which sounds more like putting a yoke on than taking it off. JPS also understands the verse this way, translating: "I seemed to them as one who imposed a yoke on their jaws, though I was offering them food." That translation offers its own problems.

28. Smith follows neither of the common interpretations, although he takes a position similar to the parent-child metaphor. He understands the chapter in terms of kinship language, but translates על as "yoke." This does not refer to cattle imagery, however, but should be seen in terms of binding and oath language related to covenant terminology, as something a superior imposes on an inferior ("Kinship and Covenant," 45–46).

29. The imagery in 11:10 will be discussed further below, as it is employs animal imagery, with the parent lion calling the bird children home from Egypt and Assyria, not quite the relationship pictured in the first part of the chapter.

30. While he may become the good farmer, the general consensus is that whatever the final translation, YHWH is showing tender care. Those who admit to sitting on the fence include Landy, *Hosea*, 139; Beeby, *Grace Abounding*, 143; Linzy Howard Hill Jr., "Hosea 11: Yahweh's Persistant Love," *SwJT* 36 (1993): 28. There is some debate about whether the parent imagery is specifically of a father, or if the imagery is more descriptive of a mother. I will consider this issue in ch. 5.

31. Bruce K. Waltke and M. O'Connor, *An Introduction to Biblical Hebrew Syntax* (Winona Lake, IN: Eisenbrauns, 1990), 221. A. E. Cowley, *Gesenius' Hebrew Grammar* (2d English ed.; ed. and enl. by E. Kautzsch; Oxford: Oxford University Press, 1910), 377. See Gen 6:13. Cf. Kelle, *Hosea 2*, 160. See also Judg 9:21; 1 Sam 21:11; Jer 35:11; 37:11; 41:9; 50:16.

32. The number switches between the singular child in 11:1 and the multiple children in 11:2.

33. Melnyk suggests that the punishment in this chapter could extend to slavery in Egypt and Assyria, as slavery was also a punishment for a rebellious adoptee ("When Israel Was a Child," 257).

34. Braaten makes this point ("Parent-Child Imagery," 309), which is also noted by Eidevall (*Grapes in the Desert*, 154).

35. Some commentators suggest that this is divorce language (*e.g.,* Macintosh, *Hosea*, 377; Sweeney, *Twelve Prophets*, 101), but marriage imagery does not occur elsewhere outside of chs. 1–3, whereas there are several scattered references to parent-child relationships. Norbert Lohfink sees political language here, with the "House of YHWH" analogous to the House of Omri as a way to speak of the monarchy ("Hate and Love in Osee 9,15," *CBQ* 25 [1963]: 417). While I think that the parent-child imagery is used toward political ends, direct political language here seems somewhat awkward.

36. The second half translates literally "at the breaking place of sons."

37. Macintosh thinks that Ephraim is portrayed as the mother here, not the son (*Hosea*, 543).

38. See Isa 13:8; Isa 26:17–18; Jer 13:21; Jer 22:23; Jer 49:24. When the metaphor is used for men, the implication is usually that the men are greatly afraid, rather than in great pain. This may reflect a male perception of the birthing process. When used of cities (personified as women), it sometimes refers to distress and sometimes to fear. It generally represents some crisis point (see Bergmann, "We Have Seen the Enemy").

39. Seow, "Hosea 14:10," 222. Cf. Mays, *Hosea*, 120; Wolff, *Hosea*, 228.

40. Sweeney, *Twelve Prophets*, 134; Andersen and Freedman, *Hosea*, 638.

41. See Deut 10:17–18; Ps 10:14, 18; Ps 68:6; Ps 82:3; Ps 146:9; Jer 49:11. Human oppression is often indicated by mistreatment of widows and orphans, *e.g.*, Mal 3:5; Ezek 22:7; Jer 5:28; Isa 1:23, 10:12; Ps 94:6; Deut 27:19; Exod 22:21. Cf. Eidevall, *Grapes in the Desert*, 221; Wolff, *Hosea*, 235.

42. Mays, *Hosea*, 187; Sweeney, *Twelve Prophets*, 139. Macintosh sees also an allusion to YHWH's adoption of Israel in Egypt. The relationship was later disrupted, so that Israel is now fatherless (*Hosea*, 567).

43. Most commentators do not know what to do with the destruction of the mother in 4:5. Eidevall (*Grapes in the Desert,* 56) and Mays (*Hosea*, 68) prefer to emend to "clan." Macintosh thinks it is a reference to the wife in ch. 2 (*Hosea*, 138), while Sweeney links her to Gomer, the mother of the children, symbolizing Israel (*Twelve Prophets*, 47). Landy, after weighing various possibilities, states: "Primarily, however, she is a figure for the return to origins, the desire to reverse time and eradicate evil before its inception, that frequently recurs in Hosea (cf. 9.10–17). The destruction of the mother adumbrates a wish that the priest had never been born" (*Hosea,* 55). Wolff suggests that she is the priest's mother and is either a specifically bad person, or is symbolic of the destruction of the priestly dynasty (*Hosea*, 78). Jack R. Lundbom suggests that the oracle is directed to the king, and it is his mother that will be destroyed with him, like Jehoiachin and his mother (Jer 13:18, 22:26). He observes that the monarchy and the priesthood are closely related ("Contentious Priests and Contentious People in Hosea 4:1–10," *VT* 26 [1986]: 61). Rather than assigning a specific identity, I propose that she represents the powerlessness of the priest to protect his dependents. The destruction of the sons may indicate an end to the hereditary succession of the priesthood (Macintosh, *Hosea*, 139; Wolff, *Hosea*, 80; Mays, *Hosea*, 71) or the wicked nature of the sons, as well as the father's inaction, similar to the expulsion of Eli's sons in 1 Sam 3:11–14 (Andersen and Freedman, *Hosea*, 354). Again in this case I see a failing on the father's part to properly raise and educate his sons, even endangering them by his own actions.

44. As is usual when the text uses נאף or זנה with female subjects, most commentators treat it literally. Macintosh pictures some sort of orgy under the trees (*Hosea*, 160). Eidevall also imagines literal sexual activity (*Grapes in the Desert*, 59). Andersen and Freedman think that these daughters are the priests'

daughters, which makes it worse, because priests are forbidden to prostitute their daughters (*Hosea*, 370). Sweeney seems to understand the harlotry as figurative, representing apostasy. Since the priests have, through lack of proper education and guidance, led the people into apostasy, they will be the ones punished (*Twelve Prophets*, 49). Like Sweeney, I see no reason to treat the sexual activity literally.

45.   The usual interpretation is that this represents apostasy. The foreign children are children of an adulterous union, i.e. that the children are begotten by a foreign god. Yet many commentators have difficulty letting go of a literal interpretation. Landy suggests that these may be the children of the fornicating daughters in 4:13 (*Hosea*, 71). Wolff, while he concedes that there is a metaphorical side, that of Israel bearing children outside of her [*sic*] intimate relationship with YHWH, is also still married to his proposal of the bridal initiation rites, and concludes that they must be children of strangers (*Hosea*, 101).

46.   Eidevall, *Grapes in the Desert*, 73.

47.   Several commentators suggest that the barrenness and bereavement pictured here is an ironic punishment for participation in the fertility cult (Mays, *Hosea*, 137; Macintosh, *Hosea*, 367; Sweeney, *Twelve Prophets*, 100). Given the language of war and exile in 9:13, 15, however, a political explanation seems more likely.

48.   Macintosh, *Hosea*, 374; Eidevall, *Grapes in the Desert*, 153; Mays, *Hosea*, 134; Wolff, *Hosea*, 166, though I am not convinced by the latter idea.

49.   Eidevall, *Grapes in the Desert*, 153; Mays, *Hosea*, 134; Wolff, *Hosea*, 166.

50.   Stephen G. Burnett rather idiosyncratically understands 9:13 as referring to child sacrifice for the purpose of agricultural fertility, then interprets the whole second half of the chapter as a critique of this, expressing YHWH's anger that the children he has provided are being sacrificed to Baal ("Hosea 9:10–17," *TJ* 6 [1985]: 211–14).

51.   David R. Tasker observes that the role of YHWH as father in the Hebrew Bible includes both that of creation and adoption (*Ancient Near Eastern Literature and the Hebrew Scriptures About the Fatherhood of God* [Studies in Biblical Literature 69; New York: Peter Lang, 2004], 87).

52.   Parpola and Watanabe, *Neo-Assyrian Treaties*, 46.

53.   This may serve as an appellative of the Assyrian king, also known as the Great King (cf. Sweeney, *Twelve Prophets*, 67).

54.   Some commentators propose that 6:1–3 represents part of a cultic liturgy, and may indicate here "lip service." See Wolff, *Hosea*, 116–17; Sweeney, *Twelve Prophets*, 69–72. Buss notes the similarity to Deut 32:39, which may indicate liturgical language here (*Prophetic Word*, 85). Macintosh follows the proposal that these lines represent the prophet's hoped for result, which is not fulfilled (*Hosea*, 217–19). Andersen and Freedman see no reason to consider the prayer of repentance as hypocritical (*Hosea*, 426).

55.   Michael L. Barré makes a good case for the healing from sickness perspective, arguing that the pair קום and חיה occur frequently as metaphors for healing in biblical and ANE texts ("New Light on the Interpretation of Hosea VI 2," *VT*

28 [1978]: 129–41). The link between the pair has a parallel in the "Prayer of Lamentation to Ishtar": "Where thou dost look, one who is dead lives; one who is sick rises up" (*ANET*, 384).

56.   J. Wijngaards, "Death and Resurrection in Covenantal Context (Hos. VI 2)," *VT* 17 (1967): 226–39.

57.   Macintosh, *Hosea*, 211; Sweeney, *Twelve Prophets*, 67. Mays says that health cannot be obtained through political maneuvers, because they are the symptoms, not the cause of the disease. "Yahweh, not the Assyrian, is the ultimate source of their wound (vv. 12, 14), and he alone can heal them" (*Hosea*, 91). Similarly Beeby: "As though it were not bad enough to go to the butcher when one needs a doctor, the ultimate madness was in thinking that anyone could conquer an illness which had been brought on by God" (*Grace Abounding*, 67). Eidevall, on the contrary, links 11 with 13 and 12 with 14, and thus does not see a causal linkage between 12 and 13 (*Grapes in the Desert*, 85).

58.   עש is often translated as "moth," but "pus" has become a standard alternative (KB; Wolff, *Hosea*, 115; Mays, *Hosea*, 85) parallel to the bone-rot of Judah (cf. Hab 3:16). רקב can also be related to maggot-ridden corpses (KB; cf. JArm.; MHeb.). Andersen and Freedman translate עש as larvae, noting that the word occurs frequently with רקב, with the latter as the sore or rottenness, and the former as that which is eating at it. In the case of humans, the image is of maggots consuming flesh of open sores on either live or dead bodies (*Hosea*, 412; cf. NRSV). Sweeney prefers moth for its connotations of slow decay, often unnoticed until it is too late, but suggests that the image of gnats or small moths attracted to a festering wound, as in a gangrenous limb, could also be supported (*Twelve Prophets*, 67). Macintosh hedges by translating "emaciating disease" (*Hosea*, 207). I prefer maggot, because it indicates the cause of, or exacerbation of, the injury, rather than pus, which is a surface symptom. It better parallels the putrefication of the second half, eating away at the flesh or bones. Esarhaddon's Succession Treaty holds a similar curse: "Just as a worm eats..., so may the worm eat, while you are (still) alive, your own flesh and the flesh of your wives, your sons and your daughters" (Parpola and Watanabe, *Neo-Assyrian Treaties*, 53).

59.   אהי is an unusual form, and has been alternately translated as the coming from היה, in which case the translation would be "I am your plagues," so that YHWH would be standing in for death (Rashi, ibn Ezra, Kimchi), and as a variant form of אי or איה, "Where are your plagues" (*e.g.*, BDB; Mays, *Hosea*, 178; Wolff, *Hosea*, 221).

60.   NRSV; Wolff, *Hosea*, 228; Sweeney, *Twelve Prophets*, 134; Davies, *Hosea*, 296. Buss understands this verse in the positive sense, of YHWH's power over Sheol, and "can only be read as a declaration of victory over it." He observes that this hope is overturned in the next verse (*Prophetic Word*, 98). Andersen and Freedman prefer not to take a position either way (*Hosea*, 639–40).

61.   Note that in some of the Neo-Assyrian loyalty oaths, including Esarhaddon's Succession Treaty, one of the curses is for a god to cause illness: "May Gula,

the great physician, put sickness and weariness [in your hearts] and an unhealing wound in your body. Bathe in [blood and pus] as if in water!" (Parpola and Watanabe, *Neo-Assyrian Treaties*, 48).

62. Sarah J. Melcher observes that wounds and sickness can be the means of both punishment and reconciliation ("With Whom Do the Disabled Associate? Metaphorical Interplay in the Latter Prophets," in *This Abled Body: Rethinking Disabilities in Biblical Studies* [ed. Hector Avalos, Sarah J. Melcher, and Jeremy Schipper; Semeia 55; Atlanta: SBL, 2007], 115–129).

63. שטים is a disputed word. KB indicates a corruption of שִׁטִים [Shittim], cf. Buss, *Prophetic Word*, 13; Mays, *Hosea*, 79; Stuart, *Hosea*, 88; Wolff, *Hosea*, 94. I translate as a participle from שטה which means to stray or deviate, usually with implications of sexual straying (see Num 5:12, 19, 20, 29; Pr 7:5 [to a strange woman]). This sense ties in well with 5:3, which accuses Ephraim of fornicating and Israel of defiling itself [נטמא], especially because the Numbers passages link שטה and טמא: 5:29b: אשר תשטה אשה תחת אישה נטמאה [when a woman strays from under her husband and defiles herself.] Macintosh translates "perverse men" from שוט "to deviate" (*Hosea*, 179). Sweeney notes that the MT translates literally as "the slaughter of those who revolt has become deep," which he then would associate with the slaughter of the fornicators at Baal-Peor, but he rejects this translation and emends to the usual pit at Shittim (*Twelve Prophets*, 54). In any case, העמיקו in the MT is a hiphil form, and thus should be translated in an active, not passive sense. The same difficulty apples to Andersen and Freedman's translation: "The rebels are deep in slaughter" (*Hosea*, 380), though they also note the parallels with Numbers 5 (388).

64. Most emend שחטה to שחתה [pit], (cf. Buss, *Prophetic Word*, 13; Mays, *Hosea*, 79; Stuart, *Hosea*, 88; Wolff, *Hosea*, 94), which fits with digging deeply, but it is likely that a play on words is intended, as the chapter as a whole seems to relate to war (cf. 5:8–9), and chs. 6 and 7 deal with murder, ambush, betrayal, and assassination. Macintosh translates as a qal infinitive construct from שחת, claiming that the author deliberately used a variant spelling, but for phonological, rather than punological, reasons.

65. Some propose reading מוֹסֵר [fetter] which would maintain the hunting imagery, rather than מוּסָר [chastisement] (Buss, *Prophetic Word*, 13; Stuart, *Hosea*, 90). Perhaps a pun is intended here also.

66. *E.g.*, Pss 7:16; 9:16–17; 57:7; 64:6; 119:110; 140:6; 141:9; 142:4. See Buss, *Prophetic Word*, 84; Paul A. Kruger, "The Divine Net in Hosea 7,2," *ETL* 68 (1992): 136. The ambush the wicked set for the Psalmist can be seen in Pss 56:7; 59:4.

67. The usage here has a parallel in 9:6, where Egypt gathers them and Moph buries them. Thus קבץ has negative connotations. Macintosh, noting the parallel with קבר in 9:6, translates as "put an end to" (*Hosea*, 320). While he does not draw on hunting imagery, his interpretation better expresses the usually fatal end of the gathered prey than do the more usual positive interpretations, understanding

a gathering either to salvation or to judgment (Wolff, *Hosea*, 153; Sweeney, *Twelve Prophets*, 90).

68. *E.g.*, Pss 9:16; 10:9; 31:5; 35:7.

69. For further references see Buss, *Prophetic Word*, 84.

70. Jeremy Black, "The Imagery of Birds in Sumerian Poetry," in *Mesopotamian Poetic Language: Sumerian and Akkadian* (ed. M. E. Vogelzang and H. L. J. Vanstiphout; Cuneiform Mongraphs 6; Groningen: Styx, 1996), 26.

71. Black, "Imagery of Birds," 27.

72. Black, "Imagery of Birds," 28.

73. Parpola and Watanabe, *Neo-Assyrian Treaties*, 53.

74. Parpola and Watanabe, *Neo-Assyrian Treaties*, 54.

75. Parpola and Watanabe, *Neo-Assyrian Treaties*, 58.

76. Kuan, *Neo-Assyrian Historical Inscriptions*, 172, from Layard 72b +73a l.203.

77. Carole R. Fontaine, *With Eyes of Flesh: The Bible, Gender, and Human Rights* (The Bible in the Modern World 10; Sheffield: Sheffield Phoenix, 2008), 49, 58.

78. Cf. Black, "Imagery of Birds," 26.

79. There are no directional prepositions in this verse, so there is ambiguity about whether Ephraim is going to or departing from Assyria.

80. The word translated testimony עדה, resembles the Aramaic word (and its Akkadian cognate) עדי "treaty."

81. Eidevall, *Grapes in the Desert*, 119.

82. Landy, *Hosea*, 99. Macintosh observes that this association "may suggest that here the state approaches Egypt and Assyria with the easy optimism of a loose woman (cf. Ezek 23) just as *mutatis mutandis* the gullible youth is easy prey to the seductress of Prov 7" (*Hosea*, 274). While I disagree with his assessment, the representation of Ephraim as a vacillating female bird ties into the theme of gender reversal.

83. Black, "Imagery of Birds," 37.

84. Black, "Imagery of Birds," 38.

85. Kuan, *Neo-Assyrian Inscriptions*, 177, from a summary inscription discovered by Layard in 1849 at Nimrud.

86. "Imagery of Birds," 42.

87. See Eidevall, *Grapes in the Desert*, 134; Andersen and Freedman, *Hosea*, 505. Macintosh, translates rather freely that the wild ass is following its nose (*Hosea*, 318). Sweeney reads this verse in light of Jer 2:24 which portrays an ass in its lust, snuffing the wind for a mate (*Twelve Prophets*, 90). In the Jer passage, however, the ass is a female, whereas here it is male. Wild asses are commonly invoked in the potency incantations, but if the ass is wandering alone, its potency is futile.

88. Kuan, *Neo-Assyrian Historical Inscriptions*, 177.

89. While most people have understood "going up to Assyria" as Israel making positive advances or treaties, the verb עלה is often used to describe a military attack (*e.g.*, Judg 20:18, 23, 28; Isa 7:1; 21:2). Many of the images in ch. 8 are

shared with those in the Assyrian political inscriptions describing the defeat of those whose rebellions have been crushed.

90.   Parpola and Watanabe, *Neo-Assyrian Treaties*, 45.

91.   This may mean the farmer yoked the heifer or that her good features attracted his attention.

92.   So Paul A. Kruger, "'I Will Hedge Her Way with Thornbushes' (Hosea 2,8): Another Example of Literary Multiplicity?" *BZ* 43 (1999): 99.

93.   Macintosh cites this verse to claim that heifer is used as "a term of affection for a wife/daughter," and also notes that David's wife is named Eglah in 2 Sam 3:5 (*Hosea*, 420). Given the context of Samson's rage in Judges, however, this extrapolation seems highly unlikely. If anything, it is a disparaging term in that passage.

94.   Luigi Cagni, *The Poem of Erra* (SANE 1/3; Malibu: Undena, 1977), 54, tablet 4, ll. 91–92.

95.   Joan Goodnick Westenholz, "Symbolic Language in Akkadian Narrative Poetry: The Metaphorical Relationship between Poetical Images and the Real World," in *Mesopotamian Poetic Language: Sumerian and Akkadian* (ed. M. E. Vogelzang and H. L. J. Vanstiphout; Cuneiform Mongraphs 6; Groningen: Styx, 1996), 191. For example: "To kill the Dark-headed (people and) to slaughter Šakkan's herds" *Erra* I:43; "You govern men, you shepherd the herds," *Erra* III:D6. Others see these as a literal reference to cattle, commonly associated with humans because they are important to human well-being (Cagni, *Erra*, 29).

96.   Joan Goodnick Westenholz, *Legends of the Kings of Akkade* (Mesopotamian Civilizations 7; Winona Lake, IN: Eisenbrauns, 1997), 67.

97.   Westenholz, *Legends*, 85.

98.   For a detailed study of this imagery, see Brent A. Strawn, *What Is Stronger than a Lion? Leonine Image and Metaphor in the Hebrew Bible and the Ancient Near East* (OBO 212; Göttingen: Vandenhoeck & Ruprecht, 2005).

99.   Cf. Gören Eidevall, "Lions and Birds as Literature: Some Notes on Isaiah 31 and Hosea 11," *SJOT* 7 (1993): 82; J. Cheryl Exum, "Of Broken Pots, Fluttering Birds, and Visions in the Night: Extended Simile and Poetic Technique in Isaiah," *CBQ* 43 (1981): 336–38.

100.   Westenholz, *Legends*, 99–101.

101.   *ANET*, 578.

102.   *ANET*, 384.

103.   *ANET*, 374.

104.   *ANET*, 245.

105.   *ANET*, 247.

106.   Šulgi Hymn C ll. 1,10 in G. R. Castellino, *Two Šulgi Hymns (BC)* (Studi Semitici 42; Rome: Istituto di studi del Vicino Oriente, 1972), 249.

107.   This is often translated as vulture. Macintosh notes that נשר can refer to a number of large predatory birds (*Hosea*, 291). Because vultures are often thought of as eaters of carrion rather than as predators, I chose the generic term raptor.

The circling of carrion-eating vultures, however, is often even more ominous than that of a predator, because of the imminence, or actual occasion, of death.

108. Parpola and Watanabe, *Neo-Assyrian Treaties*, 46, 51.

109. Jörg Jeremias observes that YHWH's attack on Ephraim and Judah in 5:14 is an intensification of YHWH's role as disease in 5:12. The sickness could have been healed, if Ephraim had turned to the right doctor (i.e. YHWH), but since they did not recognize YHWH as the disease, they were not healed. He argues that as a lion, YHWH's identity as the source of their ailments can no longer be denied, but at that point, it is too late—the lion rends and there is no one to deliver ("'Ich bin wie ein Löwe für Efraim...' (Hos 5,14): Aktualität und Allgemeingültigkeit im prophetischen Reden von Gott am Beispiel von Hos 5,8–14," in *"Ich will euer Gott werden": Beispiele biblischen Redens von Gott* [ed. Helmut Merklein and Erich Zenger; SBS 100; Stuttgart: Katholisches Bibelwerk, 1981], 89).

110. Eidevall, "Lions and Birds," 83.

111. Westenholz quotes a passage from Babylonian wisdom literature: "The lion, the enemy of the herds" ("Symbolic Language," 191).

112. See *e.g.*, Pss 7:3; 10:9; 17:12; 22:14; 57:4. Cf. Buss, *Prophetic Word*, 85.

113. Parpola and Watanabe, *Neo-Assyrian Treaties*, 27.

114. Fitzmyer, *Aramaic Inscriptions*, 123.

115. Strong wind storms such as whirlwinds and hurricanes are used by the Assyrians to describe their assaults on cities. One example is from the annals of Tiglath-Pileser III (Layard 29b), which seems to report on his campaign in Palestine in 733–732 BCE: "(229) [...like] a hurricane [...(230) prisoners of...] districts of Bit-[...I] took away [...prisoners of...]bara, 625 prisoners of A[..., prisoners of] Hinatuna, 650 prisoners of Ku[..." (Kuan, *Neo-Assyrian Inscriptions*, 168). Other biblical texts use storms and whirlwinds to symbolize war and destruction. Ps 83:15 implores YHWH to chase foreign enemies with his storm; Prov 1:27 compares tribulation with a whirlwind; Chariot wheels are likened to a whirlwind in Isa 5:28; 66:15; Jer 4:13.

116. Jer 48:38 also uses the phrase ככלי אין־חפץ בו in its description of how Moab will be destroyed, broken [שברתי] like a pot. That this imagery was not uncommon as a way of discussing the defeat of a country is supported by a line in the Azekah Inscription, describing the Assyrian campaign against Judah and Ashdod in 712 BCE. The siege of the city (whose exact identity is unknown—Galil proposes Ekron) is described and finally something (presumably its wall) is broken: "(18')...all the units of Amurru; I caused them to carry earth...(19')...against them. In the seventh time, its mighty...[I smashed] like a pot [of clay...(20') [...shee]p I carried out from it, [and counted as] spo[il]" (Gershon Galil, "A New Look at the 'Azekah Inscription,'" *RB* 102 [1995]: 321–29).

117. The rain is essential to the growth of the crops. Calling on the gods who witness a treaty to withhold rain is a common treaty curse. The Esarhaddon Succession Treaty, Section 63, ll. 526–529 reads: "Ditto, ditto, may all the gods that are

[mentioned by name] in th[is] treaty tablet make the ground as narrow as a brick for you. May they make your ground like iron (so that) nothing can sprout from it" (Parpola and Watanabe, *Neo-Assyrian Treaties*, 51).

118. See Wolff, *Hosea*, 153–54; Andersen and Freedman, *Hosea*, 522–23. They go so far as to translate 9:1 as "You have made love for a fee by every threshing floor" (514).

119. That this is sexual imagery is not in doubt. However, as in the other occurrences, both male and female, the imagery is figurative, not literal.

120. See Macintosh for a discussion of this translation of ענה with the connotation of "taking care of things," (*Hosea*, 86).

121. See, *e.g.*, "A Hymn to Ninurta as God of Vegetation" (*ANET*, 576).

122. See Mays, *Hosea*, 145. Jer 51:33 describes Babylon as a threshing floor, ready to be trodden. More explicitly Mic 4:13 implores Zion to thresh her enemies: קומי ודושי בת־ציון כי־קרנך אשים ברזל ופרסתיך אשים נחושה והדקות עמים רבים [Get up and thresh, daughter Zion, for I make your horns iron and your hooves bronze, and you will crush many peoples]; cf. Jer 50:11.

123. See Macintosh, *Hosea*, 419; Mays, *Hosea*, 145.

124. See Macintosh, *Hosea*, 419; Mays, *Hosea*, 145; Wolff, *Hosea,* 185; Buss comments: "He gave the nation a profitable and promising task of plowing—as a calf—in Palestine (10:11)" (*Prophetic Word*, 112).

125. Jer 6:9; 51:33; Joel 3:13.

126. The latter verse is often considered an addition, because of the reference to Judah, and of its somewhat awkward position in the surrounding context. See *e.g.*, Macintosh, *Hosea*, 247. Judah is mentioned earlier in the chapter, however, and the theme of judgment fits the context with 6:5 providing a parallel hewing of the prophets.

127. See Pss 1:4, 35:5; Isa 17:13; Zeph 2:2; Job 21:18.

128. The slippage of gender from male in Hos 1 to female in Hos 2 will be discussed further in ch. 5.

129. The animal imagery in 13:5–6 is unspecified, indicated by the terms מרעיתם [pasturage] and שבע [have one's fill of], presumably of grass in this verse. Though cattle are also grazed, language of shepherds and sheep is more common in the HB, and Israel was, after all, turned into a sheep in 4:16.

130. Nwaoru, *Imagery*, 170.

131. Eidevall, *Grapes in the Desert*, 150. See Mic 7:1–2; Jer 8:13; Isa 5:1–7.

132. Kirsten Nielsen, *There is Hope for a Tree: The Tree as Metaphor in Isaiah* (JSOTSup 65; Sheffield: Sheffield Academic Press, 1989), 77.

133. Human reproduction is symbolized by שרש in Isa 11:1, 5:24; Mal 3:19.

134. See Cornelis van Leeuwen, "Meaning and Structure of Hosea X 1–8," *VT* 53 (2003): 370.

135. Nwaoru, *Imagery,* 171; JPS: ravaged.

136. Van Leeuwen, "Meaning and Structure," 370.

137. For the association of cedars with Lebanon see Ps 104:16, which also calls them the "trees of YHWH"; Judg 9:15; 1 Kgs 5:20; Isa 2:13, 14:8.

138.   See 5:12, with the possible translation as moth. Judg 9:15, 2 Kgs 14:9, and Isa
        2:3 indicate an association of cedars with height and arrogance.
139.   For use of שׁיב with another verb to indicate repetition of an action, see KB, also
        Macintosh, *Hosea*, 573.
140.   Robert B. Coote has suggested that a series of scribal errors occurred and the
        phrase should be "and those who are filled with grain shall live," ("Hos 14:8:
        They Who Are Filled with Grain Shall Live," *JBL* 93 [1974]: 170). This does
        not obviously solve the problem of context, except for the idea of provision
        under YHWH's shadow. He classifies it as banquet imagery (172).
141.   Cf. Paul A. Kruger, who associates the image with a return from exile
        ("Yahweh's Generous Love: Eschatological Expectations in Hosea 14:2–9,"
        OTE 1 [1983], 42).
142.   Cf. Oestreich, *Metaphors and Similes*, 220; Kruger, "Yahweh's Generous Love,"
        41.
143.   Several commentators follow the LXX, "makes his sons as prey for the hunter."
        See Mays, *Hosea*, 131; Davies, *Hosea*, 228; Wolff, *Hosea*, 160.
144.   NRSV; see also Macintosh, *Hosea*, 370.
145.   Buss, *Prophetic Word*, 19.
146.   Jeffrey K. Kuan, "Hosea 9.13 and Josephus *Antiquities* IX, 277–287," *PEQ* 123
        (1991): 103–8.
147.   The translation requires several minor modifications: Ephraim, a masculine
        entity must be the subject of a feminine verb form, and ל must take the
        otherwise unattested meaning "on." It also presupposes, to some extent, a
        proverb juxtaposing rock and meadow, which is impossible to attest.
148.   Douglas R. Edwards, "Tyre," *ABD* 6:687, 689.
149.   For a discussion of Assyrian images of gods and kings pollinating female date
        palms with the male cones and their implications for general issues of
        prosperity, see W. G. Lambert, "The Background of the Neo-Assyrian Sacred
        Tree," in *Sex and Gender in the Ancient Near East* (ed. Simo Parpola and R.M.
        Whiting; Helsinki: Neo-Assyrian Text Corpus Project, 2002), 321–26.
150.   David Allan Hubbard writes: "His desire to wipe the land clean of the fertility
        cult has led him to strong, almost risky, language. He borrowed the enemy's
        sword to make his final thrust" (*Hosea: An Introduction and Commentary* [TOTC;
        Downers Grove, IL: Inter-Varsity, 1989], 233). See also Beeby, *Grace Abounding*,
        184; Wolff, *Hosea,* 237; Mays, *Hosea*, 189. Macintosh proposes that this verse
        represents a dialogue between Ephraim and YHWH, so that it is Ephraim who
        claims himself the luxuriant cypress, and YHWH responds that he is the source
        of the fruit (*Hosea*, 576–79).
151.   See K. Arvid Tångberg, "'I am like an Evergreen Fir; From Me Comes Your
        Fruit': Notes on Meaning and Symbolism in Hosea 14, 9b (MT)," *SJOT* 2
        (1989): 88, 92; Kruger, "Yahweh's Generous Love," 42.
152.   Several biblical verses depicts YHWH as the one who cuts down the trees
        representing kings in judgment (Isa 10:18–19, 33–34; Isa 2:13, Zech 11:1–2).
153.   Oestreich, *Metaphors and Similes*, 224.

154. Isa 5:6, 7:23, 27:4, 32:13; Judg 9:14–15 indicates that thorns and thistles were not well thought of.
155. Esarhaddon Succession Treaty, Section 64 ll. 530–533 (Parpola and Watanabe, *Neo-Assyrian Treaties*, 51).
156. The translation of קֶצֶף is not at all certain. For the purposes of this analysis, however, the exact nature of what is carried away on the water is not important.
157. Gary A. Rendsburg, "Hebrew rhm='Rain,'" *VT* 33 (1983): 357–62.
158. Rendsburg translates Ps 110:3b as "In holy splendor from the rain of your dawn. For you the dew of your youth." Isa 49:10: "They shall not hunger nor thirst, And hot wind and sun shall not strike them, For he that causes rain will lead them, To the springs of water he will guide them." He does not intend to exclude the traditional "have compassion" reading, but to add another layer. The meaning of rain he finds particularly apropos in Hos 2:6, "And I will not have pity on/cause rain upon her sons," which immediately follows the threat to turn their mother into a dry land. He cites Rabbi Yohanan, Ashi, a blessing used to combat drought, and a story about Rabbi Honi, which pair רחם and rain ("Hebrew rhm= 'Rain,'" 359–60).
159. Rendsburg, "Hebrew rhm='Rain,'" 360.
160. Oestreich, *Metaphors and Similes,* 159.
161. Oestreich, *Metaphors and Similes*, 160–69.
162. More literal references to the east wind drying up land and crops include Gen 41:6, Exod 14:21; Jon 4:8. The east wind brings locusts in Exod 10:13. Symbolic use of the drying power of the wind occurs in Ezek 17:10, 19:12. The power of the east wind to sweep things away and to wreck ships is used mostly symbolically in Job 27:21; Ps 48:7; Isa 27:8; Jer 18:17; Ezek 27:26. Nah 1:3 provides another example of YHWH coming as wind and storm to dry up the rivers.
163. Katherine M. Hayes, *"The Earth Mourns": Prophetic Metaphor and Oral Aesthetic* (SBLAB 8; Leiden: Brill, 2002), 47.
164. See Michael DeRoche, "The Reversal of Creation in Hosea," *VT* 31 (1981): 400–409. He also observes that the three categories of animals listed, in order, beasts, birds, and fish, represent the three spheres of life and reverse the order of creation.
165. Many passages discuss YHWH's control of water either in giving rain, *e.g.*, Lev 26:4; 1 Kgs 18:1; Jer 5:24; Job 38:28; Joel 2:23; Ezek 34:26; Ps 68: 9–10; or withholding rain, *e.g.*, Deut 11:17 ; Amos 4:7; Ps 105:32; Jer 3:3; Hag 1:10.

5 Syntheses and Subversions

1. Various of these attributes are ascribed to good rulers (in the HB often to YHWH), wise men, and heroes in the narrative/epic texts.
2. As observed in ch. 3, while women can also commit adultery against their husbands, the preponderance of uses of נאף, especially outside of the prophets, refers to men.

3.   Strawn observes that although the lion is a popular image to represent kings in the ANE, especially with regard to their military endeavors, it is never used this way for Israelite kings in the HB (*What Is Stronger,* 236).

4.   This example is not directly attributed to YHWH, but does represent the punishment for Ephraim's actions.

5.   Chapman, *Gendered Language,* 24–28.

6.   Yvonne Sherwood has examined some of the ways the tensions and contradictions in Hosea work to subvert Israel's conception of itself, its practices, and its history, ultimately deconstructing itself in several places (*The Prostitute and the Prophet: Hosea's Marriage in Literary-Theoretical Perspective* [JSOTSup 212; GCT 2; Sheffield: Sheffield Academic Press, 1996).

7.   Ben Zvi observes that the rhetoric of Hosea generally works to support prevailing hegemonic models: "The education or socialization of the subordinate partner is a pervading theme in these texts. In fact, rhetorically the texts are most often construed as a persuasive effort by the hegemonic partner, or those who identified with it/him, to educate the readership of the text, that is, to convince subordinates to accept the control and viewpoint of the hegemonic partner, in this case to convince 'the wife' that the 'husband' is right." ("Marital Metaphor," 372).

8.   Cornwall and Lindisfarne, "Dislocating Masculinity," 20.

9.   Carrigan et al. suggest that this type of instability is always a part of a power structure: "The fissuring of the categories of 'men' and 'women' is one of the central facts about patriarchal power and the way it works. In the case of men, the crucial division is between hegemonic masculinity and various subordinated masculinities" ("New Sociology," 90).

10.   Gilmore, "Above and Below," 63. Playing with inversions of hierarchies, gendered or otherwise, does not necessarily change the hierarchical system itself. Rituals or festivals in which these types of relationships are inverted— men dressing as women and vice versa—can serve as a type of safety-valve to release tensions and, in fact, reinforce the existing order. At times, however, such reversals do create opportunities for a change in conceiving society and power relations. See Natalie Zemon Davis, "Women on Top: Symbolic Sexual Inversion and Political Disorder in Early Modern Europe," in *The Reversible World* (ed. Barbara A. Babcock; Ithaca: Cornell University Press, 1978), 153–55.

11.   Deborah F. Sawyer observes that if one recognizes that people exist along a continuum of gender and sex and not in bipolar categories, this type of gender play is normal ("Gender Criticism: A New Discipline in Biblical Studies or Feminism in Disguise?" in Deborah W. Rooke, ed. *A Question of Sex? Gender and Difference in the Hebrew Bible and Beyond* [ed. Deborah W. Rooke; Hebrew Bible Monographs 14; Sheffield: Sheffield Phoenix, 2007], 7).

12.   Dramatic inversions, such as the male-female role reversals celebrated during designated festivals, as discussed in the previous note and in Brandes, *Metaphors of Masculinity,* may be less likely to encourage a questioning of the status quo because the intention is clearly to mock. Smaller changes are harder to dismiss

because they conform more closely to experiential norms. I am also focusing on the subversions related to hegemonic masculinity, which places a particular type of masculinity in opposition to any other kind of masculinity or femininity. Hegemonic masculinity tends to emphasize the differences between its own norm and other ways of conceiving gender. A separate analysis of the subordinate masculinities and femininities may show that the latter categories are not polar opposites, but are in many respects orthogonal to each other and to hegemonic masculinity.

13. The text shows a separation in the concepts of masculinity and men. As Cornwall and Lindisfarne observe, the equation of men and masculinity is one of the hallmarks of hegemonic masculinity ("Dislocating Masculinity," 20).

14. BHS; Macintosh, *Hosea*, 92.

15. Sweeney, *Twelve Prophets*, 37.

16. Calvin, *Twelve Minor Prophets*, 1:120.

17. He states: "to see beneath the male control, undercut by uncertainty, revisions and impossibility, a desire for surrender of power, knowledge and discourse…it is also a fantasy of the transfer of gender, of slippage between male and female personae. This can be illustrated at the end of the chapter where the male child, Jezreel, is suddenly feminized" ("Fantasy and Displacement," 146).

18. This is not necessarily to aggressively sexualize YHWH, but it highlights the point that Jezreel is no longer in the position to perform this masculine action.

19. Herbert B. Huffmon, "Gender Subversion in the Book of Jeremiah," in *Sex and Gender in the Ancient Near East* (ed. Simo Parpola and R.M. Whiting; Helsinki: The Neo-Assyrian Text Corpus Project, 2002), 246.

20. Biggs, *ŠÀ.ZI.GA*, 18, incantation no. 2.

21. Biggs, *ŠÀ.ZI.GA*, 19, incantation no. 3.

22. Biggs, *ŠÀ.ZI.GA*, 20, incantation no. 4.

23. Kamionkowski, *Gender Reversal*.

24. Kamionkowski, *Gender Reversal*, 132.

25. Kamionkowski, *Gender Reversal*, 110–26.

26. Kamionkowski notes that 16:34 explicitly states that the woman Jerusalem is "the opposite" [הפך] of other women, because she paid her lovers, rather than being paid (*Gender Reversal*, 126–27).

27. Kamionkowski, *Gender Reversal*, 127–31.

28. Kamionkowski, *Gender Reversal*, 132.

29. Kamionkowski, *Gender Reversal*, 152. Galambush also makes this point, noting that the male audience is able to use the metaphor to project its own humiliation on the "other," and can interpret the destruction of Jerusalem as a way for YHWH to restore his honor and potency after the wife's betrayal (*Jerusalem*, 161).

30. See Hayes and Hooker, *A New Chronology*, 67; John H. Hayes and Jeffrey K. Kuan, "The Final Years of Samaria (730–720 BC)," *Biblica* 72 (1991): 153–81.

31. Kamionkowski notes the analogous point in Ezekiel (*Gender Reversal*, 131).

32. Braaten, "Parent-Child Imagery," 228–29.

33. The idea that YHWH had ordered Hosea to marry a woman who he knew was promiscuous scandalized many generations of interpreters and led to many of the alternative explanations mentioned in ch. 1. At least part of the difficulty was that Hosea's authority as a prophet would be undermined if he knew (along with everyone else) that he was marrying a woman with a tainted reputation. If she was "pure" when he married her, then later went astray, it was her fault. If he knowingly married her "tainted" then his own status was immediately lowered. While the commentators do not speak in terms of masculinity, it is clear that knowledge of and seeming acceptance of his wife's improprieties affected a man's own reputation.

34. Stone, "Lovers and Raisin Cakes," 138.

35. See Catlett, "Reversals," 269. The husband appears to be making threats, however, rather than taking actual measures, and thus is not as active as he could be.

36. Helen Schüngel-Straumann perhaps takes this idea the farthest, translating תרגלתי as "nursed" based on an Arabic cognate, and לחיהים as breasts. She tightly links compassion to the womb, emending the word נחומי in 11:8 to רחמי to make this connection more obvious and, perhaps, linking it to the daughter in ch. 1 ("God as Mother in Hosea 11," in *A Feminist Companion to the Latter Prophets* [ed. Athalya Brenner; FCB 8; Sheffield: Sheffield Academic Press, 1995], 200–202, 208).

37. See especially Braaten, "Parent-Child Imagery," 305–6; Siegfried Kreuzer, "Gott als Mutter in Hosea 11?" *TQ* 169 (1989): 123–32; Landy, *Hosea*, 137.

38. Chapman, *Gendered Language*, 23–24.

39. See Strawn, *What is Stronger*, 58–65. He describes two other biblical texts where the image of YHWH as lion has at least some positive connotations: Joel 4:16 and Isa 31:4, but both of these carry much ambiguity.

40. At least if YHWH is only one maggot. Large groups of maggots can very rapidly consume a carcass.

41. Carol Meyers observes that in Ancient Israel, it was likely that several overlapping hierarchies existed, so that a person could occupy different positions in different hierarchies simultaneously. She refers to this as a system of heterarchy, which opens up more complex interpretations of social status ("Contesting the Notion of Patriarchy: Anthropology and the Theorizing of Gender in Ancient Israel," in *A Question of Sex? Gender and Difference in the Hebrew Bible and Beyond* [ed. Deborah W. Rooke; Hebrew Bible Monographs 14; Sheffield: Sheffield Phoenix, 2007], 97).

42. Because of the political situation in Israel, a legitimate, properly appointed king is largely absent in Hosea. The king would ordinarily be the position with the most potential for a high position in the activity/potency/goodness octant, the one clearly occupied by YHWH. There are a few hints that such a position can be acceptable for a human. One is 2:2: "The sons of Israel and the sons of Judah will gather together and appoint one head over them and they will go up from the land because great is the day of Jezreel." The second is 3:5: "Afterward the

sons of Israel will return and seek YHWH their God and David their king and they will rejoice over YHWH and his bounty in the following days." These cases suggest that a properly appointed and recognized king can occupy an active, potent, and good position, if the king remains under the authority of YHWH. It is possible for a human leader to occupy the same octant as YHWH, but he must be closer to the origin of the axes than YHWH. Such a position is only hinted at, however, and Hosea makes repeated reference to the non-legitimacy of the current kings in Samaria.

43.   This suggests that there is a difference in what may be acceptable masculinity in human-human relations and in human-divine relations. Hosea criticizes the idea that humans can occupy the same position in both types of relations. In relation to YHWH a proper masculinity has a large receptive (less active, less powerful) element and would constitute a subordinate masculinity to the hegemonic norm.

44.   Cornwall and Lindisfarne, "Introduction," 10.

6 Conclusion

1.   In this project I am only considering the implications the figure of the wife has for masculinity. I am not discussing any implications the portrayal of the wife may have for construction of femininity, which is not simply the inverse of masculinity, nor am I making any generalizations about the conception of women based on the portrayal of the wife in this passage.

2.   Relationships between real people, especially in domestic settings, tend to show much more variability.

3.   As noted in ch. 3, foreign policy, especially that including war, is often couched in terms of masculinity, with the Assyrian king bragging that he is a man. Defeated parties, on the other hand, have their masculinity brought low in relation to the victors.

4.   The introduction of each additional axis doubles the number of divisions of social space, so that while including more factors in the analysis captures more of the nuance of the imagery, it exponentially complicates the space, decreasing the ability to detect general trends.

❖BIBLIOGRAPHY❖

Aaron, David H. *Biblical Ambiguities: Metaphor, Semantics and Divine Imagery*. Brill Reference Library of Ancient Judaism 4. Leiden: Brill, 2001.

Abma, Richtsje. *"Bonds of Love": Methodic Studies of Prophetic Texts with Marriage Imagery*. Studia semitica neerlandica. Assen: Van Gorcum, 1999.

Ackerman, Susan. "The Personal is Political: Covenantal and Affectionate Love (אהב, אהבה) in the Hebrew Bible." *Vetus Testamentum* 52 (2002): 437–58.

Albertz, Rainer. *From the Beginnings to the End of the Monarchy*. Vol. 1 of *A History of Israelite Religion in the Old Testament Period*. Translated by John Bowden. Old Testament Library. Louisville: Westminster John Knox, 1994.

Alter, Robert. *The Art of Biblical Narrative*. New York: Basic Books, 1981.

———. "From Line to Story in Biblical Verse." *Poetics Today* 4 (1983): 615–37.

Andersen, Francis I., and David Noel Freedman. *Hosea*. Anchor Bible 24. New York: Doubleday, 1980.

Aristotle. *The "Art" of Rhetoric*. Translated by John Henry Freese. Loeb Classical Library. Cambridge: Harvard University Press, 1926.

———. *The Poetics*. Translated by W. Hamilton Fyfe. Loeb Classical Library. Cambridge: Harvard University Press, 1927.

Bailey, Randall. "They're Nothing but Incestuous Bastards." Pages 121–38 in *Social Location and Biblical Interpretation in the United States*. Vol. 1 of *Reading from This Place*. Edited by Fernando F. Segovia and Mary Ann Tolbert. Minneapolis: Fortress, 1995.

Bal, Mieke. *Death and Dissymmetry: The Politics of Coherence in the Book of Judges*. Chicago: University of Chicago Press, 1988.

Barré, Michael L. "New Light on the Interpretation of Hosea VI 2." *Vetus Testamentum* 28 (1978): 129–41.

Bartsch, Renate. "Generating Polysemy: Metaphor and Metonymy." Pages 49–71 in *Metaphor and Metonymy in Comparison and Contrast*. Edited by René Dirven and Ralf Pörings. Cognitive Linguistics Research 20. Berlin: de Gruyter, 2002.

Baumann, Gerlinde. *Love and Violence: Marriage as Metaphor for the Relationship between YHWH and Israel in the Prophetic Books*. Translated by Linda M. Maloney. Collegeville, MN: Liturgical Press, 2003.

Beardsley, Monroe C. "The Metaphorical Twist." Pages 105–21 in *Philosophical Perspectives on Metaphor*. Edited by Mark Johnson. Minneapolis: University of Minnesota Press, 1981.

Bechtel, Lyn M. "Shame as a Sanction of Social Control in Biblical Israel: Judicial, Political, and Social Shaming." *Journal for the Study of the Old Testament* 49 (1991): 47–76.

Beeby, H. D. *Grace Abounding*. Grand Rapids: Eerdmans, 1989.

Ben Zvi, Ehud. "Observations on the Marital Metaphor of YHWH and Israel in its Ancient Israelite Context: General Considerations and Particular Images in Hosea 1:2." *Journal for the Study of the Old Testament* 28 (2004): 363–84.

Bergant, Dianne. "'My Beloved is Mine and I am His' (Song 2:16): The Song of Songs and Honor and Shame." *Semeia* 68 (1994): 23–40.

Berger, Maurice, Brian Wallis, and Simon Watson, eds. *Constructing Masculinity*. New York: Routledge, 1995.

Bergmann, Claudia D. "'We Have Seen the Enemy, and He is Only a "She"': The Portrayal of Warriors as Women." Pages 129–142 in *Writing and Reading War: Rhetoric, Gender, and Ethics in Biblical and Modern Contexts*. Edited by Brad E. Kelle and Frank Ritchel Ames. Symposium 42. Atlanta: Society of Biblical Literature, 2008.

Bidlack, Beth A. "Imagery in Ezekiel's Oracles against Foreign Nations and Rulers (Ezekiel 25–32)." Ph.D. diss., Boston University, 2000.

Biggs, Robert D. *ŠÀ.ZI.GA: Ancient Mesopotamian Potency Incantations*. Texts from Cuneiform Sources 2. Locust Valley, NY: J. J. Augustin, 1967.

Binkley, Timothy. "On the Truth and Probity of Metaphor." Pages 136–53 in *Philosophical Perspectives on Metaphor*. Edited by Mark Johnson. Minneapolis: University of Minnesota Press, 1981.

Bird, Phyllis A. "'To Play the Harlot': An Inquiry into an Old Testament Metaphor." Pages 75–94 in *Gender and Difference in Ancient Israel*. Edited by Peggy L. Day. Minneapolis: Fortress Press, 1989.

Bjørndalen, Anders Jørgen. *Untersuchen zur allegorischen Rede der Propheten Amos und Jesaja*. Beihefte zur Zeitschrift für die alttestamentliche Wissenschaft 165. Berlin: de Gruyter, 1986.

Black, Jeremy. "The Imagery of Birds in Sumerian Poetry." Pages 23–46 in *Mesopotamian Poetic Language: Sumerian and Akkadian*. Edited by M. E. Vogelzang and H. L. J. Vanstiphout. Cuneiform Monographs 6. Groningen: Styx, 1996.

Black, Max. *Models and Metaphors*. Ithaca: Cornell University Press, 1962.

Bly, Robert. *Iron John: A Book About Men*. Reading, MA: Addison-Wesley, 1990.

Bons, Eberhard. *Das Buch Hosea*. Neuer Stuttgarter Kommentar Altes Testament 23/1. Stuttgart: Katholisches Bibelwerk, 1996.

———. "Zwei überlegungen zum Verständnis von Hosea XI." *Vetus Testamentum* 45 (1995): 286–93.

Booth, Wayne. "Metaphor as Rhetoric: The Problem of Evaluation." Pages 47–70 in *On Metaphor*. Edited by Sheldon Sacks. Chicago: University of Chicago Press, 1978.

Braaten, Laurie J. "Parent-child Imagery in Hosea." Ph.D. diss., Boston University, 1987.

Brandes, Stanley. *Metaphors of Masculinity: Sex and Status in Andalusian Folklore*. Publications of the American Folklore Society New Series 1. Philadelphia: University of Pennsylvania Press, 1980.

———. "Reflections on Honor and Shame in the Mediterranean." Pages 121–34 in *Honor and Shame and the Unity of the Mediterranean*. Edited by David D. Gilmore. Special

Publication of the American Anthropological Association 22. Washington, DC: American Anthropological Association, 1987.

Brassey, Paul Del. *Metaphor and the Incomparable God in Isaiah 40–55.* BIBAL Dissertation Series 9. North Richland Hills, TX: BIBAL, 2001.

Brenner, Athalya, ed. *A Feminist Companion to the Latter Prophets.* Feminist Companion to the Bible 8. Sheffield: Sheffield Academic Press, 1995.

———. "On Prophetic Propaganda and the Politics of 'Love': The Case of Jeremiah." Pages 256–74 in *A Feminist Companion to the Latter Prophets.* Edited by Athalya Brenner. Feminist Companion to the Bible 8. Sheffield: Sheffield Academic Press, 1995.

———. "Pornoprophetics Revisited." *Journal for the Study of the Old Testament* 70 (1996): 63–86.

Brettler, Marc Zvi. *God is King: Understanding an Israelite Metaphor.* Journal for the Study of the Old Testament Supplement Series 76. Sheffield: Sheffield Academic Press, 1989.

Brod, Harry. "Introduction and Theses of Men's Studies." Pages 1–17 in *The Making of Masculinities: The New Men's Studies.* Edited by Harry Brod. Boston: Allen & Unwin, 1987.

Brown, Sydney Lawrence. *The Book of Hosea.* London: Methuen, 1932.

Brown, William P. *Seeing the Psalms: A Theology of Metaphor.* Louisville: Westminster John Knox, 2002.

Brownmiller, Susan. *Against Our Will: Men, Women and Rape.* New York: Simon & Schuster, 1975.

Bucher, Christina. "The Origin and Meaning of ZNH Terminology in Hosea." Ph.D. diss., Claremont Graduate School, 1988.

Budde, Karl. "Eine folgenschwere Redaktion des Zwölfprophetenbuchs." *Zeitschrift für die alttestamentliche Wissenschaft* 39 (1922): 218–26.

Burke, Kenneth. *The Philosophy of Literary Form: Studies in Symbolic Action.* 3d ed. Berkeley: University of California Press, 1973.

Burnett, Stephen G. "Hosea 9:10–17." *Trinity Journal* 6 (1985): 211–14.

Buss, Martin J. *The Prophetic Word of Hosea.* Beihefte zur Zeitschrift für die alttestamentliche Wissenschaft 111. Berlin: Alfred Töpelmann, 1969.

———. "Tragedy and Comedy in Hosea." *Semeia* 32 (1984): 71–82.

Cagni, Luigi. *The Poem of Erra.* Sources from the Ancient Near East 1/3. Malibu: Undena, 1977.

Calvin, John. *Commentaries on the Twelve Minor Prophets.* Translated by John Owen. 5 vols. Grand Rapids: Eerdmans, 1950.

Cameron, Lynne, and Graham Low, eds. *Researching and Applying Metaphor.* Cambridge: Cambridge University Press, 1999.

Camp, Claudia V., and Carole R. Fontaine, eds. *Women, War, and Metaphor. Semeia* 61 (1993).

Carrigan, Tim, Bob Connell, and John Lee. "Toward a New Sociology of Masculinity." Pages 63–100 in *The Making of Masculinities: The New Men's Studies.* Edited by Harry Brod. Boston: Allen & Unwin, 1987.

Carroll, Robert P. "Desire Under the Terebinths: On Pornographic Representation in the Prophets—A Response." Pages 275–307 in *A Feminist Companion to the Latter Prophets*. Edited by Athalya Brenner. Feminist Companion to the Bible 8. Sheffield: Sheffield Academic Press, 1995.

Casson, David. "'The Mountain Shall Be Most Holy': Metaphoric Mountains in Ezekiel's Rhetoric." Ph.D. diss., Emory University, 2004.

Castellino, G. R. *Two Šulgi Hymns (BC)*. Studi Semitici 42. Rome: Istituto di Studi del Vicino Oriente, 1972.

Catlett, Michael Lee. "Reversals in Hosea." Ph.D. diss., Emory University, 1988.

Chance, John K. "The Anthropology of Honor and Shame: Culture, Values, and Practice." *Semeia* 68 (1994): 139–51.

Chapman, Cynthia R. *The Gendered Language of Warfare in the Israelite-Assyrian Encounter*. Harvard Semitic Monographs 62. Winona Lake, IN: Eisenbrauns, 2004.

Cheyne, T. K. *Hosea*. Cambridge Bible for Schools and Colleges. Cambridge: Cambridge University Press, 1889.

Clines, David J. A. "He-Prophets: Masculinity as a Problem for the Hebrew Prophets and Their Interpreters." Pages 311–28 in *Sense and Sensitivity: Essays on Reading the Bible in Memory of Robert Carroll*. Edited by David J. A. Clines and Philip R. Davies. Journal for the Study of the Old Testament Supplement Series 348. Sheffield: Sheffield Academic Press, 2002.

———. *Interested Parties: The Ideology of Writers and Readers of the Hebrew Bible*. Journal for the Study of the Old Testament Supplement Series 205. Gender, Culture, Theory 1. Sheffield: Sheffield Academic Press, 1995.

Connally, Tristanne J. "Metaphor and Abuse in Hosea." *Feminist Theology* 18 (1998): 55–66.

Connell, R. W. *Masculinities*. 2d ed. Berkeley: University of California Press, 2005.

Cook, H. J. "Pekah." *Vetus Testamentum* 14 (1964): 121–35.

Cook, Stephen L. "The Lineage Roots of Hosea's Yahwism." *Semeia* 87 (1999): 145–61.

Coote, Robert B. "Hosea XII." *Vetus Testamentum* 21 (1973): 389–402.

———. "Hos 14:8: They Who Are Filled with Grain Shall Live." *Journal of Biblical Literature* 93 (1974): 161–73.

Cornwall, Andrea, and Nancy Lindisfarne, eds. *Dislocating Masculinity: Comparative Ethnographies*. Male Orders. New York: Routledge, 1994.

———. "Dislocating Masculinity: Gender, Power, and Anthropology." Pages 11–47 in *Dislocating Masculinity: Comparative Ethnographies*. Edited by Andrea Cornwall and Nancy Lindisfarne. Male Orders. New York: Routledge, 1994.

Cowley, A. E. *Gesenius' Hebrew Grammar*. 2d English ed. Edited and enlarged by E. Kautzsch. Oxford: Oxford University Press, 1910.

Cross, Frank Moore. *Canaanite Myth and Hebrew Epic*. Cambridge: Harvard University Press, 1973.

Davidson, Donald. "What Metaphors Mean." Pages 200–220 in *Philosophical Perspectives on Metaphor*. Edited by Mark Johnson. Minneapolis: University of Minnesota Press, 1981.

Davies, G. I. *Hosea*. The New Century Bible Commentary. Grand Rapids: Eerdmans, 1992.

Davis, Natalie Zemon. "Women on Top: Symbolic Sexual Inversion and Political Disorder in Early Modern Europe." Pages 147–90 in *The Reversible World: Symbolic Inversion in Art and Society*. Edited by Barbara A. Babcock. Ithaca: Cornell University Press, 1978.

Day, John. "Pre-deuteronomic Allusions to the Covenant in Hosea and Psalm LXXVIII." *Vetus Testamentum* 36 (1986): 1–12.

Dearman, Andrew. "YHWH's House: Gender Roles and Metaphors for Israel in Hosea." *Journal of Northwest Semitic Languages* 25 (1999): 97–108.

Delaney, Carol. "Seeds of Honor, Fields of Shame." Pages 35–48 in *Honor and Shame and the Unity of the Mediterranean*. Edited by David D. Gilmore. Special Publication of the American Anthropological Association 22. Washington, DC: American Anthropological Association, 1987.

Denham, A. E. *Metaphor and Moral Experience*. Oxford: Clarendon, 2000.

DeRoche, Michael. "The Reversal of Creation in Hosea." *Vetus Testamentum* 31 (1981): 400–409.

Dijk-Hemmes, Fokkelien van. "The Metaphorization of Woman in Prophetic Speech: An Analysis of Ezekiel 23." Pages 244–55 in *A Feminist Companion to the Latter Prophets*. Edited by Athalya Brenner. Feminist Companion to the Bible 8. Sheffield: Sheffield Academic Press, 1995.

Doorly, William J. *Prophet of Love: Understanding the Book of Hosea*. New York: Paulist Press, 1991.

Doyle, Brian. *The Apocalypse of Isaiah Metaphorically Speaking: A Study of the Use, Function and Significance of Metaphors in Isaiah 24–27*. Bibliotheca ephemeridum theologicarum lovaniensium 151. Leuven: Leuven University Press, 2000.

Dressler, Harold. "Is the Bow of Aqhat a Symbol of Virility?" *Ugarit-Forschungen* 7 (1975): 217–25.

Driver, G. R. *Canaanite Myths and Legends*. Old Testament Studies 3. Edinburgh: T & T Clark, 1956.

Durham, Deborah, and James W. Fernandez. "Tropical Dominions: The Figurative Struggle over Domains of Belonging and Apartness in Africa." Pages 190–210 in *Beyond Metaphor: The Theory of Tropes in Anthropology*. Edited by James W. Fernandez. Stanford, CA: Stanford University Press, 1991.

Edwards, Douglas R. "Tyre." Pages 686–91 in vol. 6 of *The Anchor Bible Dictionary*. Edited by David Noel Freedman. 6 vols. New York: Doubleday, 1992.

Eidevall, Gören. *Grapes in the Desert: Metaphors, Models, and Themes in Hosea 4–14*. Coniectanea biblica: Old Testament Series 43. Stockholm: Almqvist & Wiksell, 1996.

———. "Lions and Birds as Literature: Some Notes on Isaiah 31 and Hosea 11." *Scandinavian Journal of the Old Testament* 7 (1993): 78–87.

Eilberg-Schwarz, Howard. *God's Phallus: And Other Problems for Men and Monotheism*. Boston: Beacon, 1994.

Eldredge, John. *Wild at Heart*. Nashville: Thomas Nelson, 2001.

Emmerson, Grace I. *Hosea: An Israelite Prophet in Judean Perspective*. Journal for the Study of the Old Testament Supplement Series 28. Sheffield: Sheffield University Press, 1984.

Exum, J. Cheryl. "Of Broken Pots, Fluttering Birds, and Visions in the Night: Extended Simile and Poetic Technique in Isaiah." *Catholic Biblical Quarterly* 43 (1981): 331–52.

Farrell, Warren. *The Myth of Male Power*. New York: Simon & Schuster, 1993.

Fensham, F. C. "The Marriage Metaphor in Hosea for the Covenant Relationship Between the Lord and His People." *Journal of Northwest Semitic Languages* 12 (1984): 71–78.

Fernandez, James W. *Persuasions and Performances*. Bloomington, IN: Indiana University Press, 1986.

Fitzmyer, Joseph A. *The Aramaic Inscriptions of Sefire*. Rev. ed. Biblica et orientalia 19/A. Rome: Pontifical Bible Institute, 1995.

Fontaine, Carole R. "'Be Men, O Philistines!' (1 Samuel 4:9): Iconographic Representations and Reflections on Female Gender as Disability in the Ancient World." Pages 61–72 in *This Abled Body: Rethinking Disabilities in Biblical Studies*. Edited by Hector Avalos, Sarah J. Melcher, and Jeremy Schipper. Semeia 55. Atlanta: Society of Biblical Literature, 2007.

———. "Hosea." Pages 40–59 in *A Feminist Companion to the Latter Prophets*. Edited by Athalya Brenner. Feminist Companion to the Bible 8. Sheffield: Sheffield Academic Press, 1995.

———. *With Eyes of Flesh: The Bible, Gender, and Human Rights*. The Bible in the Modern World 10. Sheffield: Sheffield Phoenix, 2008.

Foucault, Michel. *Histoire de la sexualité*. 3 vols. Paris: Gallimard, 1976.

Franklyn, Paul N. "Prophetic Cursing of Apostasy: The Text, Forms, and Traditions of Hosea 13." Ph.D. diss., Vanderbilt University, 1986.

Friedrich, Paul. "Polytropy." Pages 17–55 in *Beyond Metaphor: The Theory of Tropes in Anthropology*. Edited by James W. Fernandez. Stanford, CA: Stanford University Press, 1991.

Frymer-Kensky, Tikva. *In the Wake of the Goddesses: Women, Culture, and the Biblical Transformation of Pagan Myth*. New York: Free Press, 1992.

———. "Virginity in the Bible." Pages 79–96 in *Gender and Law in the Hebrew Bible and the Ancient Near East*. Edited by Victor H. Matthews, Bernard M. Levinson, and Tikva Frymer-Kensky. Journal for the Study of the Old Testament Supplement Series 262. Sheffield: Sheffield Academic Press, 1998.

Galambush, Julie. *Jerusalem in the Book of Ezekiel: The City as Yahweh's Wife*. Society of Biblical Literature Dissertation Series 130. Atlanta: Scholars Press, 1992.

Galil, Gershon. "A New Look at the 'Azekah Inscription.'" *Revue Biblique* 102 (1995): 321–29.

Galloway, Lincoln E. *Freedom in the Gospel: Paul's Exemplum in 1 Cor 9 in Conversation with the Discourses of Epictetus and Philo*. Contributions to Biblical Exegesis and Theology 38. Leuven: Peeters, 2004.

Garrett, Duane A. *Hosea, Joel*. New American Commentary 19A. Nashville: Broadman & Holman, 1997.

Gilmore, David D. "Above and Below: Toward A Social Geometry of Gender." *American Anthropologist* 98 (1996): 54–66.

———. ed. *Honor and Shame and the Unity of the Mediterranean*. Special Publication of the American Anthropological Association 22. Washington, DC: American Anthropological Association, 1987.

———. "Honor, Honesty, Shame: Male Status in Contemporary Andalusia." Pages 90–103 in *Honor and Shame and the Unity of the Mediterranean*. Edited by David D. Gilmore. Special Publication of the American Anthropological Association 22. Washington, DC: American Anthropological Association, 1987.

Ginsberg, H. L. "Lexigraphical Notes." Pages 71–82 in *Hebräische Wortforschung*. Edited by James Barr. Vetus Testamentum Supplement Series 16. Leiden: Brill, 1967.

Giovannini, Maureen J. "Female Chastity Codes in the Circum-Mediterranean: Comparative Perspectives." Pages 61–74 in *Honor and Shame and the Unity of the Mediterranean*. Edited by David D. Gilmore. Special Publication of the American Anthropological Association 22. Washington, DC: American Anthropological Association, 1987.

Gitay, Yehoshua. "Why Metaphors: A Study of the Texture of Isaiah." Pages 57–65 in *Writing and Reading the Scroll of Isaiah: Studies of an Interpretive Tradition*. Edited by Craig C. Broyles and Craig A. Evans. Vetus Testamentum Supplement Series 70. Leiden: Brill, 1997.

Goldingay, John. "Hosea 1–3, Genesis 1–4 and Masculist Interpretation." Pages 161–68 in *A Feminist Companion to the Latter Prophets*. Edited by Athalya Brenner. Feminist Companion to the Bible 8. Sheffield: Sheffield Academic Press, 1995.

Goldstein, Elizabeth W. "Genealogy, Gynecology, and Gender: The Priestly Writer's Portrait of a Woman." Pages 74–86 in *Embroidered Garments: Priests and Gender in Biblical Israel*. Edited by Deborah W. Rooke. Sheffield: Sheffield Phoenix, 2009.

Good, Edwin M. "The Composition of Hosea." *Svensk Exegetisk Årsbok* 31 (1966): 21–63.

Goodman, Nelson. "Languages of Art." Pages 123–35 in *Philosophical Perspectives on Metaphor*. Edited by Mark Johnson. Minneapolis: University of Minnesota Press, 1981.

Gordon, Pamela, and Harold C. Washington. "Rape as a Military Metaphor in the Hebrew Bible." Pages 308–25 in *A Feminist Companion to the Latter Prophets*. Edited by Athalya Brenner. Feminist Companion to the Bible 8. Sheffield: Sheffield Academic Press, 1995.

Graetz, Naomi. "God is to Israel as Husband is to Wife: The Metaphoric Battering of Hosea's Wife." Pages 126–45 in *A Feminist Companion to the Latter Prophets*. Edited by Athalya Brenner. Feminist Companion to the Bible 8. Sheffield: Sheffield Academic Press, 1995.

Green, Josef. "Hosea and Gomer Revisited." *Jewish Bible Quarterly* 31 (2003): 84–89.

Gruber, Mayer I. "Marital Fidelity and Intimacy: A View from Hosea 4." Pages 169–79 in *A Feminist Companion to the Latter Prophets*. Edited by Athalya Brenner. Feminist Companion to the Bible 8. Sheffield: Sheffield Academic Press, 1995.

Haddox, Susan E. "(E)Masculinity in Hosea's Political Rhetoric." Pages 174-200 in *Israel's Prophets and Israel's Past*. Edited by Brad E. Kelle and Megan Bishop Moore. New York: T&T Clark, 2006.

———. "Favoured Sons and Subordinate Masculinities." Pages 2-19 in *Men and Masculinity in the Hebrew Bible and Beyond*. Edited by Ovidiu Creangă. The Bible in the Modern World 33. Sheffield: Sheffield Phoenix, 2010.

Harper, William Rainey. *Amos and Hosea*. International Critical Commentary 23. Edinburgh: T&T Clark, 1905.

Harris, Rivkah. *Gender and Aging in Mesopotamia: The Gilgamesh Epic and Other Ancient Literature*. Norman: University of Oklahoma Press, 2000.

Hart, Angie. "Missing Masculinity? Prostitutes' Clients in Alicante, Spain." Pages 48–65 in *Dislocating Masculinity: Comparative Ethnographies*. Edited by Andrea Cornwall and Nancy Lindisfarne. Male Orders. New York: Routledge, 1994.

Hayes, John H., and Paul K. Hooker. *A New Chronology for the Kings of Israel and Judah and Its Implications for Biblical History and Literature*. Atlanta: John Knox, 1988.

Hayes, John H., and Jeffrey K. Kuan. "The Final Years of Samaria (730–720 BC)." *Biblica* 72 (1991): 153–81.

Hayes, Katherine M. *"The Earth Mourns": Prophetic Metaphor and Oral Aesthetic*. Society of Biblical Literature Academia Biblica 8. Leiden: Brill, 2002.

Hendriks, Hans Jurgens. "Juridical Aspects of the Marriage Metaphor in Hosea and Jeremiah." Ph.D. diss., University of Stellenbosch, 1982.

Henle, Paul. "Metaphor." Pages 173–95 in *Language, Thought, and Culture*. Edited by Paul Henle. Ann Arbor: University of Michigan Press, 1958.

Henry, Matthew. *An Exposition of the Old and New Testament. III. The Prophetical Books*. New York: Robert Carver, 1827.

Herzfeld, Michael. "'As in Your Own House': Hospitality, Ethnography, and the Stereotype of Mediterranean Society." Pages 75–89 in *Honor and Shame and the Unity of the Mediterranean*. Edited by David D. Gilmore. Special Publication of the American Anthropological Association 22. Washington, DC: American Anthropological Association, 1987.

Hill, Linzy Howard, Jr. "Hosea 11: Yahweh's Persistent Love." *Southwestern Journal of Theology* 36 (1993): 27–31

Hillers, Delbert R. *Treaty-Curses and the Old Testament Prophets*. Biblica et orientalia 16. Rome: Pontifical Bible Institute, 1964.

Hoffner, Harry A. Jr. "Symbols of Masculinity and Femininity: Their Use in Ancient Near Eastern Sympathetic Magic Rituals." *Journal of Biblical Literature* 85 (1966): 326–34.

Holt, Else Kragelund. *Prophesying the Past: The Use of Israel's History in the Book of Hosea*. Journal for the Study of the Old Testament Supplement Series 194. Sheffield: Sheffield Academic Press, 1995.

Hornsby, Teresa J. "Israel Has Become a Worthless Thing: Rereading Gomer in Hosea 1–3." *Journal for the Study of the Old Testament* 82 (1999): 115–28.

Hubbard, David Allan. *Hosea: An Introduction and Commentary*. Tyndale Old Testament Commentaries. Downers Grove, IL: Inter-Varsity, 1989.

Huber, Lynn R. *Like a Bride Adorned: Reading Metaphor in John's Apocalypse.* Emory Studies in Early Christianity. New York: T&T Clark, 2007.

Huffmon, Herbert B. "Gender Subversion in the Book of Jeremiah." Pages 245–53 in *Sex and Gender in the Ancient Near East: Proceedings of the 47th Rencontre Assyriologique Internationale, Helsinki, July 2–6, 2001.* Edited by Simo Parpola and R. M. Whiting. Helsinki: The Neo-Assyrian Text Corpus Project, 2002.

Israel, Richard D. "Prophecies of Judgment: A Study of the Protasis-Apodosis Text Structures in Hosea, Amos and Micah." Ph.D. Diss., Claremont Graduate School, 1989.

Jakobson, Roman. "The Metaphoric and Metonymic Poles." Pages 41–47 in *Metaphor and Metonym: Metonymy in Comparison and Contrast.* Edited by René Dirven and Ralf Pörings. Cognitive Linguistics Research 20. Berlin: de Gruyter, 2002.

Jennings, Theodore W. Jr. *Jacob's Wound: Homoerotic Narrative in the Literature of Ancient Israel.* New York: Continuum, 2005.

Jeremias, Jörg. "Die Anfänge des Dodekapropheton: Hosea und Amos." Pages 34–54 in *Hosea und Amos: Studien zu den Anfängen des Dodekapropheton.* Forschungen zum Alten Testament 13. Tübingen: J. C. B. Mohr, 1996.

———."Hosea 4–7. Beobachtungen zur Komposition des Buches Hosea." Pages 55–66 in *Hosea und Amos: Studien zu den Anfängen des Dodekapropheton.* Forschungen zum Alten Testament 13. Tübingen: J. C. B. Mohr, 1996.

———."'Ich bin wie ein Löwe für Efraim...' (Hos 5,14): Aktualität und Allgemeingültigkeit im prophetischen Reden von Gott am Beispiel von Hos 5, 8–14." Pages 75–95 in *"Ich will euer Gott werden": Beispiele biblischen Redens von Gott.* Edited by Helmut Merklein and Erich Zenger. Stuttgarter Bibelstudien 100. Stuttgart: Katholisches Bibelwerk, 1981.

Jones, W. T. *The Romantic Syndrome.* The Hague: Martinus Nijhoff, 1961.

Joosten, Jan. "Targumic Aramaic מְרוֹעָא—'Oppression' (Isa. LXVII 2, Hos. XI 7, Mic. VI 3)." *Vetus Testamentum* 51 (2001): 552–55.

Kamionkowski, S. Tamar. *Gender Reversal and Cosmic Chaos: A Study on the Book of Ezekiel.* Journal for the Study of the Old Testament Supplement Series 368. London: Sheffield Academic Press, 2003.

Kaufmann, Yehezkel. *The Religion of Israel: From Its Beginnings to the Babylonian Exile.* Translated and Abridged by Moshe Greenberg. Chicago: University of Chicago Press, 1960.

Keefe, Alice A. "Family Metaphors and Social Conflict in Hosea." Pages 113–127 in *Writing and Reading War: Rhetoric, Gender, and Ethics in Biblical and Modern Contexts.* Edited by Brad E. Kelle and Frank Ritchel Ames. Symposium 42. Atlanta: Society of Biblical Literature, 2008.

———. "The Female Body, the Body Politic, and the Land: A Sociopolitical Reading of Hosea 1–2." Pages 70–100 in *A Feminist Companion to the Latter Prophets.* Edited by Athalya Brenner. Feminist Companion to the Bible 8. Sheffield: Sheffield Academic Press, 1995.

————. *Woman's Body and the Social Body in Hosea*. Journal for the Study of the Old Testament Supplement Series 338. Gender, Culture, Theory 10. Sheffield: Sheffield Academic Press, 2001.

Keen, Sam. *Fire in the Belly: On Being a Man*. New York: Bantam, 1991.

Kelle, Brad E. *Hosea 2: Metaphor and Rhetoric in Historical Perspective*. Atlanta: Society of Biblical Literature, 2005.

————. "Wartime Rhetoric: Prophetic Metaphorization of Cities as Female." Pages 95–111 in *Writing and Reading War: Rhetoric, Gender, and Ethics in Biblical and Modern Contexts*. Edited by Brad E. Kelle and Frank Ritchel Ames. Symposium 42. Atlanta: Society of Biblical Literature, 2008.

Kinet, Dirk. *Ba'al and Jahwe: Ein Beitrag zur Theologie des Hoseabuches*. Europäische Hochschulschriften 23/87. Frankfurt: Peter Lang, 1977.

Kittay, Eva Feder. *Metaphor: Its Cognitive Force and Linguistic Structure*. Oxford: Clarendon, 1987.

Kleven, Terence. "The Cows of Bashan: A Single Metaphor at Amos 4:1–3." *Catholic Biblical Quarterly* 58 (1996): 215–27.

Kreuzer, Siegfried. "Gott als Mutter in Hosea 11?" *Theologische Quartalschrift* 169 (1989): 123–32.

Kruger, P.A. "The Divine Net in Hosea 7,2." *Ephemerides theologicae lovanienses* 68 (1992): 132–36.

————. "'I Will Hedge Her Way with Thornbushes' (Hosea 2,8): Another Example of Literary Multiplicity?" *Biblische Zeitschrift* 43 (1999): 92–99.

————. "Israel, the Harlot (Hos. 2:4–9)." *Journal of Northwest Semitic Languages* 11 (1983): 107–16.

————. "Yahweh's Generous Love: Eschatological Expectations in Hosea 14:2–9." *Old Testament Essays* 1 (1983): 27–48.

Kuan, Jeffrey Kah-jin. "Hosea 9.13 and Josephus *Antiquities* IX, 277–287." *Palestine Exploration Quarterly* 123 (1991): 103–8.

————. *Neo-Assyrian Historical Inscriptions and Syria-Palestine: Israelite/Judean-Tyrian-Damascene Political and Commercial Relations in the Ninth-Eighth Centuries BCE*. Jian Dao Dissertation Series 1. Bible and Literature 1. Hong Kong: Alliance Bible Seminary, 1995.

Kuhl, Curt. *The Prophets of Israel*. Translated by Rudolf J. Ehrlich and J. P. Smith. Richmond, VA: John Knox, 1960.

Lakoff, George and Mark Johnson. *Metaphors We Live By*. Chicago: University of Chicago Press, 1980.

————. *More Than Cool Reason: A Field Guide to Poetic Metaphor*. Chicago: University of Chicago Press, 1989.

Lambert, W. G. "The Background of the Neo-Assyrian Sacred Tree." Pages 321–26 in *Sex and Gender in the Ancient Near East: Proceedings of the 47th Rencontre Assyriologique Internationale, Helsinki, July 2–6, 2001*. Edited by Simo Parpola and R. M. Whiting. Helsinki: The Neo-Assyrian Text Corpus Project, 2002.

Landy, Francis. "Fantasy and the Displacement of Pleasure: Hosea 2:4–17." Pages 146–60 in *A Feminist Companion to the Latter Prophets*. Edited by Athalya Brenner. Feminist Companion to the Bible 8. Sheffield: Sheffield Academic Press, 1995.

———. *Hosea*. Readings. Sheffield: Sheffield Academic Press, 1995.

Lapsley, Jacqueline E. "Shame and Self-Knowledge: The Positive Role of Shame in Ezekiel's View of the Moral Self." Pages 143–73 in *The Book of Ezekiel: Theological and Anthropological Perspectives*. Edited by Margaret S. Odell and John T. Strong. Society of Biblical Literature Symposium Series 9. Atlanta: Society of Biblical Literature, 2000.

Leeuwen, Cornelis van. "Meaning and Structure of Hosea X 1–8." *Vetus Testamentum* 53 (2003): 367–78.

Leith, Mary Joan Winn. "Verse and Reverse: The Transformation of the Woman, Israel, in Hosea 1–3." Pages 95–108 in *Gender and Difference in Ancient Israel*. Edited by Peggy L. Day. Minneapolis: Fortress, 1989.

Levine, Baruch A. "'Seed' versus 'Womb': Expressions of Male Dominance in Biblical Hebrew." Pages 337–43 in *Sex and Gender in the Ancient Near East: Proceedings of the 47th Rencontre Assyriologique Internationale, Helsinki, July 2–6, 2001*. Edited by Simo Parpola and R. M. Whiting. Helsinki: The Neo-Assyrian Text Corpus Project, 2002.

Lévi-Strauss, Claude. *The Savage Mind*. Chicago: University of Chicago Press, 1962.

Lewis, R. L. "The Persuasive Style and Appeals of the Minor Prophets Amos, Hosea, and Micah." Ph.D. diss., University of Michigan, 1958.

Lindisfarne, Nancy. "Variant Masculinities, Variant Virginities: Rethinking Honor and Shame." Pages 82–96 in *Dislocating Masculinities*. Edited by Andrea Cornwall and Nancy Lindisfarne. Male Order. New York: Routledge, 1994.

Lipshitz, Abe. *The Commentary of Rabbi Abraham Ibn Ezra on Hosea*. New York: Sepher-Hermon, 1988.

Locke, John. *An Essay Concerning Human Understanding*. Edited by Peter H. Nidditch. Oxford: Clarendon, 1975.

Loewenberg, Ina. "Identifying Metaphors." Pages 154–81 in *Philosophical Perspectives on Metaphor*. Edited by Mark Johnson. Minneapolis: University of Minnesota Press, 1981.

Lohfink, Norbert. "Hate and Love in Osee 9,15." *Catholic Biblical Quarterly* 25 (1963): 417.

Loizos, Peter. "A Broken Mirror: Masculine Sexuality in Greek Ethnography." Pages 66–81 in *Dislocating Masculinity: Comparative Ethnographies*. Edited by Andrea Cornwall and Nancy Lindisfarne. Male Orders. New York: Routledge, 1994.

Lundbom, Jack R. "Contentious Priests and Contentious People in Hosea 4:1–10." *Vetus Testamentum* 26 (1986): 52–70.

Maasen, Sabine, and Peter Weingart. *Metaphors and the Dynamics of Knowledge*. New York: Routledge, 2000.

Mac Cormac, Earl R. *A Cognitive Theory of Metaphor*. Cambridge: MIT Press, 1985.

Macintosh, A. A. *A Critical and Exegetical Commentary on Hosea*. International Critical Commentary. Edinburgh: T&T Clark, 1997.

Macwilliam, Stuart. "Ideologies of Male Beauty and the Hebrew Bible." *Biblical Interpretation* 17 (2009): 265–287.

Magdalene, F. Rachel. "Ancient Near Eastern Treaty-Curses and the Ultimate Texts of Terror: A Study of the Language of Divine Sexual Abuse in the Prophetic Corpus." Pages 326–52 in *A Feminist Companion to the Latter Prophets*. Edited by Athalya Brenner. Feminist Companion to the Bible 8. Sheffield: Sheffield Academic Press, 1995.

Malamat, A. "The Politics of Bipolarity in the Guise of Sexual Relations: The Case of Ezekiel 16 and 23." Pages 355–57 in *Sex and Gender in the Ancient Near East: Proceedings of the 47th Rencontre Assyriologique Internationale, Helsinki, July 2–6, 2001*. Edited by Simo Parpola and R. M. Whiting. Helsinki: The Neo-Assyrian Text Corpus Project, 2002.

Malul, Mier. *The Comparative Method in Ancient Near Eastern and Biblical Legal Studies*. Alter Orient und Altes Testament 227. Neukirchen-Vluyn: Neukirchener Verlag, 1990.

Margalit, Baruch. "On Canaanite Fertility and Debauchery." Pages 177–192 in *"He Unfurrowed His Brow and Laughed."* Edited by Wilfred G. E. Watson. Altes Orient und Altes Testament 299. Münster: Ugarit-Verlag, 2007.

Marks, Herbert. "The Twelve Prophets." Pages 207–33 in *The Literary Guide to the Bible*. Edited by Robert Alter and Frank Kermode. Cambridge: Belknap of Harvard University Press, 1987.

Marti, Karl. *Das Dodekapropheton: Hosea*. Kurzer Hand-Commentar zum Alten Testament 13. Tübingen: J. C. B. Mohr, 1904.

Matthews, Victor H. "Honor and Shame in Gender-Related Legal Situations in the Hebrew Bible." Pages 97–112 in *Gender and Law in the Hebrew Bible and the Ancient Near East*. Edited by Victor H. Matthews, Bernard M. Levinson, and Tikva Frymer-Kensky. Journal for the Study of the Old Testament Supplement Series 262. Sheffield: Sheffield Academic Press, 1998.

Matthews, Victor H., and Don C. Benjamin, eds. *Honor and Shame in the World of the Bible*. Semeia 68 (1994).

Mays, James Luther. *Hosea*. Old Testament Library. Philadelphia: Westminster, 1969.

McCaffrey, Kathleen. "Reconsidering Gender Ambiguity in Mesopotamia: Is a Beard just a Beard?" Pages 379–91 in *Sex and Gender in the Ancient Near East: Proceedings of the 47th Rencontre Assyriologique Internationale, Helsinki, July 2–6, 2001*. Edited by Simo Parpola and R. M. Whiting. Helsinki: The Neo-Assyrian Text Corpus Project, 2002.

Melcher, Sarah J. "With Whom Do the Disabled Associate? Metaphorical Interplay in the Latter Prophets." Pages 115–129 in *This Abled Body: Rethinking Disabilities in Biblical Studies*. Edited by Hector Avalos, Sarah J. Melcher, and Jeremy Schipper. Semeia 55. Atlanta: Society of Biblical Literature, 2007.

Melnyk, Janet L. R. "When Israel Was a Child." Pages 245–59 in *History and Interpretation*. Edited by M. Patrick Graham, William P. Brown, and Jeffrey K. Kuan. Journal for the Study of the Old Testament Supplement Series 173. Sheffield: Sheffield Academic Press, 1993.

Meyers, Carol. "Contesting the Notion of Patriarchy: Anthropology and the Theorizing of Gender in Ancient Israel." Pages 84–105 in *A Question of Sex? Gender and Difference in the Hebrew Bible and Beyond*. Edited by Deborah W. Rooke. Hebrew Bible Monographs 14. Sheffield: Sheffield Phoenix, 2007.

Miller, Geoffrey P. "A Riposte Form in The Song of Deborah." Pages 113–27 in *Gender and Law in the Hebrew Bible and the Ancient Near East*. Edited by Victor H. Matthews, Bernard M. Levinson, and Tikva Frymer-Kensky. Journal for the Study of the Old Testament Supplement Series 262. Sheffield: Sheffield Academic Press, 1998.

Miller, J. Maxwell, and John H. Hayes. *A History of Ancient Israel and Judah*. Philadelphia: Westminster, 1986.

Moore, Stephen D. *God's Beauty Parlor: And Other Queer Spaces Around the Bible*. Contraversions. Stanford, CA: Stanford University Press, 2001.

Moore, Stephen D., and Janice Capel Anderson, eds. *New Testament Masculinities*. Semeia Studies 45. Atlanta: Society of Biblical Literature, 2003.

Moran, William L. "The Ancient Near Eastern Background of the Love of God in Deuteronomy." *Catholic Biblical Quarterly* 25 (1963): 77–87.

Morris, Gerald. *Prophecy, Poetry, and Hosea*. Journal for the Study of the Old Testament Supplement Series 219. Sheffield: Sheffield Academic Press, 1996.

Naumann, Thomas. *Hoseas Erben: Strukturen der Nachinterpretation im Buch Hosea*. Beitrage zur Wissenschaft vom Alten und Neuen Testament 11 (131). Stuttgart: Kohlhammer, 1991.

Nesbitt, James H. "Metaphor and Metonomy and the Nations in Isaiah." Th.D. diss., Grace Theological Seminary, 1991.

Newsom, Carol A. "A Maker of Metaphors: Ezekiel's Oracles against Tyre." Pages 191–204 in *"The Place is Too Small for Us": The Israelite Prophets in Recent Scholarship*. Edited by Robert P. Gordon. Sources for Biblical and Theological Studies. Winona Lake: Eisenbrauns, 1995. Repr. from *Interpretation* 38 (1984): 151–64.

Niditch, Susan. "Eroticism and Death in the Tale of Jael." Pages 43–57 in *Gender and Difference in Ancient Israel*. Edited by Peggy L. Day. Minneapolis: Fortress, 1989.

Nielsen, Kirsten. *There is Hope for a Tree: The Tree as Metaphor in Isaiah*. Journal for the Study of the Old Testament Supplement Series 65. Sheffield: Sheffield Academic Press, 1989.

North, Francis Sparling. "Hosea's Introduction to His Book." *Vetus Testamentum* 8 (1958): 429–32.

Nwaoru, Emmanuel O. *Imagery in the Prophecy of Hosea*. Ägypten und Altes Testament 41. Wiesbaden: Harrassowitz, 1999.

———. "The Role of Images in the Literary Structure of Hosea VII 8 –VIII 14." *Vetus Testamentum* 54 (2004): 216–22..

Nyberg, H. S. *Studien zum Hoseabuch. Zugleich ein Beitrag zur Klärung des Problems der alttestamentlichen Textkritik*. Uppsala: A. B. Lundequistska, 1935.

Odell, Margaret S. "I Will Destroy Your Mother: The Obliteration of a Cultic Role in Hosea 4:4–6." Pages 180–93 in *A Feminist Companion to the Latter Prophets*. Edited by Athalya Brenner. Feminist Companion to the Bible 8. Sheffield: Sheffield Academic Press, 1995.

Oestreich, Bernard. *Metaphors and Similes for Yahweh in Hosea 14:2–9 (1–8): A Study of Hoseanic Pictorial Language*. Friedensauer Schriftenreihe. Frankfurt: Peter Lang, 1998.

Olyan, Saul M. "'And with a Male You Shall Not Lie the Lying Down of a Woman': On the Meaning and Significance of Leviticus 18:22 and 20:13." Pages 398–414 in

Que(e)rying Religion: A Critical Anthology. Edited by Gary David Comstock and Susan E. Henking. New York: Continuum, 1997. Repr. from *Journal of the History of Sexuality* 5 (1994): 179–206.

———. "Honor, Shame, and Covenant Relations in Ancient Israel and Its Environment." *Journal of Biblical Literature* 115 (1996): 201–18.

Ortner, Sherry B., and Harriet Whitehead, eds. *Sexual Meanings: The Cultural Construction of Gender and Sexuality.* Cambridge: Cambridge University Press, 1981.

Ortony, Andrew, ed. *Metaphor and Thought.* 2d ed. Cambridge: Cambridge University Press, 1993.

Osgood, Charles E., George Suci, and Percy H. Tannenbaum. *The Measurement of Meaning.* Urbana: University of Illinois Press, 1967.

Parpola, Simo, and Kazuko Watanabe. *Neo-Assyrian Treaties and Loyalty Oaths.* State Archives of Assyria 2. Helsinki: Helsinki University Press, 1988.

Paul, Shalom M. "The Image of the Oven and the Cake in Hosea VII 4–10." *Vetus Testamentum* 18 (1968): 114–20.

Peiser, Felix E. *Hosea.* Philologische Studien zum Alten Testament. Leipzig: J. C. Hinrichs'sche, 1914.

Pentiuc, Eugen J. *Long Suffering Love: A Commentary on Hosea with Patristic Annotations.* Brookline, MA: Holy Cross Orthodox Press, 2002.

Peristiany, Jean G., ed. *Honour and Shame: The Values of Mediterranean Society.* London: Weidenfeld and Nicolson, 1965.

Pitt-Rivers, Julian A. *The Fate of Shechem, or, The Politics of Sex: Essays in the Anthropology of the Mediterranean.* Cambridge Studies in Social Anthropology 19. Cambridge: Cambridge University Press, 1977.

———. "Honour and Social Status." Pages 19–78 in *Honour and Shame: The Values of Mediterranean Society.* Edited by Jean G. Peristiany. London: Weidenfeld and Nicolson, 1965.

Pritchard, James B., ed. *Ancient Near Eastern Texts Relating to the Old Testament.* 3d ed. Princeton: Princeton University Press, 1969.

Quinn, Naomi. "The Cultural Basis of Metaphor." Pages 56–93 in *Beyond Metaphor: The Theory of Tropes in Anthropology.* Edited by James W. Fernandez. Stanford, CA: Stanford University Press, 1991.

Rendsburg, Gary A. "Hebrew rhm= 'Rain.'" *Vetus Testamentum* 33 (1983): 357–62.

Ricoeur, Paul. "The Metaphorical Process as Cognition, Imagination, and Feeling." Pages 228–47 in *Philosophical Perspectives on Metaphor.* Edited by Mark Johnson. Minneapolis: University of Minnesota Press, 1981.

———. *The Rule of Metaphor.* Translated by Robert Czerny with Kathleen McLaughlin and John Costello. University of Toronto Romance Series 37. Toronto: University of Toronto Press, 1977.

Richards, I. A. *The Philosophy of Rhetoric.* New York: Oxford University Press, 1936.

Rooke, Deborah W. "Breeches of the Covenant: Gender, Garments, and the Priesthood." Pages 19–37 in *Embroidered Garments: Priests and Gender in Biblical Israel.* Edited by Deborah W. Rooke. Sheffield: Sheffield Phoenix, 2009.

Ross, J. F. "Bread." Pages 461–64 in vol. 1 of *The Interpreter's Dictionary of the Bible*. Edited by G. A. Buttrick. 4 vols. Nashville: Abingdon, 1962.

Rowley, H. H. *Men of God: Studies in Old Testament History and Prophecy*. London: Thomas Nelson, 1963.

Rudolph, Wilhelm. *Hosea*. Kommentar zum Alten Testament 13. Gütersloh: Gerd Mohn, 1966.

Sanders, Susan J. "Baal au Foudre: The Iconography of Baal of Ugarit." Pages 249–265 in *"He Unfurrowed His Brow and Laughed."* Edited by Wilfred G. E. Watson. Altes Orient und Altes Testament 299. Münster: Ugarit-Verlag, 2007.

Sawyer, Deborah F. "Gender Criticism: A New Discipline in Biblical Studies or Feminism in Disguise?" Pages 2–17 in *A Question of Sex? Gender and Difference in the Hebrew Bible and Beyond*. Edited by Deborah W. Rooke. Hebrew Bible Monographs 14. Sheffield: Sheffield Phoenix, 2007.

Schmitt, John J. "Gender Correctness and Biblical Metaphors: The Case of God's Relation to Israel." *Biblical Theology Bulletin* 26 (1996): 96–106.

———. "The Gender of Ancient Israel." *Journal for the Study of the Old Testament* 26 (1983): 115–25.

Schüngel-Straumann, Helen. "God as Mother in Hosea 11." Pages 194–218 in *A Feminist Companion to the Latter Prophets*. Edited by Athalya Brenner. Feminist Companion to the Bible 8. Sheffield: Sheffield Academic Press, 1995.

Sedgwick, Eve Kosofsky. "'Gosh, Boy George, You Must Be Awfully Secure in Your Masculinity.'" Pages 11–20 in *Constructing Masculinity*. Edited by Maurice Berger, Brian Wallis, and Simon Watson. New York: Routledge, 1995.

Seow, C. L. "Hosea 14:10 and the Foolish People Motif." *Catholic Biblical Quarterly* 44 (1982): 212–24.

Setel, T. Drorah. "Prophets and Pornography: Female Sexual Imagery in Hosea." Pages 86–95 in *Feminist Interpretation of the Bible*. Edited by Letty M. Russell. Philadelphia: Westminster, 1985.

Sherwood, Yvonne. "Boxing Gomer: Controlling the Deviant Woman in Hosea 1–3." Pages 101–25 in *A Feminist Companion to the Latter Prophets*. Edited by Athalya Brenner. Feminist Companion to the Bible 8. Sheffield: Sheffield Academic Press, 1995.

———. *The Prostitute and the Prophet: Hosea's Marriage in Literary-Theoretical Perspective*. Journal for the Study of the Old Testament Supplement Series 212. Gender, Culture, Theory 2. Sheffield: Sheffield Academic Press, 1996.

Siebert-Hommes, Jopie. "'With Bands of Love': Hosea 11 as Recapitulation of the Basic Themes in the Book of Hosea." Pages 167–73 in *Unless some one guide me...* Edited by J. W. Dyk, P. J. van Midden, K. Spronk, G. J. Venema, and R. Zuurmond. Amsterdamse Cahiers voor Exegese van de Bijbel en zijn Tradities Supplement Series 2. Maastricht: Shaker, 2001.

Smith, Duane Andre. "Kinship and Covenant in Hosea 11:1–4." *Horizons in Biblical Theology* 16 (1994): 41–53.

Smith, S. H. "'Heel' and 'Thigh': The Concept of Sexuality in the Jacob-Esau Narratives." *Vetus Testamentum* 40 (1990): 464–73.

Smoak, Jeremy D. "Assyrian Siege Warfare Imagery and the Background of a Biblical Curse." Pages 83–91 in *Writing and Reading War: Rhetoric, Gender, and Ethics in Biblical and Modern Contexts.* Edited by Brad E. Kelle and Frank Ritchel Ames. Symposium 42. Atlanta: Society of Biblical Literature, 2008.

Soskice, Janet Martin. *Metaphor and Religious Language.* Oxford: Oxford University Press, 1985.

Stansell, Gary. "Honor and Shame in the David Narratives." *Semeia* 68 (1994): 55–79.

Stienstra, Nelly. *YHWH is the Husband of His People: Analysis of a Biblical Metaphor with Special Reference to Translation.* Kampen, The Netherlands: Kok Pharos, 1993.

Stone, Ken. "Gender Criticism: The Un-Manning of Abimelech." Pages 183–201 in *Judges and Method: New Approaches in Biblical Studies.* Edited by Gale A. Yee. 2d ed. Minneapolis: Fortress Press, 2007.

———. "Lovers and Raisin Cakes: Food, Sex, and Divine Insecurity in Hosea." Pages 116–39 in *Queer Commentary and the Hebrew Bible.* Edited by Ken Stone. Cleveland: Pilgrim Press, 2001.

———. *Practicing Safer Texts: Food, Sex and Bible in Queer Perspective.* New York: T&T Clark/Continuum, 2005.

———. *Sex, Honor, and Power in the Deuteronomistic History.* Journal for the Study of the Old Testament Supplement Series 234. Sheffield: Sheffield Academic Press, 1996.

Strathern, Marilyn. *The Gender of the Gift: Problems with Women and Problems with Society in Melanesia.* Studies in Melanesian Anthropology 6. Berkeley: University of California Press, 1988.

Strawn, Brent A. *What Is Stronger than a Lion? Leonine Image and Metaphor in the Hebrew Bible and the Ancient Near East.* Orbis biblicus et orientalis 212. Göttingen: Vandenhoeck & Ruprecht, 2005.

Strek, Maximilian. *Assurbanipal und die letzten assyrischen Könige bis zum Untergange Ninevehs.* Leipzig: Hinrichs, 1916.

Stuart, Douglas. *Hosea-Jonah.* Word Biblical Commentary 31. Waco: Word Books, 1987.

Sweeney, Marvin A. *The Twelve Prophets.* Berit Olam 1. Collegeville, MN: Liturgical Press, 2000.

Tadmor, Hayim. "The Campaigns of Sargon II of Assur: A Chronological-Historical Study." *Journal of Cuneiform Studies* 12 (1958): 22–40

Tångberg, K. Arvid. "'I am like an Evergreen Fir; From Me Comes Your Fruit': Notes on Meaning and Symbolism in Hosea 14, 9b (MT)." *Scandinavian Journal of the Old Testament* 2 (1989): 81–93.

Tarlin, Jan William. "Utopia and Pornography in Ezekiel: Violence, Hope, and the Shattered Male Subject." Pages 175–83 in *Reading Bibles, Writing Bodies: Identity and The Book.* Edited by Timothy K. Beal and David M. Gunn. Biblical Limits. New York: Routledge, 1997.

Tasker, David R. *Ancient Near Eastern Literature and the Hebrew Scriptures About the Fatherhood of God.* Studies in Biblical Literature 69. New York: Peter Lang, 2004.

Thistlethwaite, Susan Brooks. "Every Two Minutes: Battered Women and Feminist Interpretation." Pages 96–107 in *Feminist Interpretation of the Bible.* Edited by Letty M. Russell. Philadelphia: Westminster, 985.

Thompson, J. A. "Israel's Lovers." *Vetus Testamentum* 27 (1977): 475–81.

Törnkvist, Rut. *The Use and Abuse of Female Sexual Imagery in the Book of Hosea: A Feminist Critical Approach to Hosea 1–3.* Uppsala Women's Studies A: Women in Religion 7. Uppsala: Gotab, 1998.

Turner, Mark. *Death is the Mother of Beauty: Mind, Metaphor, Criticism.* Chicago: University of Chicago Press, 1987.

Turner, Terence. "'We are Parrots,' 'Twins are Birds': Play of Tropes as Operational Structure." Pages 121–58 in *Beyond Metaphor: The Theory of Tropes in Anthropology.* Edited by James W. Fernandez. Stanford, CA: Stanford University Press, 1991.

Wacker, Marie-Theres. "Traces of the Goddess in the Book of Hosea." Pages 219–41 in *A Feminist Companion to the Latter Prophets.* Edited by Athalya Brenner. Feminist Companion to the Bible 8. Sheffield: Sheffield Academic Press, 1995.

Waltke, Bruce K. and M. O'Connor. *An Introduction to Biblical Hebrew Syntax.* Winona Lake, IN: Eisenbrauns, 1990.

Ward, James M. *Hosea: A Theological Commentary.* New York: Harper and Row, 1966.

Washington, Harold C. "Violence and the Construction of Gender in the Hebrew Bible: A New Historicist Approach." *Biblical Interpretation* 5 (1997): 324–63.

Watson, Wilfred G. E. "Reflexes of Akkadian Incantations in Hosea." *Vetus Testamentum* 34 (1984): 242–47.

Weems, Renita J. *Battered Love: Marriage, Sex, and Violence in the Hebrew Prophets.* Overtures to Biblical Theology. Minneapolis: Fortress, 1995.

―――. "Gomer: Victim of Violence or Victim of Metaphor?" *Semeia* 47 (1989): 87–104.

Wellhausen, Julius. *Prolegomena to the History of Israel.* Repr. of 1885 ed. Atlanta: Scholars Press, 1994.

Westenholz, Joan Goodnick. *Legends of the Kings of Akkade.* Mesopotamian Civilizations 7. Winona Lake, IN: Eisenbrauns, 1997.

―――. "Symbolic Language in Akkadian Narrative Poetry: The Metaphorical Relationship between Poetical Images and the Real World." Pages 183–205 in *Mesopotamian Poetic Language: Sumerian and Akkadian.* Edited by M. E. Vogelzang and H. L. J. Vanstiphout. Cuneiform Mongraphs 6. Groningen: Styx, 1996.

White, Roger M. *The Structure of Metaphor.* Oxford: Blackwell, 1996.

Wijngaards, J. "Death and Resurrection in Covenantal Context (Hos. VI 2)." *Vetus Testamentum* 17 (1967): 226–39.

Willi-Plein, Ina. *Vorformen der Schriftexegese innerhalb des Alten Testaments.* Beihefte zur Zeitschrift für die alttestamentliche Wissenschaft 123. Berlin: Walter de Gruyter, 1971.

Wolfe, Rolland Emerson. "The Editing of the Book of the Twelve." *Zeitschrift für die Alttestamentliche Wissenschaft* 53 (1935): 90–129.

―――. *Meet Amos and Hosea.* New York: Harper, 1945.

Wolff, Hans Walter. *Hosea.* Translated by Gary Stansell. Edited by Paul D. Hanson. Hermeneia. Philadelphia: Fortress, 1974.

Wood, Leon J. "Hosea." Pages 161–225 in vol. 7 of *The Expositor's Bible Commentary.* Edited by Frank E. Gaebelein. 12 vols. Grand Rapids: Zondervan, 1985.

Wu, Kuang-Ming. *On Metaphoring: A Cultural Hermeneutic.* Leiden: Brill, 2001.

Yamauchi, Edwin M. "Cultic Prostitution: A Case Study in Cultural Diffusion." Pages 213–22 in *Orient and Occident*. Edited by H. A. Hoffner. Alter Orient und Altes Testament 22. Neukirchen-Vluyn: Neukirchener Verlag, 1973.

Yee, Gale A. *Composition and Tradition in the Book of Hosea: A Redaction Critical Investigation*. Society of Biblical Literature Dissertation Series 102. Atlanta: Scholars Press,1987.

———. "Hosea." Pages 195–297 in vol. 7 of *The New Interpreter's Bible*. 12 vols. Nashville: Abingdon, 1996.

———. "Hosea." Pages 207–15 in *Women's Bible Commentary*. Exp. ed. Edited by Carol A. Newsom and Sharon H. Ringe. Louisville: Westminster John Knox, 1998.

———. *Poor Banished Children of Eve*. Minneapolis: Fortress, 2003.

Zock, Hetty. "The Predominance of the Feminine Sexual Mode in Religion: Erikson's Contribution to the Sex and Gender Debate in the Psychology of Religion." *International Journal for the Psychology of Religion* 7 (1997): 187–198.

Studies in Biblical Literature

This series invites manuscripts from scholars in any area of biblical literature. Both established and innovative methodologies, covering general and particular areas in biblical study, are welcome. The series seeks to make available studies that will make a significant contribution to the ongoing biblical discourse. Scholars who have interests in gender and sociocultural hermeneutics are particularly encouraged to consider this series.

For further information about the series and for the submission of manuscripts, contact:

Peter Lang Publishing
Acquisitions Department
P.O. Box 1246
Bel Air, Maryland 21014-1246

To order other books in this series, please contact our Customer Service Department:

(800) 770-LANG (within the U.S.)
(212) 647-7706 (outside the U.S.)
(212) 647-7707 FAX

or browse online by series at:

WWW.PETERLANG.COM